The scope of child analysis

The scope of child analysis

by
Victor Smirnoff

Foreword by
M. Masud R. Khan

Translated from the French
by Stephen Corrin and revised
by the author

International Universities Press, Inc.
New York

First published in The United States of America in 1971
by International Universities Press
New York
Translated from the French
La Psychanalyse de l'enfant
© Presses universitaires de France 1966
Revised edition 1968
English translation by Stephen Corrin,
revised and brought up to date by the author
© Routledge & Kegan Paul Ltd 1971

ISBN 0 8236 6010 9

Library of Congress Catalog Card No. 70 – 160286

Printed in Great Britain

Contents

Foreword

In the past thirty years, most of the significant research in psycho-analysis has been the contribution of analysts who were or are actively engaged in child analysis. The names of Anna Freud, Melanie Klein, Donald Winnicott, Ernst Kris, Margaret Mahler and René Spitz stand out prominently in this field, and the twenty-five volumes of *The Psychoanalytic Study of the Child* bear ample testimony to the range and quality of the researches published. Furthermore, each of these creative thinkers has given an explicit and detailed account of his or her own point of view. Yet an anomolous situation persists in so far as no integrated account of this vast, varied and often militantly controversial data of research exists. Factional zeal and partisan loyalties have hindered a unification of the various clinical approaches and theoretical points of view.

Dr V. Smirnoff, a distinguished training analyst of the Association Psychanalytique de France, has undertaken to remedy this lacuna in the analytic literature. In his book, *The Scope of Child Analysis*, he not only gives us a judicious, non-partisan and lucid account of most of the significant researches in child analysis, but also places it correctly in the larger perspective of child psychiatry. It was a daunting undertaking which he succeeds in accomplishing with an enviable sagacity and erudition.

It is natural that Dr Smirnoff should discuss the researches of Anna Freud and Melanie Klein at greater length than those of any other analyst. Both Anna Freud and Melanie Klein were not only the pioneers of child analysis, but the influence they have exerted on their colleagues has created a definite split among child analysts. Dr Smirnoff's is the first book, to my knowledge, that gives a balanced account of the issues at stake and evaluates each with unbiased criticalness.

That Anna Freud's point of view comes out more in harmony with the researches of others is largely due to the extreme and dogmatic position that the Kleinian school has taken up regarding the role of death instinct and unconscious fantasy. Anna Freud had from the beginning respected and allowed for the maturational and developmental *lack* in the child patient, and also included the role of the actual familial environment as an inevitable auxiliary to the analytic work. Researches of Winnicott, Erikson and Spitz, as well as of M. Mannoni, have endorsed the veracity of this point of view.

All too often analysts writing in one language disregard the researches in other countries. This has been woefully true of analysts writing in English. Dr Smirnoff has given us the first truly integrative, as well as an almost encyclopedic, account of the essential research in child analysis in England, France, America and Germany.

When one has finished reading *Scope of Child Analysis*, one is convinced that it is no less than the scope of the whole of psychoanalysis and all debates about child analysis as a sub-speciality of psychoanalysis are more socio-political in character than germane to the nature and range of the subject itself. This is a book that one hopes everyone interested in learning about child analysis, or teaching it, will read with care and pleasure.

June 1971   M. MASUD R. KHAN

Preface

In presenting this introduction to child analysis it is necessary to specify its purpose. It is not intended as a textbook for psychotherapeutic or psychoanalytic practice, but rather as a presentation of basic facts, in order to clarify present approaches to child analysis.

It is important to delineate the scope of this discipline and its relation to the allied fields of child psychiatry and psychology. Psychoanalysis has considerably influenced psychological and psychiatric thinking and methods, and many psychoanalytic concepts have been integrated into present-day psychological thought and psychiatric practice.

More space has been devoted to the theoretical basis of psychoanalysis than to technical considerations, which could be of interest only to the practising analyst. On the other hand, the theoretical concepts behind the practice of psychoanalysis are indispensable to anyone professionally interested in the area of child development, paediatrics and mental hygiene. For this reason I have attempted to present the basic concepts and methodology of psychoanalysis.

Is it feasible to maintain, as some do, that one approach is more 'modern' than another? I do not think so, for the foundations of this discipline have not changed. No doubt, with a widening scope of experience there has come a refinement in our understanding and a greater precision in our concepts. We also have begun to expect more from psychoanalysis.

Of course, the situation has changed since the publication of Freud's seminal work, *The Interpretation of Dreams* (1900). Many psychoanalytic concepts and expressions are now part of the cultural heritage, although, of course, this process of integration into various national cultures has taken place in different ways. All in all, the Freudian discovery, with all its consequences, has probably had an effect analogous to that produced in its day by the Copernican revolution or the advent of dialectical materialism in the social sciences. Whatever one's attitude to these discoveries, it is not possible to ignore the tremendous breakthrough which they represent.

In the process of becoming part of the public domain, and as knowledge of it becomes more and more widespread, all theory tends to move away from its core and suffers an ever-increasing distortion. Thus its original acuity is blunted, its erstwhile revolutionary sweep blurred, and its general content disfigured. But its progressive dilution has in no way reduced the fundamental misconceptions about psychoanalysis. On the contrary, fresh prejudices have replaced the old ones, with as little basis and as tenacious as ever. Ignorance of the elementary principles of psychoanalysis is evident in the misuse and abuse of the word itself which thus gets reduced to absurdity. Serge Moscovici (1961) makes abundantly clear the extent to which the public image of psychoanalysis and analysts remains vague, inconsistent and blatantly unreal. The fault lies not in a lack of published material, there being numerous works on the subject for the edification of the so-called cultivated public. Ignorance arises from other causes, as Freud (1925) clearly recognized in his article 'Resistance to Psycho-Analysis'.

Admittedly this misunderstanding is to some extent engendered by the nature of the subject matter. For psychoanalysis concerns each and every one of us in precisely those areas in which we would like to remain ignorant: the unveiling of the repressed, even in the most tenuous and intellectualized way, can only provoke resistance, conscious and unconscious.

The criticism which psychoanalysis has encountered has been of two sorts. The first is a methodological criticism, essential to the advance of every science, which entails a scrutiny of the Freudian hypotheses through, and by contact with, the facts which they seek to explain. A critical approach of this nature signifies a widening of the psychological horizons.

Psychoanalysis has also come up against a polemical criticism based on certain ethical and metaphysical principles which challenge it on the grounds that Freudian theory is unacceptable *a priori*. Criticism of this sort would be a fruitless expenditure of energy leading only to barren debate.

I hope, therefore, that this volume will not be read in any polemical spirit, as no kind of apologia has been intended in the writing of it. My aim is to inform those who wish to enquire, and to present an account of child analysis, which would dispel certain misunderstandings that have arisen around it. It has been almost to present an account of child analysis which would dispel certain formulations. In an effort to present a common corpus of knowledge I have often found it necessary to state conclusions instead of providing explanations. Freud (1938) has stated that 'the teachings of psychoanalysis are based on an uncalculable number of observations and experiences and only someone who has repeated those observations on himself and on others is in a position to arrive at a judgement of his own upon it'. Hence some statements may well seem arbitrary to those not in a position to refer to their own experience or their own analytical practice, but this hazard has been preferred to that of offering over-simplified explanations.

The work of Freud is a unique example of the elaboration of theory pursued over a period of more than fifty years. The integrity which is characteristic of Freud appears in his continuous readiness to evaluate critically and revise his own ideas whenever they did not fit the facts. His work has inspired an enormous amount of further research which has brought an enrichment of our knowledge and should not be ignored.

The present volume claims to be no more than an introduction to the subject of child analysis and I hope it will encourage and help the reader to pursue his own investigations further.

For the English edition I have wholly rewritten the preface and conclusion and I have added sections IV, V and VI of Chapter five. All the other chapters have been revised, and the bibliography brought up to date.

Paris, 1971   V. SMIRNOFF

I Definition

Over the years the word psychoanalysis has been used and mis-used. Some of the confusion can be traced back to a basic misunder-standing inherent to the various meanings of the word used: it designates a therapeutic method, a psychological theory, and also a specific approach to social and cultural phenomena. Thus it appears necessary to define the different meanings with greater precision.

(a) Originally psychoanalysis was the name given by Freud (1896) to a method in which the therapeutic process was carried out exclusively by psychological means. As in any other type of psychotherapy the analytical technique builds upon the doctor-patient relationship, but with one essential difference: the relation-ship does not make use of any kind of suggestion, but uses interpretation to clarify and remove the patient's complaints.

Psychoanalysis thus works through interpretations which strive to bring to the consciousness the *unconscious* content of symptoms and behaviour. The verbal material produced by the patient dur-ing each analytic session (free associations) is interpreted by the analyst, who is in an essentially neutral position, offering no advice and passing no judgment. This very neutrality promotes a special relationship, and induces a *transference*: a process by which the patient displaces his feelings onto the analyst, specifically those feelings which derive from his relationships in earlier life, i.e. all the emotions and phantasies connected with his parents, siblings (or parent-substitutes). Such projections on the analyst of uncon-scious, infantile attitudes are new versions of infantile tendencies and phantasies which have been awakened and made conscious by the process of analysis. Thus the characteristic feature of this relationship is the replacement, in the patient's imagination, of a previously known person by the analyst. Psychic states are relived, not as states belonging to the past, but as present emotions. In this 'imaginary' relationship the patient reproduces and re-enacts situations from his previous life-experience. Transference has been described as 'an ecmnesic[1] re-enactment, in the analytical situation, of an unconscious psychic conflict belonging to the past' (Lagache, 1950).

As early and unresolved conflicts are thus revived in the trans-ference, memories which are connected with earlier psychic conflicts are released. With the help of interpretation the patient

---

[1] Ecmnesia is a psychiatric term defined as the ability to recall *intensively* old and forgotten memories and to experience them as present feelings and events: the patient often talks and acts as if, for a short period of time, he was actually taken back to a remote part of his life.

can recognize these conflicts, as well as his unconscious defences which were once effective in dealing with them. The analyst's neutral attitude and unobtrusiveness, his refusal to play along with or to respond to the patient's phantasies, creates a new situation in which *interpretation* becomes possible. In other words, the analytic setting allows the patient to bring to the fore the unconscious climate and reactions to earlier psychic conflict (transference), and to recognize the unconscious basis for his present behaviour and his symptoms: the patient thus becomes able to set up new mechanisms of defence, which are less stereotyped, and compatible with non-neurotic functioning.

In child analysis the problem of transference is a major issue and is at the centre of the debate between two different conceptions of analytic child therapy.[1]

Psychoanalysis strives to achieve *structural changes*:

(i) it allows the ego to satisfy instinctual demands according to the pleasure principle, while respecting the limitations imposed by the reality principle;

(ii) it destroys the rigid neurotic mechanisms of the ego, enabling it to accept unconscious impulses while accommodating them and mitigating the demands of the super-ego;

(iii) it uncovers, behind symptoms, dreams and behaviour patterns, the unconscious phantasies so as ultimately to admit them to consciousness.

(b) The word *psychoanalysis* is also used to define a psychological theory of mental functioning; but clinical experience and psychoanalytic theory are inseparable, since all theoretical concepts are derived from 'clinical' facts and observations which have been theorized through conceptual elaboration (generalization, systematization, verification). Hence psychoanalysis may be considered as systematized psychotherapy (Palmade, 1951). If the practice of psychoanalysis has made possible the elaboration of theory, theory has, in turn, led to the understanding of pathological mechanisms and of the therapeutic process.

As a psychological theory, psychoanalysis is based on three major propositions:

(i) *Psychic determinism* is one of the basic assumptions of psychoanalysis: mental phenomena are seen as having causes and as taking place in the general psychic development. Thus psychoanalysis is concerned with interrelationship of psychological facts.

[1] See Chapter six.

The concrete character of analytic theory, which describes mental phenomena in terms of living experience, and not as abstract entities, has been emphasized by the Marxist philosopher George Politzer (1928).

Specific to psychoanalytic theory is its attempt to describe and explain forms of concrete, individual human behaviour considered as mediating between the organism and its environment, especially the social environment (Lagache, 1949).

(ii) Psychoanalytical experience, moreover, introduces the notion that this causality confronts us with *unconscious* psychological facts. The psychoanalyst is reluctant to consider consciousness as forming the essence of the psychic life but sees in consciousness a simple quality of this psychic life (Freud). This is tantamount to saying that all human behaviour, and *a fortiori* the neurotic symptom, is to a great extent influenced by motivations which elude our conscious knowledge. A 'latent' meaning has to be wrested from our manifest actions, our dreams and our phantasies. All the efforts of the psychoanalysts are aimed at discovering this unconscious meaning by using various techniques, such as free association, which enable seemingly fortuitous and unrelated events to be meaningfully linked together.

Freud was not the first to recognize the idea of the unconscious. There were others before him, notably the nineteenth-century German writers, Jean-Paul Richter, Schopenhauer and E. von Hartmann (who published his *Philosophie des Unbewusten* in 1868); but their approach was closer to metaphysical speculation based on some intuitive perception rather than to any scientific inquiry.

At the turn of the century Pierre Janet claimed to have 'discovered' the unconscious before Freud. But his work clearly shows that what Janet called *unconscious* was a vague unformulated mental activity and had nothing to do with the unconscious Freud was talking about: a specific mode of psychic functioning. This basic confusion exemplifies the misunderstanding with which analysis met during the first years, and to a certain extent still meets today. There is no doubt that it is to Freud that we owe the discovery of the 'the ways and laws' of the unconscious: it was he who introduced the unconscious, not as some meaningless mental automatism, but as an operational concept.[1]

This is particularly true of Chapter VI of *The Interpretation of Dreams* (1900), in which Freud expounds the different modalities

[1] For the history of the discovery of the unconscious see Lancelot Law Whyte, *The Unconscious before Freud* (1960).

B

of unconscious 'coding'. Freud talks about a new way of investigating the relation between the *manifest content of the dream* and the *latent dream thoughts*. He also describes the process by which the latter have been changed into the former (*dreamwork*). The two main processes are those of *condensation* and *displacement*.

> The dream content seems like a transcript of dream thoughts into another mode of expression, whose character and syntactic laws it is our business to discover. . . . The dream thoughts are immediately comprehensible; the dream content is expressed as it were in a pictographic script, the characters of which have to be transposed individually into the language of the dream thoughts. If we attempted to read those characters according to their pictorial value instead of according to their symbolic relation we should clearly be led into error.

(iii) Freud emphasizes that the psychic life is regulated by dynamic and economic factors. Because of this, psychic motivation amounts to a conflict between instinctual drive and their gratification, which must be compatible with the conditions imposed by the external world (*reality principle*). All behaviour must be understood in dynamic terms, that is, in terms of the interplay between drives and repression. Freud thus introduces the notion of psychical energy which

> is not designated to explain phenomena such as mental fatigue, difference in vitality, etc. . . . but to elucidate problems of shifts in attention, interest and attachment from one object or activity to another. These are explained by postulating that *quanta* of energy are invested in the mental representations of objects and that these quanta vary in their mobility (Rycroft, 1968).

Freud thus introduces quantitative aspects of drives and repression, together with the pleasure and reality principles. These phenomena Freud described under the heading of 'economic' effects. Our mental life proceeds by following directed lines of energy, and all behaviour takes account of these forces, their origin and direction, their nature and intensity. The unconscious is thus conceived as a structurally determined and dynamically oriented mode of functioning. The economic viewpoint provides the rationale for the basic principles of psychoanalytic psychology (as will be explained later) and they form the groundwork of what Freud called the *mental apparatus*. The model of the mental apparatus is a structural one, as first described in the *Project for a*

Scientific Psychology[1] and over the years this model was replaced by others, none of them definitive but intended to deal with concepts based on the current state of Freud's clinical experience and knowledge.

But one should keep in mind that Freud's theory of energy has little to do with the concept of energy as used by the other natural sciences, but that it is really a *theory of meaning* in disguise.

(c) Many disciplines—sociology, anthropology, literary criticism, linguistics and even ethology—have sought to make use of ideas and concepts borrowed from psychoanalysis in order to interpret the unconscious factors, e.g. those which might underlie social attitudes and prejudices, the formation of myth and ritual, etc. Freud himself was the first to attempt 'applied psychoanalysis' when he undertook to clarify the unconscious meaning of certain works of art, and of creativity, as in *Delusions and Dreams in Jensen's Gradiva* (1906), *Leonardo da Vinci and a Memory of his Childhood* (1910), *The Moses of Michelangelo* (1914), and also the basis of cultural phenomena, such as the prohibition of incest in *Totem and Taboo* (1913). He tried to apply his method to moral, social and religious problems—*The Future of an Illusion* (1927), *Civilisation and its Discontents* (1929), *Moses and Monotheism* (1934-8).

But two questions must be raised concerning this type of research:

(i) The first one is a question of methodology. Lagache (1956) issued a warning to workers in these fields who attempt to apply the hypotheses of psychoanalysis without submitting themselves to the methodological constraints of their new field of enquiry. He observes that though systematic ostracism of psychoanalysis may be the sign of prejudice or of irrational resistance, psychoanalytic fanaticism, on the other hand, may coincide with a neglect of the fundamental principles of scientific research and lead to unwarranted generalizations. He emphasizes that the origin of a working hypothesis is no guarantee of its value: its worth must be demonstrated.

Frequent abuse and misinterpretations have brought authentic psychoanalytic approach into disrepute. This is partly due to the superficial understanding of analytic concepts, by using them out of context and disregarding their exact place in a coherent pre-

[1] The *Project for a Scientific Psychology* (1895) is part of Freud's correspondence with Wilhelm Fliess. This first draft is in much of his vocabulary and certain of its conceptions largely inspired by the psycho-physiological theories of his time and based on the work of Herbart, Brücke, Meynert and Fechner. See Peter Amacher, *Freud's Neurological Education* (1965).

sentation of analytic theory. Also there seems to be an eagerness to use certain notions in an over-simplified way and thus neglecting to consider that analysis itself has been built following strict rules and methods of (clinical) research. It is important to remember that psychoanalysis ought to be used rather as a method than as an established body of knowledge which can be extrapolated from its proper domain. Their conclusions, accordingly, are often speculative and are marred by a high coefficient of uncertainty. It remains true, none the less, that psychoanalysis has brought new variables into these various fields.

(ii) The second question concerns analytic terminology. The use of analytic vocabulary is not sufficient to confer an analytic character on works of this kind, the words being often superimposed upon new concepts, which, though bearing a faint resemblance to the original word, are only remotely related, if at all, to the concept as it is used by psychoanalysts. Thus terms like 'ego', 'superego', 'identification', often lose their specific psychoanalytic meaning and do nothing but increase the existing misunderstanding and add to the confusion that so often is being found between workers in the various fields.

The task of circumventing psychoanalytic jargon has been for several years a major preoccupation and several authors have recently published critical dictionaries to clarify the precise use of analytic terms and concepts (Laplanche and Pontalis, 1967; Rycroft, 1968).

But as crucial as this might be, it is even of greater importance to promote a multi-disciplinary approach, by creating a close co-operation of workers in the various fields of research. If psychoanalysis is to cross the boundaries of its specific, clinical purpose and to contribute to research in the human sciences, without in this process being over-simplified or totally disfigured, it must establish a scientific dialogue with all workers of adjoining fields.

Freud's discovery has radically changed our approach to human sciences. The *unconscious* is obviously the foundation not only of a new psychology but also of a new evaluation of knowledge itself.

2   The scope of child analysis

A definition of psychoanalysis does not tell us much about where its enquiries begin or where they end. It is therefore essential to define the limits of its investigations, especially in those areas where they impinge upon related disciplines and borderline concepts.

I. The nosological and structural approaches to mental illness

The nosological propensities have restricted nineteenth-century psychiatry to a purely descriptive approach. Minute symptomatological analysis made it possible to identify the major syndromes which even today represent, as it were, the framework of so-called classical psychiatry: schizophrenia, manic depressive psychosis, chronic hallucinatory psychoses, etc. Psychiatric research, from Griesinger to Kraepelin, from Pinel to Clérambault, often based on neuro-anatomy and pathology, attempted to establish the aetiology of mental illness in terms of constitutional or organic factors.[1]

In its early days, child psychiatry inherited this orientation. Psychiatry bequeathed to this rising discipline the rigid framework of its theoretical preconceptions and the dead hand of its own prejudices. In trying to model the psychiatric symptomatology of the child upon that of the adult, it not only strove to discover in the child the major syndromes already mentioned but it also borrowed the aetiological pattern, and by trying to squeeze mental disorder into a straitjacket of anatomical deficiency or functional disorder, it thereby discounted any dynamic or psychological explanation. It nevertheless soon became obvious that psychopathological manifestations in the child were not the same as those in the adult, if only because, in the adult, mental illness comes at a time when maturational potential is at its limit, whereas in the child it takes its course during the peak period of affective and intellectual development.

Essential differences divide child psychiatry from that of the adult:

(a)   Mental disturbance in the adult may be defined by reference to the notion of maladjustment, by the subjective perception with which the adult experiences his mental disturbance or his anxiety

[1] The evolution and development of psychiatric thinking has been remarkably presented by G. Zilboorg and G. W. Henry, *A History of Medical Psychology* 1941).

(M. Foucault, 1954), or by the social ostracism directed against the mental patient (T. Szasz, 1962). Such criteria are not adequate for child psychiatry. The social adjustment of a child has quite a different meaning: behaviour disorders are mostly thought of as a disturbance of family life and as a possible danger for the child's subsequent development and learning capacities. The diagnostic criteria may well belong to the external world but this does not necessarily imply a greater objectivity. Although the disturbance involves the future well-being of the child, *the locus of recognition* of that disturbance may well lie elsewhere; it is the parents, rather than the child, who find themselves asking for help.

This misunderstanding presided at the very birth of child psychiatry. The major syndromes which were looked for, on a mistaken cue from adult psychiatry, were rarely found, and the almost exclusive preoccupation of nineteenth-century child psychiatry with mental retardation and delinquent behaviour may be explained by its being alarmed only by the major disorders of conduct, learning and adaptation. The advent of psychoanalysis led to a broadening of the idea of mental illness and to a study of so-called 'minor' deviations of behaviour. School and learning difficulties, phobias, obsessions, enuresis, nail-biting or *pavor nocturnus*, assumed a new significance as they suggested the existence of deep-rooted psychological disturbances, the emphasis being shifted from the symptom itself to its underlying cause and significance.

Psychoanalysis replaced descriptive diagnosis by a structural clarification of the psychological disturbance. A symptom or a behaviour disturbance cannot be tackled simply with a view to its radical suppression. All psychoanalytic treatment is aimed at changing or removing the underlying psychic cause. To the extent that psychotherapy can act upon the aetiological (unconscious) factors of the disturbance and not on its obvious clinical manifestations—the suppression of which would leave the root cause intact—to that extent it demonstrates its effectiveness.

The precise significance of the symptom must be made explicit. A clear-cut distinction between the 'reactive' and the 'neurotic' is essential to the psychoanalytic approach. *Reactive* (secondary) *disorders* correspond to symptoms or behaviour patterns which arise under stress and disappear when conditions are normalized. *Neurosis*, on the other hand, is a manifestation of an unresolved inner conflict, repressed and thus unconscious, and 'returning' as a symptom. On closer examination, this distinction between neurosis and reactive disorders may lose something of its sharpness. From the prognostic and therapeutic point of view, however, it none the less seeks to go beyond a descriptive nosology, with the aim of revealing, behind the apparently banal and non-specific symptom, either the neurotic structure of the patient or the sometimes latent determining circumstances.

(b) Because of his close dependence on his immediate environment, and more specifically on the family, the child finds himself in conditions far different from those of the adult. The influence exerted by the parents and the important part they play in the life of the child are obvious. Nevertheless, it should be emphasized that in the course of development the child-parent relation undergoes constant changes which are a reflection of the various phases in object-relations. Every symptom is therefore bound to reflect basic disturbances in this relation, and the symptom will also have its impact on the emotional interactions within the family.

Furthermore, parents have an educational part to play and this profoundly modifies the 'natural' emotional bonds. Their dual role of parent and educator invests them with an authority which confers a new meaning, that of parental approval or disapproval to all the affectivity and activity of the child. This authority, external to begin with, is rapidly internalised and contributes to superego formation.

Whatever part the parents have played in the past of the adult neurotic patient, their influence in the case of child neurosis is intensified by their actual presence in the child's daily life. The importance of this real relation has been variously estimated. Some regard it as fundamental and attribute to it the prime responsibility in the origins of the child's psychological disturbances. Others see the real relation only as a reinforcement, since they consider the parental image in the child's phantasies, the 'interiorized' parents —which may or may not be true to the parents in real life—to be a decisive factor.

(c) A third point to be emphasized is that the developmental particularities of the child must be taken into account. Whereas in the adult we are dealing with the terminal stage of a long process, in the child we are faced with a process in the course of development. This is true both of neurobiological maturation (that is, the progressive growth of the motor skills and of perceptual and cognitive capacities) as well as of emotional development, where the setting up of more and more differentiated relations, due to the emergence of speech, continually modify the child's interaction with the external world.

Among the various factors in this development we should note: the libidinal phases and the fluctuation and adaptability of the child's instinctual drives; his object-relations on which will ultimately depend his place in a structured society; and, last but not least, the development of his defence mechanisms and character traits. In order to maintain a dynamic approach, one should keep in mind that the development history and maturational potential are of utmost importance; and that all symptoms are the products of progressive integration of instinctual drives, unconscious phantasies and object-relations.

II. Orthopsychiatry and psychotherapy

The development of child psychiatry runs parallel with psychoanalysis. The latter helped the former by enriching it with a certain number of basic concepts. Nevertheless the psychological and pedagogical approach to the child had already begun in the eighteenth century under the influence of John Locke, David Hume, Condillac and Rousseau. Education was no longer considered as a scholastic drill, but as a method aimed at developing the child's 'natural' intelligence: all learning must be motivated by a wish to learn and this wish must be awakened in the child rather than imposed by coercive means. Sensory psychology laid the foundations for experiments in the education of the so-called abnormal child: these were the first steps towards child psychiatry.

At the end of the nineteenth and the beginning of the twentieth centuries, child psychiatry can be regarded as mainly directed towards re-education, as shown by the important work of Ebbinghaus published in 1887. This trend towards 'normalization' is apparent in the importance attached to educational problems. At the very beginning of the nineteenth century, Pestalozzi, at his school of 'intuitive education' in Yverdon; Froebel, initiator of the first kindergartens; and Itard, founder of the first institutions for abnormal children, promoted methods of re-educating backward children. These methods were predominantly empirical, but the teaching was still aimed at the progressive improvement and an almost mechanical fostering of intelligence. Educators strove to develop the natural learning 'capacities' which were thought to be inhibited by some functional defect or failing of the natural endowments. Froebel recommended 'sensory education': he used geometrical shapes to lead to a gradually increasing complexity in perception. With Itard it was physiological and functional education, which he tried to demonstrate by educating the 'wild boy from Aveyron' (1801). Edouard Seguin recognized the importance of functional defect in the child and the considerable contributions that could come from the use of toys and play in learning (1846). But they all approached this learning deficiency as being 'physiological' rather than psychological, a conception which was reflected in the methods applied to deal with it.

At the same time Maria Montessori was evolving special educational methods for backward children. Her methods were soon generalised and applied to normal children. Despite a certain theoretical rigidity and the rather artificial aspect of the material and the exercises proposed, the Montessori method did promote a certain freedom for the child and encouraged free expression through spontaneous drawing. It may thus be regarded as the beginning of the so-called 'active education' which was later to be developed by Decroly, who advocated the idea of *'centres of interest'* in the education of young children, demanding from each child an individual participation leading him to the gradual acquisition of knowledge. But more important still, Decroly's method effectively tried to put into practice an education made to fit the individuality of each child.[1] Thus play, bodily experience, creative activity and free expression were promoted to the status of educational methods and enlarged the field of learning which had hitherto been confined to the area of cognition.

But it was John Dewey who, by emphasizing the child's need to solve new problems and to organize the facts of his experience, introduced a behaviourist and materialist orientation into traditional teaching methods.[2] Dewey's attachment to liberalism and the principles of democracy made him an advocate of the idea of adjustment to environment. Education, considered essentially as social learning, aims to integrate the individual into a community and to familiarize him with a mode of life in which the social group sets both the goal and the limits. It was Dewey's work that gave rise to the growth of children's villages and republics and which performed a useful function in helping young delinquents to adjust

[1] It is not intended to examine the various educational methods, all of which raise highly important issues. For a more detailed account of the history of education and educational methods, see W. O. Lester Smith, *Education* (Penguin Books, 1969) and S. J. Curtis and Boultwood, *A Short History of Educational Ideas* (1965).
[2] The opposition between traditional and modern teaching methods should not be pushed too far. Ancient education was obviously far from being as rigid as an over-simplified view might suggest (see Castle, *Ancient Education and Today*, Penguin Books, 1961).

to normal social life.[1] It was Dewey too who emphasized that the aim of education is not only the preparation of the child for adulthood but to encourage his full development at *each* period of his life. Active teaching took over from traditional passive methods.

Educational methods are closely connected with general conceptions of human development and psychology. It is therefore not amazing that changing educational methods reflect changing aims in education. At the beginning of the twentieth century the growing awareness of psychological factors in child development was to exert a deep and lasting influence in the field of 'special education' and in that of child psychiatry. Education was taking on an orthopsychiatric orientation and aimed at compensating for an intellectual or social deficiency. Very soon the 'psychotherapeutic' approach found its way into the practice of child psychiatry as well as into the educational system.

By introducing new methods and through prolonged observation, child psychiatry was able to break down the major nosological categories such as mental backwardness, insanity, dementia and constitutional psychopathy. By extending its field to cover behaviour disturbances, formerly neglected or considered as mere non-specific oddities of character, psychoanalysis profoundly modified existing classification. Henceforth, when faced by psychopathological symptoms, diagnosed as behaviour problems, the re-educative approach was gradually replaced by attempts to get at the very root of the disorder. The problem became not one of remedial teaching or of relieving unfavourable home conditions, but of tracking down the aetiology. Thus, under the influence of psychoanalysis, psychological investigation assumed a more important place in the 'mental health' clinics.

This new approach led to the opening of *child-guidance clinics* which, at the outset, were intended to trace the causes of juvenile delinquency and to provide treatment. The scope of the clinics, however, extended very rapidly to treatment of various behaviour disorders and learning difficulties—in short, an extensive part of child psychiatry.

The first child-guidance clinic was set up by William Healey and Augusta Bronner in Chicago in 1909. This clinic, the Juvenile Psychopathic Institute, which was to be the prototype of a whole series of other such centres, specialized at first in identifying the

---

[1] Something akin to this is to be found in the experience of the U.S.S.R. in its treatment of homeless children, the *bezprizornyi*, based on Makarenko's pedagogical theories. The Soviet film, *The Road to Life*, directed by Nicholas Ekk (1931), is a fictionalized but honest account of the methods employed to deal with the problem of adolescent maladjustment.

psychological factors in juvenile delinquency but went on to deal with the whole range of children's psychological disturbances. In 1915, Dr Healey opened at Boston the Judge Baker Foundation, and at the same time Dr Bernard Glueck was establishing the School of Social Work at Smith College for the training of social workers. Soon afterwards, Marion Kenworthy, the first American child psychiatrist to receive a psychoanalytic training, became director of the school and thus contributed to the specifically psychoanalytic orientation of social case-work in the United States.

Among psychoanalytic circles in Vienna, there was a growing interest in child psychology, and in 1922 Siegfried Bernfeld, head of a residential school for abandoned children, the Kinderheim Baumgarten, delivered a course of lectures on analytical psychology as applied to infants.[1] August Aichhorn tried to re-educate young delinquents at his institution at Ober-Hollabrun on psychoanalytical principles.[2] In 1924, a child-guidance clinic was linked to the Lehrinstitut of the Psychoanalytical Institute of Vienna. In order to understand the development of the Viennese group it may be useful to specify the nature of its activities and to appreciate the importance attached by psychoanalysts to the diffusion of their views among educationists. The lectures delivered by Anna Freud to the primary school-teachers of Vienna in 1929,[3] the numerous articles by Alice Balint, Edith Sterber, Herta Fuchs, Fritz Redl,[4] the seminars directed by Sterba and Aichhorn, the courses inaugurated by W. Hoffer to encourage educationists to revise their teaching methods in the light of psychoanalysis—all this bears witness to the development of their numerous and varied activities in teaching circles. Constantly recurring terms like *Grundlagen eines Erziehungssystems, psychoanalytische Pädagogik*,[5] convey the general orientation. The aim was to lay the foundation of a psychoanalytical theory of education and this same concern was later to permeate the work of Anna Freud.

In France, Georges Heuyer was to invite in 1936 a child psychoanalyst, Sophie Morgenstern, as consultant to the Clinique de Neuropsychiatrie Infantile. It is thanks to Georges Heuyer that psychoanalysis became accepted by child psychiatry at a time when 'Freudian' doctrines were still facing deeply entrenched prejudices in French psychiatric circles.

[1] This appeared under the title *Psychologie des Säuglings* (1925).
[2] The author related his experiences in his book, *Wayward Youth* (1925).
[3] Published under the title *Introduction to Psychoanalysis for Teachers* (1931).
[4] A relevant bibliography will be found in the work of Anna Freud, *The Psychoanalytical Treatment of Children* (1945).
[5] Foundations of an educational system; psychoanalytical pedagogy.

In spite of these obstacles, some of which still persist, psycho-analysis has won an established place as a therapeutic method in most mental hospitals and institutions.[1] Even its opponents have adopted certain of its formulations; the concepts of the unconscious, of infantile sexuality, of psychic trauma, have been incorporated as current notions in psychopathology. Psychoanalytic theories have thus made possible the expansion of child-guidance clinics by laying the conceptual foundations of a psychotherapeutic approach. These clinics, in their turn, have greatly helped psychoanalytic theory to gain general recognition.

The aim of child-guidance clinics is to lead the child to a better adjustment, not by merely changing his surroundings but by concentrating effort on the child's emotional problems. The clinics do not intend to mould the child into some form of pre-established social ideal, but to clarify and remove the obstacles encountered by the individual child in the course of his develop-ment. The therapeutic measures follow the general line of analytic practice and aim at enabling the child to modify the underlying personality structure and, by resolving the intrapsychic conflicts, to find a more satisfactory means of adjustment. It is not, therefore, a question of adjusting the child to external circumstances but of allowing him to improve his self-awareness and to gain some understanding of his relationship to others.

The methods of child guidance are an application of analytical theory.[2] Given the physical and emotional immaturity of the child, and his natural tendencies to normal development, the situation becomes not dissimilar to that encountered in psychoanalysis. By the working through of the transference it is hoped to achieve a structural readjustment.

The attitude towards the family, on the other hand, must take into account the necessity of using short-term measures in order to carry on the child's psychotherapy under the best possible conditions, and with as little parental resistance as possible. The therapy aimed at the parents would not, of course, satisfy the criteria of psychoanalysis. Because of the pattern of the weekly, sometimes only monthly, sessions, and also because of deep-seated parental attitudes, structural change of the parents becomes un-likely as an immediate goal. An attempt, however, is made to

[1] Following the Second World War, under the influence of Henri Duchêne, a growing number of psychoanalysts came to practise in child-guidance clinics sponsored by the Mental Health Board of the City of Paris (O.P.H.S.).
[2] It is true that many clinics use techniques of functional re-education, speech therapy, etc., in addition to psychotherapy. We have discussed only the psychotherapeutic activities.

render parents aware of their relation to their children, to make them grasp the significance of this relation, having regard to the child's feelings, and to get the parents to disclose the unconscious repetitiveness in their behaviour patterns. The term 'guidance' is thus rather confusing. Advice or teaching is not relevant here; the idea is to enable parents to perceive certain underlying motives behind their attitudes towards the family but also towards themselves. The task of achieving these aims falls either upon the child psychiatrist in the course of his meetings with the parents or upon the psychiatric social case-worker.

Although, of course, this is not psychoanalysis in the strict sense of the word, there is no doubt that these methods of psychotherapy and the idea of social case-work derive directly from the theories of psychoanalysis since they depend on an analytic conception of personality-structure and on the principles of a dynamic psychology. They have no pedagogic purpose and are not mandatory. They do not seek to indoctrinate or to advise but to arrive at a clearer understanding of inner conflicts and motives.

III. Constitution, maturation and environment

Nineteenth-century psychiatry had made an essential distinction between psychiatric disorders of *organic origin* and those which were looked upon as the result of mental *constitution*, either innate or hereditary.

Dynamic psychiatry was an attempt to elucidate the so-called constitutional factors. The range of organic affections in psychiatry was soon limited to a few precise entities—epilepsy, paresis, degenerative brain diseases, senile dementia—all relatively rare by comparison with the considerable size of the mentally ill population. The biological origin of many mental illnesses remains obscure in spite of advances in biochemistry, neuropathology and genetics.

However, once the problem of the somatic origin is put aside, psychoanalysis is still confronted by the question of mental illness which has no obvious cause. It is important to determine the part attributed to innate factors as opposed to environmental ones.[1]

1 *Hereditary factors*

Genetic transmission is due to hereditary factors (or *genes*) which

[1] The extent of this debate can be judged from the symposium, held at Bonneval in 1946, published under the title *Le problème de la psychogénèse des névroses et des psychoses* (Desclée de Brouwer, 1950).

are located in the chromosomes. An individual genetic constitution is called 'genotype'; the actual appearance, which is the product of the genotype and the influence of environment, is called 'phenotype'. Due to considerable advances in genetic research over the last forty years human heredity has become a highly specialized field. The popular conception that children resemble their parents may be sufficient to establish the fact that the inheritance of various physical characteristics or malformations does exist, but it is far from accounting for the complexities of genetic transmission.[1]

The study of heredity requires a great deal of statistical data which is easy to collect if hereditary transmission is being studied in viruses, insects or small animals. However, in human genetics samples are rather limited and investigations rarely go beyond the study of two or three generations. Even so, medical genetics (investigations of metabolic disorders, mongolism, muscular dystrophy) are a relatively simple matter when compared with genetic investigation of mental illness.

In psychology and psychiatry, the hereditary transmission of a character trait, intelligence, psychiatric syndromes, or even a predisposition to disease, is more difficult to assert. Freud, from the outset of his career, waged a fierce struggle against the 'hereditary' theory of neurosis. It must, however, be emphasized that Freud was not opposed to genetic theories but to the use of a word not employed in its strictly scientific sense and devoid of any concrete supporting evidence.[2] Freud was therefore opposed to the myth of hereditary mental disease, and to the oversimplification implicit in a word which was an excuse for a resigned and impotent acceptance of social irresponsibility. He could not accept

[1] Genetic transmission is a complicated matter and has been becoming more so since the discovery of dominant and recessive genes, of linkage and crossing over, of gene mutations, of chromosome abnormalities (trisomics or monosomics), etc. The chemical basis of genetic transmission was recently discovered in the nucleotides of D.N.A. (nucleic acid). The physical arrangements of those molecules are fixed in each gene like the letters in a word, but the order of units in a single column of nucleotide must determine the order in its partner. Thus any chromosome carries a code capable of determining the diversities of heredities in different organisms. For further reading see C. D. Darlington, *Genetics and Man* (1966), and Robert P. Levine, *Genetics* (1968).

[2] *Only that which is transmitted according to genetic laws, through successive generations, is hereditary.* The fate that has befallen the theory of 'hereditary' syphilis is particularly illuminating in this respect. Belief in a vague 'hereditary transmission' has given way to the discovery of *congenital* syphilis resulting from contamination *in utero* or in the utero-vaginal passage. Thus, far from being some inescapable act of fate or the mark of an atavistic defect, syphilis can be looked upon as the consequence of a direct mother-to-child contamination and thus amenable to appropriate treatment of the mother before or during pregnancy. The notorious brandmarks of 'hereditary' syphilis thus lose their ethical stigma and this has obvious repercussions on the psycho-social level.

that the fate of an individual was already sealed even before conception.

The idea of innate factors seems better suited to explain mental illness than the notion of heredity. This idea embraces all innate factors which are part of a child's equipment at birth. As well as purely genetic elements they would also include intra-uterine influences. Pre-natal factors are a function of the mother's physiological condition, but, to a certain extent, her psychological state during pregnancy cannot be ignored. During intra-uterine life, certain psychophysiological patterns in the child are already being formed, although it is difficult to talk of 'psychic traumata' in the usual sense of the term.

In psychology, it is often impossible to make a sharp distinction between genetic and congenital factors. If one attempts to draw a clear line of demarcation between the two, one encounters methodological problems. One might say that in psychoanalytic research the innate factors (including factors operating *in utero*) supersede the genetic ones.

2 *Maturation*

The role of psychophysiological maturation is a dynamic element in the individual development. Development depends on many different factors, and specific areas of development—such as acquisition of motor skills, sensory perception, linguistic abilities and emotional response—follow their own pace due to the gradual unfolding of maturational processes.[1] Thus various manifestations and behaviour patterns cannot make their appearance until certain levels of the physiological, neural and sensory organization, as well as levels of the cortical integration, are attained. Until the various systems have reached a certain level of maturation, all education remains ineffective. Maturation brings with it a certain learning potential but the fulfilment of this potential depends largely on motivation for learning provided by environmental stimulation. Mastering the ability to walk, for example, cannot be achieved before the myelinization of the pyramidal tract is sufficiently advanced (usually by the end of the first year). To teach a child to walk before this period is useless but when it is reached, *learning to*

[1] A clear definition of these terms has been proposed by Hartmann, Kris and Loewenstein (1946). *Maturation* is defined as the unfolding of inborn functions (phylogenetically evolved) which emerge in the course of embryonic development and can be carried forward after birth as *Anlage* (predisposition) and become manifest at later stages in life. *Development* is the emergence of functions and of behaviour which are the outcome of exchanges between organism and his (inner and outer) environment.

walk does, in fact, become necessary for the child. A capacity which seems so natural to man may fail to be achieved in circumstances where the child receives no stimulation from the environment.[1] Although it is possible to speak of biological maturation, it is difficult to consider that psychological maturation can be attributed to an innate regulation only. One is struck, however, 'by the universality of the biological pre-maturation which puts the child in a state of dependency on his environment over a long period' (Lagache, 1955). This dual aspect of physiological immaturity and of dependency on others is the basis of the child's entire development and constitutes what Freud called *helplessness*.

The question has, however, been raised whether certain phases of libidinal development are not, to some extent, cultural artefacts and can only in part be attributed to maturation in the physiological sense. In other words, it is possible to consider that neurobiological maturation does not determine, but merely makes possible, the establishment of object-relations, by providing the child with a certain endowment; and that the means whereby these relations are established depend on external factors which may be called 'cultural'.

We can define, from this point of view, the role of maturation in personality formation: 'maturation is innate *but it becomes effective* only through the influence of the environment. Maturation cannot be considered as a *direct* factor in personality development; it operates as part of a complex interaction and depends both on early influences as well as on the present environmental conditions' (J. C. Filloux, 1957).

3 Constitution and environment

The respective roles of constitution and environment in determining personality traits and mental illness have long been a subject of debate. The opposition of *nature* and *nurture* polarized the discussion, part of which may be recalled here.

(a)   One line of research dealt with mental deficiency and social maladjustment. The studies by Goddard (1912) on the two branches of the Martin Kallikak family—the one legitimate and mentally normal, the other illegitimate and feeble-minded—pur-

[1] See, with reference to this, the studies of cases of *wolf-children* whose deprivation of stimulation, in conditions approximating those of experimentation, resulted in their inability to walk upright. Since Itard's study of Victor, the wild boy of the Aveyron (1801) many cases have been reported. A general review of the subject can be found in Gesell's *Wolf Child and Human Child* (1941), Singh and Zinng, *Wolf Children and Feral Man* (1942), and Malson's *Les Enfants sauvages* (1964).

ported to demonstrate that intelligence is genetically determined·
However, as numerous critics have observed, nobody knows what
might have happened to the illegitimate line if it had enjoyed the
social advantages of the other: 'despised, social rejects on the
fringe of society, the luckless relatives of the more fortunate
Kallikaks suffered the destiny which society meted out to them'
(Malson, 1964). A similar fate seem to have befallen the descendants of Max Jukes, a tramp and a drunk, or, to use the American
term, a bum. A rather depressing account of this man's family was
given by Dugdale in 1877; in 1916, numerous descendants of his
were traced by Estabrook. Among them, he recorded 300 prosti-
tutes, 600 mental defectives, 140 criminals, and 310 vagrants.
Although at first sight these studies may seem to prove a constitutional predisposition, they are, in fact, a weighty argument for the
influence of environment.[1]

(b) The idea that intelligence is in part inherited has been
investigated methodically only since the introduction of intelligence
tests, which made it possible to grade children in the middle range
of intelligence.

An extensive project carried out by Freeman, Holzinger and
Mitchell (1928), clearly demonstrated the influence of environment in intellectual development. Among children placed in foster
families, the correlation between adopted children and true
children was higher than that between adopted children and their
parents. They also found significant correlations between adopted
children from distinctly different backgrounds but living in the
same family. Children of feeble-minded mothers placed in normal
families achieve average standards, whereas children brought up
by two feeble-minded parents may turn out to be decidedly backward.

Twin studies provided workers with valuable information.
Newman, Freeman and Holzinger (1937) studied identical (monozygotic) twins[2] reared together and apart. They found great

---

[1] H. H. Goddard, *The Kallikak Family, A Study in the Heredity of Feeble-
mindedness* (Macmillan, 1912); R. L. Dugdale, *A Study in Crime, Disease and
Heredity* (Putnam, 1877); A. H. Estabrook, *The Jukes in 1915* (Carnegie Institute,
1916).

[2] There are two distinct types of twins. The pairs derived from a single
fertilized egg, or zygote, are most accurately described as *monozygotic*. This term
emphasizes that they are derived from the same sperm as well as the same egg.
They are commonly called *identical*, but they are not exactly alike except for
their inheritance. This type of twinning shows no tendency to run in families.
The quite distinct type of twinning, in which the pair are derived from two
fertilized eggs, is most accurately described as *dizygotic*. They are commonly
called *fraternal*. This type of twinning shows a marked tendency to run in
families (Carter, 1962).

C

resemblances between identical twins reared together, while fraternal (dizygotic) twins were no more alike than non-twin siblings brought up in the same home. On the other hand, identical twins reared apart presented differences which can be related to different educational opportunities and, to a lesser degree, to a difference in estimated social advantage.

Such studies do not clearly prove the fact that intelligence can be considered as a genetic factor: results are not simple to interpret, since they also show environmentally caused variations even in the case of identical twins. This is fairly demonstrative of the kind of difficulties encountered in genetic studies of psychological components, even more so since 'intelligence' is one of the easier factors liable to be evaluated in a more or less objective way through intelligence-test scores. Interpretations of twin studies are even more uncertain when it comes to character traits or mental illness. These results are strong arguments in favour of explanations that intellectual functions are associated with the notion of parental models, educational similarities and unconscious identification rather than in favour of a purely genetic influence.[1]

It may be important to emphasize that psychoanalytic theory has tried to account for the growth of intellectual functions in terms of ego-functions. From Freud's initial statement that the functions of judgment and reality testing are derived from primary instinctual impulses, to Susan Isaacs' views, including intellectual development as part of the overall unfolding of the child's psychical abilities, it becomes clear that psychoanalysis does not consider intelligence as an innate or inherited potential, or rather that, whatever such a 'potential' could be, the subject's experience throughout his development is going to play a considerable role in shaping, expanding and specializing this initial 'potential'.

Thus Susan Isaacs (1943) points out that:

> if phantasy be the 'language of primary instinctual impulses it can be assumed that phantasy enters in the earliest development of the ego in its relation to reality and the development of knowledge of the external world. . . . The disappointingness of hallucinatory satisfaction is the first spur to some degree of adaptation to reality. Here is the beginning of adjustment to reality and of the development of appropriate skills and of perception of the external world.

From the very start, the infant's exploration of the external world is invested with libido. The drive towards taking things into

---

[1] See the chapter, 'Individual Differences', in Otto Kleinberg's *Social Psychology* (1954). Also Carter, *Human Heredity* (1962).

his mind, towards looking, touching, listening and exploring, satisfies some of the wishes frustrated by the original object. In order to understand phantasy, reality testing and 'intelligence', we must consider their various functions as closely interrelated. To say 'this is perception and knowledge, but *that* is something quite different and unrelated, that is mere phantasy, would be to miss the *developmental* significance of both functions'. And Susan Isaacs sees in the child's make-believe play and in the first forms of 'as if' thinking, the prototype of the future use of these elements in the growth of hypothetical reasoning.

But in the acquisition of knowledge and the development of intellectual skills others have emphasized various concomitant factors.

For instance, Melanie Klein (1932) talks of *epistemophilic tendencies*, derived from the child's sexual drive in his quest for knowledge and understanding, particularly in satisfying his sexual curiosity, and which, later on, become cathected with any kind of intellectual curiosity or pursuit. If those epistemophilic tendencies undergo repression—whether under the influence of his inner psychic conflicts or even through active parental prohibition—the result may be the child's inability to learn and even a repulsion towards anything connected with learning. Epistemophilic tendencies thus represent one of the most important factors in the ability to face and to adjust to the demands of external reality and in controlling the outer world. We should also mention M. Mannoni's concept (1964) of the *mother's unconscious desire*, which may act either as an inhibiting factor or as an encouragement in the child's learning abilities. The role played by *identification with the parents* also influences to a large extent the child's attitudes towards intellectual acquisitions and performances. It becomes clear that psychoanalysis does not take potential intellectual endowment for granted. Whatever its original importance may be (and no decisive proof has been produced so far as to the hereditary transmission of the 'average' grades of intelligence) developmental factors seem to play a decisive role both in the intellectual growth and in intellectual efficiency.

(c) Another series of research projects is concerned with schizophrenia and its hereditary transmission. Twin studies do not produce sufficient evidence to point to genetic transmission. Although there is a high degree of correlation between monozygotic twins, this could argue as strongly for pre-natal influences as for environmental ones; it has been emphasized that the environmental similarities are likely to be the stronger where the biological kinship is closer. In the genetic studies of Rosanoff, Kallmann and others, the chances for schizophrenia of identical twins were thought to be eighty to ninety per cent. Recent investigations have challenged this assumption.[1]

It is now held that the identical co-twin has no more than twenty to forty per cent chances of becoming schizophrenic. This is still higher than for fraternal twins or ordinary siblings, while these siblings in turn have a higher chance than the average population (where less than one out of 100 persons can expect to become labelled a schizophrenic). The reported incidence of schizophrenia in siblings of schizophrenic patients ranges from five to fifteen per cent. To add to the difficulties in interpreting these studies the findings of Glick (1967), who reports that in seven cases of monozygotic twins reared apart, four are concordant and three are discordant for schizophrenia, make it even more impossible to draw definite conclusions. In fact, many studies of the ability of twins separated and reared in different families suggest that the twins are less similar mentally than physically.

Psychologically speaking, twins brought up separately show traits more closely related to their educational milieu than to the families from which they have sprung. No doubt there are hints that some 'organic' basis may exist after all. But these hints seem overshadowed by the failure to nail down, until now, specific causes and factors. As a result of such developments the psychoses came into 'the twilight of controversy'. The organic had to compete with the functional point of view, which places its weight on the individual's transaction with his human environment (Stierlin, 1969). In this view the psychoses denote transaction which misfired. We are therefore obliged to reconsider the question of heredity and turn our attention to the child's family surroundings which, in any event, exert a determining influence on his personality.

Recent studies of the intrafamilial environment of the schizophrenic patient have stressed certain disorganizing factors. Lidz (1964) has explored the parental role in normal families and has described four fundamental traits the family must have if it is to provide the child with the necessary 'adaptive' pattern: (a) *parental coalition* maintains the stability of the family and gives the child *two* parents: one to identify with, one to love; (b) *maintenance of*

[1] See P. Tienari, 'Psychiatric Illness in Identical Twins', *Acta Psychiatrica Scandinavica*, Suppl. 171, *39* (1963); and E. Klinglen, 'Schizophrenia in Twins', *Psychiatry*, 29, 172–84 (1966). Also I. D. Glick *et al.*, 'Schizophrenia in Siblings Reared Apart', *Am. J. Psychiatry*, *124* (August 1967).

generation boundaries; confusion of such boundaries distorts the child's ego development since his own place within the family is invaded by childlike dependance of the parents upon each other, parental jealousy of the child and incestuous proclivities; (c) *maintenance of appropriate sexual roles*; sexual identity is an essential factor of ego-development; (d) *facilitation in the resolution of the child's oedipal situation* depends on the parents' ability to desexualize gradually the child-parent attachment.

Through careful scrutiny of the family milieu of schizophrenic patients Lidz *et al.* were able to detect some basic disturbances:
(a)   the mother's imperviousness to the feelings and needs of others;
(b)   the father's insecurity as a father and a husband: he thus fails to provide the necessary objects of masculine identification to a son and can interfere with the daughter's identity as a woman;
(c)   serious disturbances of marital relationship: in some cases, marriages were marked by severe marital schism that split the family into two opposing camps; even in those families which apparently lived together in reasonable harmony the family milieu is badly distorted or 'skewed' because the serious psychopathology of the dominant parent was accepted or shared by the other;
(d)   the family does not form an entity which serves as a protective shelter: in many cases, feelings of mistrust pervade the home, and each person has to protect himself from derision, attack or rejection by concealing feelings and motives;
(e)   schizophrenics are prone to withdraw through altering their internal representation of reality because they are reared amidst irrationality and systems of communication that distort or deny valid interpretations of the environment.

Although none of these findings by themselves can be considered as causes of schizophrenia, they are indicative of basic distortion in the family: it gives us a clue as to the serious disturbance to which a child might be exposed. The 'genetic' position today often considers that it is a secondary matter whether an individual does or does not develop clinical symptoms of schiozphrenia, but rather how hereditary and environment variables interact or coact to make for various kinds of schizophrenic outcomes (Rosenthal and Kety, 1968).

It was Freud who introduced psychological determinism into psychopathology by stressing the acquired nature of neurotic illness. In this connection the equivocal character of such empirical concepts as 'nature' and 'constitution' must be removed. Although psychoanalysis has always emphasized the powerful influence of family environment and social milieu, it has never denied the importance of constitutional factors.[1] Constitutional endowment provides a certain state of mental functioning enabling the subject, more or less, when the need arises, to resist stress and frustration and to benefit fully from the process of maturation. It is thus possible to say that within the framework of psychoanalysis, the constitution determines mainly *quantitative* factors: frustration tolerance, ability to withstand stress, etc. It has been said that the reason psychoanalysis pays little attention to these constitutional factors is that psychotherapy has no control over them. The constitutional factor lies outside the realm of both the theory and the practice of psychoanalysis, which although it does not deny its existence, is concerned only with the *historical determinants of individual experience*.

IV. Culture and historical specificity

The moderate interest shown by psychoanalysis *vis-à-vis* the 'constitutional thesis' is an indication of the importance ascribed to environmental influence. This however does not mean that the psychoanalytic viewpoint can be identified with those theories which claim that personality formation is exclusively determined by social and cultural factors.

Beyond doubt all individual behaviour is partly conditioned by the demands and laws of society. The 'culturalist' school of anthropology whose principal exponents are Ruth Benedict, Margaret Mead, A. Kardiner and R. Linton,[2] have emphasized the importance of reality factors.

[1] 'Freud's argument was based on a rigorously deterministic view. Everything that men did was determined by some property of their mind. . . . Freud's determinism, like Marx's, excluded the basis of biological determinism. But it was determinism of limited liability. One could draw on it to any amount so long as one did not touch the hereditary account. . . . Refusing to admit the genetic basis of mental characters, Freud would be quite unrestrained in his assumptions about the effects of environment' (Darlington, 1966). Although this statement contains some truth, it is still difficult to assert that mental traits or mental illness is of predominantly genetic nature. So far no really convincing evidence has been produced to show the hereditary transmission of manic-depressive psychosis or of schizophrenia. Darlington's statement that 'He [Freud] excluded every manifestation of heredity' is not quite true. The following passage from Freud in his 1905 article on the role of sexuality in the aetiology of neurosis is relevant: 'To explain the aetiology of neurosis exclusively by heredity or evolution would be as narrow as to attribute its origin solely to the accidental influences to which sexuality is subjected in the course of the patient's life.'

[2] This school has been strongly influenced by 'neo-Freudian' psychoanalysts (particularly Karen Horney and Harry Stack Sullivan) who since 1940 have

1 *Culture and society*

It is necessary to clarify the psychoanalytic position in relation to the problem of social determinants.

(a)   As defined by E. B. Taylor, culture is 'that complex whole which includes knowledge, belief, art, morals, law, custom and any other capabilities and habits acquired by man as a member of society'. A. Kardiner (1939) defines culture as the way of organizing relationships between individuals of a given group; of organizing the group's relation with the outer world in order to find ways of satisfying its own basic needs, and finally of organizing behaviour patterns and attitudes concerning childbirth, growth and development, maturity and death: in other words, whenever we encounter a *transmission* of these organized methods we are justified in referring to it as a 'culture'.[1]

Every culture is relatively independent of those who are part of it, although it exists only in virtue of them. This fact, underlined by Linton (1945), enables us to distinguish what belongs to the total culture, i.e. that which is shared by all the members of a group, for example, language, from that which belongs only to certain of its members, such as a professional group.

Every culture reflects in its ideological aspects (e.g. moral and religious principles) the adjustment of the community to the conditions of the environment. Certain conditions can be modified by man, who thus creates new conditions to which he must adjust.

(b)   It is in relation to culture thus defined that the individual's adjustment must take place. Those forms of acquired behaviour are determined by the phenomenon of *acculturation*, that is, by integrating this behaviour into the culture which is indispensable if the individual is to be a member of society. The family circle is the first and most important transmitting agent of these cultural requirements.

(c)   *Child-rearing* practices are determining factors in this process and everybody agrees that childhood experiences shape the personality. These patterns of child rearing are closely linked to

[1] We wish to mention Claude Lévi-Strauss's (1958) remark that a culture can be defined as an ethnological *ensemble* which presents significant differences when compared to any other.

---

moved away from the Freudian line. It allows a predominant role to social influences in the formation of neuroses and reduces to a minimum the part played by unconscious and libidinal factors in the development of the personality (see J. A. C. Brown, 1961).

the form of *family organization*, which varies according to the different cultures,[1] and also according to the emotional experiences of each child in face of parental acceptance, rejection, authority, permissiveness, gratification or frustration. To these determining factors, of which psychoanalysis has made its own special study, cultural anthropology adds a social dimension by attempting to establish a specific relation between parental attitudes and the cultural setting.

(d)   Kardiner (1939) tried to introduce the concept of a *basic personality type*, which would be specific to each culture.[2] This concept is based upon two contentions.

First, it is based on the notion that identical cultural standards must give rise to basic personality patterns common to all the individuals of the same culture. The basic personality is determined by those *primary institutions* represented by kinship structures, rules governing education, socio-economic organization of the family, etc.

Second, once established, the basic personality determines *secondary institutions* among which Kardiner includes religion, myth and ethics, which themselves form a superstructure. This superstructure, in its turn, modifies the primary institutions, particularly certain parental attitudes to their children.

The basic personality is thus a concomitant of the child-rearing practices. Individual variations correspond to differences in parental attitudes and in child-parent relations and determine the child-rearing pattern in the third generation. Ruth Benedict (1934) had already noted that education tends to favour and reinforce certain behaviour patterns considered necessary, and therefore desirable, in any particular culture. Frequent examples of this have been reported: differences in education among the Sioux and Yurok described by E. Erikson (1963), and among the Arapesh and the Mundugumor in New Guinea, described by Margaret Mead (1930). The authors using analytical concepts, insist on the fact that the superego arises from the internalization, not of the

[1] It is not possible to mention all the important authors in this field. We can only refer the reader to Margaret Mead, *From the South Seas* (William Morrow, 1939), D. Leighton and C. Kluckhohn, *Children of the People* (Harvard University Press, (1947), Erik E. Erikson, *Childhood and Society* (1963), J. W. M. Whiting, *Child Training and Personality* (1954) and D. Riesman, *Culture and Social Character* Free Press of Glencoe, 1961). A close scrutiny of cultural phenomena from the psychoanalytic viewpoint can be found in G. Roheim's *Psychoanalysis and Anthropology* (1950).
[2] Linton (1945) speaks of *class-linked status personalities*, related more specifically to a certain cultural modelling of the individual by his own 'class' or 'social group'.

parental image, but of the cultural norms of a given society, having regard to all the essential cultural elements.

It is to be noted, in this connection, that the pliability of individual development permits everyone to *assimilate any cultural feature* provided he feels motivated and stimulated by the prevailing environment.

The concept of the 'basic personality' has been criticized. Although nobody denies the interdependence of the personality formation and cultural norms, individual differences exist in every culture. Theories which take account only of social factor or determinants whether in terms of 'social roles' or of the notion of 'class-linked status personality' (Linton, 1945) do not take into consideration the specific individual development.

If, as can be shown, the formation of unconscious structures, of psychic agencies (the ego, the superego, the ego-ideal), or of dynamic processes (motivation, attitudes, behaviour patterns) ought to be examined in the framework of specific cultural conditions, it is nevertheless true that social pressures do exert themselves on a subject already patterned by the maturational processes and during the establishment of relations between his own self and the external world. It is hard to accept the idea of cultural influence at birth, when the infant is unable to distinguish self from nonself, unless we mean by 'cultural influence' the dyadic relation with the mother, in which case the originality of the 'culturalist' position would have to give way to other considerations.

It is clear that this position is diametrically opposed to that of the 'constitutionalists':

Henceforth the idea is established that man has no nature, only a history, or rather that he *is* history. This existentialist proposition now seems to be a truth proclaimed in all the main currents of contemporary thought. There are the behaviourists who deny the hereditary nature of mental traits, talents or capacities; the Marxists who accept that man at birth is the most helpless of all creatures—a condition of his subsequent progress; the psychoanalysts who assert that the idea of instincts developing by themselves does not correspond to any human reality. And finally, there are the culturalists who, taking their cue both from Marxism and from psychoanalysis, demolish any lingering doubts and reveal how much the individual owes to his environment in the building of the person (Malson, 1964).

2 *Reality and experience*

It is when we try to clarify the position of psychoanalysis *vis-à-vis* the concepts of 'constitution' and 'culture' that we begin to appreciate its true position. This becomes even more obvious when one considers the concept of personality where psychoanalysts have tried a new approach.

One definition, among many others, is indicative of the general viewpoint: 'Personality is the dynamic organization within the individual of those psycho-physiological systems which determine his adjustment to his environment' (Allport, 1937). Most definitions stress either the mechanisms of adaptation or the reaction to to the 'social' setting in which a given person lives and functions, whether they refer to 'character' structure, to 'ego-functions', etc. Psychoanalysts refer rather to *character* than to personality. They thus stress certain permanencies of pattern, which are represented by distinctive traits or typical ways of conducting oneself (Blos, 1968). Character thus is related to specific levels of drive development, to the defensive aspect of the ego, to fate of object libido and also to the influence of environment. 'These determinants are not mutually exclusive; on the contrary they appear in various admixtures and combinations. . . . Character originates in conflict.' Thus the concept of personality pinpoints inter-reaction of emotional factors and environment.

On the other hand, all theories, as we have said, try to evaluate the role of environment in personality formation: this is precisely where psychoanalysts disagree with the 'environmentalists'. Psychoanalysis considers that the environment only performs its function by providing the individual with a 'setting' or an 'opportunity' for experiencing and living. It may intervene to some extent, but the subject's life-history is not simply a reflection of socio-cultural conditions imposed upon him: the true determinants of object-relations and the expression of his desires are mainly fashioned by the inner psychic conflict and by the unconscious phantasies already active at an early age.

The 'historical' events of the subject's life can only gain a meaning through the prism of individual experience. Experience can *only* be concrete, 'first person singular', and this not only because of constitutional predisposition but because of the extreme variability of the circumstances, the permutations of which would make a 'basic personality' seem futile. It is not any *particular* difficulty, trauma or event which sets the seal on the person's future, but it takes its place in the total emotional context. It is this total *experience* which confers upon a particular incident the traumatic value which will set its mark on it in the subject's life, when any other incident (or even a similar one but under different circumstances) might have had an entirely different meaning.

The universal character of certain situations which occur in childhood, such as weaning, sibling rivalry, the Oedipus complex, make them potentially pathogenic and a source of frustration as they impose a brake on instinctual drives, and may result in changing the goal or the object of the instinctual drive. These situations, however, acquire a specific meaning—an inner conflict, a trauma—and become the source of subsequent neurotic problems only as a result of the particular emotional context in which they occur.

In this connection, the distinction between *reality* and *experience* must be emphasized. Attempts to confine reality to the level of external events in order to explain the child's adjustment to his family and social milieu take no account of the significance such a 'reality' could hold for each child. Reality is certainly something that can be objectified but is it the reality with which we are concerned? Maternal behaviour, family structure, a particular event which might seem decisive in early childhood—all these can be described as objective facts. But the living experience of this reality, for the person involved in it, is not reducible to statistical data which ignore the way the event was perceived and lived through in the actual situation.[1]

The originality of psychoanalysis lies in its approach to the structure and aetiology of neurosis from the point of view of *inner psychic conflict*. This is not conflict in the classical psychological sense, where the child finds itself in difficulties because of some discrepancy between his instinctual drives or needs and their relation to reality. In psychoanalysis, *intrapsychic conflict* does indeed draw its content from these situations but it does not become a conflict until the external conditions are internalized by the child, that is, when the conflicting element—instinctual drives versus environment—are represented in terms of *psychic reality*: solution of such psychic conflicts depends entirely on internal restructuring of the personality, and not on adjustment to external circumstances. The solution of these internalized conflicts leads to the shaping of behaviour patterns and a mode of reactivity which

[1] A number of studies have attempted to describe and evaluate the 'reality' of maternal behaviour, particularly the nursing situation. For instance the work of S. Brody, *Patterns of Mothering* (1956), is particularly instructive in the minutiae of its observations. But whatever the reality of the maternal behaviour, it does not really explain, or even show, the way object-relations are established.

are specific for any given personality. These behaviour patterns condition subsequent relations with the external world as well as the inner subjective reactions to the various situations according to a model formed in infancy.

Once these infantile conflicts are overcome, the child will be able to confront new situations with sufficient maturity. If the conflicts remain unresolved the child will remain fixated in a repetitive pattern of behaviour (repetition-compulsion) in an effort to solve his initial conflicts, an effort forever doomed to fail because all the energy necessary to tackle new tasks will be absorbed in sterile repetition.[1]

In its beginnings, psychoanalysis was concerned to recognize the persistence of these infantile conflicts in the adult. Later it bent all its efforts to find evidence for these conflicts in the child itself, *in statu nascendi*. The specific importance of child analysis lies in the fact that, at the time, the processes of psychological and functional maturation are actually taking place, and the effective confrontation of the child with its environment is at its most intense, so that the expression of conflicts may be captured, as it were, *live*, both in their effects (still close to their origins, and not deviated from their initial aim) as well as through the course of their attempted resolution.

---

[1] Zeigarnik (1927) has shown that unfinished tasks are remembered while tasks which have been completed are forgotten. This is also true of unconscious processes (see S. Freud, 1920b).

3   **Basic concepts**

Rather than offer a systematic presentation of psychoanalytic theory, I have preferred to give an outline of certain basic principles, which seems more suitable for bringing out the process of psychoanalytic thinking and the various problems it raises in its application to the child.[1]

I. Psychic trauma

The discovery of psychic trauma dates back to Freud's earliest works on hysterical paralysis. In their article on the formation of hysterical symptoms,[2] Freud and Breuer wrote in 1893 that

> in the great majority of cases, it is not possible to establish the point of origin by a simple interrogating of the patient, however thoroughly it may be carried out. This is in part because what is in question is often some experience which the patient dislikes discussing; but principally because he is genuinely unable to recollect it and often has no suspicion of the causal connection between the precipitating event and the pathological phenomenon.

It is the recollection of this traumatic event which was, at the outset, the aim of Freud's therapeutic efforts. This recall became possible thanks to the state of hypnosis into which the patient was plunged. But Freud soon abandoned hypnosis and replaced it by the 'free association' produced by the patient in his waking state.

The psychoanalytic technique was born and aimed at retrieving memories forgotten or unrecognized by the patient because they had been repressed and thus became unconscious. From this very first communication emerged those concepts of the unconscious, of repression and of psychic trauma which were to serve as a basis in the elaboration of a model for mental functioning.

Psychic trauma was first of all looked upon by Freud as an event barely preceding the appearance of the symptom. He soon recognized, however, that the traumatic character was not to be linked

---

[1] A comprehensive survey of psychoanalytic theory can be found elsewhere. For a well-organized presentation, one should read Robert Waelder's *Basic Theory o Ps ychoanalysis* (1960). An excellent historical introduction is offered by Marthe Robert's *The Psychoanalytic Revolution* (1964). Freud himself has tried to give an account of his work in his *Introductory Lectures on Psychoanalysis* (1916–17) and in *An Outline of Psychoanalysis* (1938). In addition, Ernest Jones's monumental *The Life and Work of Sigmund Freud* (1953–7) follows the progress of psychoanalysis as it develops throughout Freud's life and experience. (Also, in an abridged version edited by Lionel Trilling and Steven Marcus, 1962).
[2] J. Breuer and S. Freud, *Studies on Hysteria* (1895), Standard Edition, 2, p. 3.

too closely to the event as such but was in fact the reliving of a painful memory of an experience traceable to childhood. From this moment, Freud always insisted that the link between psychic trauma and the symptom to which it gave rise could not be a simple relation between the event and the consequences it involved but was, on the contrary, a symbolization of the affect which had accompanied the initial traumatic effect. In this case, the causal relation could only be elucidated by an analysis of the material yielded by free association which, by establishing a relation between the various chains of thoughts and apparently unrelated material, enables the barrier to recall (censorship) to be lifted and permits a release from repression. For a time, Freud directed his efforts to the recall of memories linked with traumas and to the discharge of emotions attached to the repressed material. The 'abreaction' thus produced by the awakening to consciousness of these memories was at that time considered to be the crucial moment of the treatment whether or not the patient understood their symbolic significance: this procedure was called the 'cathartic method'.

It was on the nature of this traumatic event that Freud brought his investigation to bear. In the early days, Freud[1] referred to trauma as to real events which actually took place: the memories and accounts given by the patient were assumed to refer to scenes dating back to early childhood at the age of three or four, and to evoke a passive sexual experience in which the child had been involved at the instigation of an adult. The consistency with which such memories were recounted could have led to the conclusion that the origin of the neuroses must be really linked to some actual event and that the child had retained an indelible, though unconscious, record of it in his mind. The painful, even unbearable, character of such a memory had caused it to be repressed.

But Freud had perforce to recognize that the account of these so-called memories was, in most cases, nothing other than the expression of a wish—a phantasy and not a reality. Since the 'seduction' was invariably, in the patient's account, the act of an adult of the opposite sex, it was a logical next step to recognize in this the wish-fulfilment of the oedipal wishes, behind which the problems posed by infantile sexuality could be traced.

It thus becomes necessary to establish the place of the psychic trauma in relation to the child's actual experience. The child's life may indeed be punctuated by more or less dramatic events which leave their imprint as repressed, and hence forgotten, memories. Even seemingly minor events may produce a cumulative effect

[1] S. Freud, *The Aetiology of Hysteria* (1896).

(Masud R. Khan, 1963). One such life may have been more 'disturbed' than another, and actual events may play a considerable part in the way a child lives through his early years, that is, in the establishing of his object-relations: for instance, the death of a parent, a disruptive family setting or a divorce, the constant presence of a psychopathic or alcoholic relative, may be experienced dramatically by the child. But it should be noted that certain circumstances, less dramatic in their expression, may leave their mark on the child in a much more definitive way, as for example, a father inadequate to ensure a paternal identification, or a mother's ostensible over-protection which reveals her unconscious rejection of the child.

Is this tantamount to saying that neurosis is the consequence of real disturbance which the child has lived through in his early years? It would be foolish to deny this possibility. But the significance of the psychic trauma can be interpreted in various ways.

Birth, as a fundamental separation from the maternal womb; weaning, as a stage on the way from complete helplessness to the first rung of independence; the Oedipus complex, a renunciation of the object of the first wish; castration anxiety, as a threat to body integrity and the loss of phallic potency—all these are crucial moments in the development of the personality. But because subsequent events will revive the affect linked to these traumas which have created unresolved and repressed psychic conflicts, they will *in later life* take on a pathogenic role.

Furthermore, the concept of a traumatic *life experience* is to be preferred to that of an actual traumatic event. This experience is not so much the result of a trauma as a reflection of a mode of parent-child relation which confers upon these various situations with which the child is confronted their traumatic impact. An over-protective mother, an emotionally distant father, the latent sado-masochistic relations of a parental couple can, in many respects, be much more damaging than those traumatic events which are rather glibly indicated to account for neuroses. The child's object-relations are more readily disturbed by an inadequate or disruptive family setting which distorts the parent-child relationship, and thus introduces the neurotic elements.

These situations, ringed by an imaginary halo, and invested with the symbolic value which gave them a meaning, are the components of what in later life *a posteriori* will assume the significance of a trauma.

Thus, starting with the concept of the trauma, the importance of the entirety of infantile experience was demonstrated. Trauma was at first considered by Freud as an environmental factor intruding on the ego. But psychic trauma can no longer be defined in terms of events but as an unavoidable part of any life-experience. It must be envisaged in terms of Freud's theory of anxiety. The essence of a traumatic situation can be considered as an experience of helplessness of the mental apparatus in dealing with the flood of large amounts of stimuli that the ego is unable to use or to deal with. The breach in the otherwise efficacious defensive barrier depends less on the real events than on the affective 'equipment' of any given individual, i.e. his tolerance to stress and frustration and the possibilities to set in motion his defence mechanisms.

II. The psychic conflict and the concept of neurosis

In order to elucidate the conception of neurosis, an essentially dynamic notion, it is necessary to clarify its origins. At the core of every neurotic formation is to be found what Freud called the intrapsychic conflict.

This is a conflict between the libidinal drives and the defence functions of the ego. If such a conflict cannot find its resolution through a compromise between the means which gratify the instinctual drive and the contingent demands of the environment antagonistic to, or restrictive of, its possibilities, the drive will be repressed, i.e. become unconscious, while still retaining its intensity. It will emerge in disguised form as a symptom—what Freud called *the return of the repressed*. Psychic conflict, repression, return of the repressed—these are the three successive terms of the formation of the neurotic symptom.

In the sense used by psychoanalysts, the psychic conflict is not just a question of the individual 'in conflict' with his environment. Reference to the theories of adaptation (Selye) and to the concept of stress will help to make this clear. A pathological condition can be viewed in terms of a disharmony between the organism and the environment: the individual is subjected to stress, a tension due to the pressure of external circumstances exerted on the organism's inadequate defences which are thus overwhelmed. Looked at in this way, the neurosis would be the result of non-adaptation, a reaction on the part of the subject to external factors.

A stress of this kind, however, does not, properly speaking, cause neurosis. The difficulties caused by environmental stress give rise to reactive disorders (or situation neurosis), that is, to symptoms which disappear when these obstacles are removed.

Psychoanalysts regard this conflict as being born within the subject himself who is confronted by the surrounding milieu. Neurosis is not the simple result of the difficulties he encounters: *for neurosis to arise conflict must be internalized*, that is, it must not be perceived as being caused by external circumstances alone. This is what the psychoanalysts call *an intrapsychic conflict*. The real difficulties met by the subject must be, as it were, metabolized; they must undergo a transformation in order to become pathogenic factors. It is to the extent that these difficulties are internalized or introjected that they become operative as factors of psychic conflict.

It is noteworthy that the intra-psychic conflict is in some way in opposition to the strain caused by actual difficulties. Clinically, it is an easy matter to establish that in difficult circumstances— inevitable or irrevocable—a person is, in fact, generally able to cope. It is in those conditions where the subject has to make a choice, or himself abandon certain aspirations or gratifications, that the inner conflict is most marked and symptoms or neurotic behaviour make their appearance.

Psychic conflict is thus defined as a confrontation of instinctual drives with ego-demands. This conflict, governed both by inner needs and the imaginary demands of its internalized love objects, is the basis of the psychoanalytical conception of neurosis.

Attempts have been made to define the nature of this conflict which is recognized as having two characteristics:

(a)   Analytical case-material has shown that the psychic con- flict is closely related to sexuality.[1] This sexual origin of neurosis is explained by the fact that sexual drives are to be distinguished from other instinctual drives by certain fundamental features. The sexual drive in fact seems to counter the subject's adjustment to external conditions since it does not involve functions essential to the self-preservation. Unlike hunger or thirst, sexual drives are capable of receiving auto-erotic gratification and can even, momen- tarily, be satisfied in a hallucinatory fashion (Freud, 1905). Thus sexual drives escape the need to adapt to the environment, and this is what marks them off from any need geared to self-preservation such as, for instance, hunger, for which obviously no auto-gratifi- cation is possible and where hallucinatory wish-fulfilment cannot replace external objects indispensable to the satisfaction of the

---

[1] The notion of *sexuality* has been and remains the least understood part of analytic theory. The usual sense of the word only partly covers the psychoanalytical meaning. In its wider sense used by the analysts, sexuality embraces the whole sphere of libidinal satisfaction.

D

need. The *object of the sexual drive* appears in quite a special position as compared with other objects.

(b) This discovery opened up the possibility of linking the neurotic states of adults with an *infantile neurosis*, as described by Freud in the *Three Essays on the Theory of Sexuality* (1905).[1]

Freud refers to the Oedipus complex and castration anxiety when he talks of the *nodal conflict* which structures neurosis and which he was able to ascertain clinically in the case of Little Hans. This phobia in a five-year-old, analysed by Freud about 1906 (and published in 1909), enabled him to check his theories of infantile sexuality *in statu nascendi*, which he had previously postulated by reconstructing childhood experiences in the light of material gathered in the course of his analysis of adults.

The resolution of this 'nodal' conflict (the Oedipus complex), whether spontaneously or through therapy, will largely condition the child's future. If this conflict cannot be overcome, and the infantile neurosis cannot be solved, it will serve as a starting point for any neurotic formations in later life. The non-resolution of this conflict may be due to several causes. There may be conflicts of such intensity as not to be susceptible to successful repression, thereby remaining active and manifesting themselves in the form of anxiety or neurotic symptoms. Alternatively, the repression may be effective for a time, the unresolved conflict remaining latent, but in certain conditions it may be overwhelmed by mental stress, leading to the manifestation of neurotic symptoms.

What, in this latter case, is often attributed to 'stress' is, in fact, the reactivation of earlier, unresolved conflicts which have remained latent for as long as the subject had sufficient energy to maintain the repression.

Because of the child's psychological immaturity, all these conflicts are experienced with great intensity. The child has little means at his disposal to alter the conditions in which he lives and so he cannot act upon the environment so as to make it conform to his wishes. On the other hand, because of the relative unorganized character of his cognitive functions and sensori-motor aptitudes, the child finds it hard to tolerate the real frustrations imposed by the outer world. These two conditions explain why the child is ill-equipped to cope with the contradictions arising from the opposition between his instinctual drives and the demand of psychic 'reality'.

[1] The concept of the 'sexual' origin of neurosis initiated the most virulent resistance to psychoanalysis which was accused of being a pansexualist theory; even today this accounts to a large extent for the resistance to be found towards the acceptance of analytic concepts.

Freud has noticed that the intensity of childhood experiences should not be evaluated according to adult standards:

The neuroses are, as we know, disorders of the ego; and it is not to be wondered at if the ego, so long as it is feeble, immature and incapable of resistance, fails to deal with tasks which it could cope with later on with utmost ease. In these circumstances, instinctual demands from within, no less than excitations from the external world, operate as 'traumas', particularly if they are met half-way by certain innate dispositions. . . . The damage inflicted on the ego by its first experiences gives us the appearance of being disproportionately great, but we have only to take as an analogy the differences in the results produced by the prick of a needle into a mass of cells in the act of cell-division and into the fully grown animal which eventually develops out of them. No human individual is spared such traumatic experiences; none escapes the repression to which they give rise.

Intrapsychic conflict is, according to Anna Freud, a normal product of development and arises as soon as ego and superego are sufficiently separated from the id and from each other. When those conflicts are not dealt with by the child's ego assisted by parental support, analytic therapy may help to reduce anxiety, dissolve defences and open up outlets for instinctual drives.

III. The concept of the unconscious

Psychoanalysis started with Freud's seminal discovery of unconscious mental processes; he described them as a constant feature of all psychic functioning. He called *'unconscious'* all mental processes whose existence is demonstrated to us by their manifestations (dreams, parapraxes) but of which we otherwise know nothing, although they take place within us. This definition was based on the existence of mental phenomena of which the subject is not consciously aware but which are revealed either by the analysis of dreams, or by the method of free associations. Thus a latent meaning can be discovered behind any manifest content of a dream, of a behaviour or of a symptom—a meaning that remains otherwise unknown.

In introducing the idea of the unconscious, Freud built up 'depth psychology'. The conscious phenomena represent only the most superficial part of mental life; the unconscious is the major part; it motivates and determines normal behaviour as well as neurotic symptoms. This was Freud's great discovery, made during the course of his work on hysteria (1893–5), when he was able to show that a patient's symptoms are but the reflexion of his unconscious mental processes, inaccessible to him under normal conditions and regardless of his expressed wish to be cured. The morbid condition, that is, the symptom, is maintained by *unconscious motivation* since this expressed the subject's unconscious wishes. A similar unconscious logic is the basis of dreams: the account which the patient gives of the *manifest* and seemingly absurd content can be interpreted by connecting the various free associations which occur to the dreamer while recounting his dream and thus a *latent* content appears which the manifest content has tried to hide from consciousness. This latent content is the expression of a wish kept concealed by the subject's defences.

The same would apply to behaviour patterns behind which analysis can reveal a latent significance often in contradiction to expressed intentions and which can lead to an explanation of neurotic symptoms as well as the unconscious motivation underlying our everyday behaviour. In this way, unbeknown to the conscious mind, and in disguised form, the unconscious meaning comes through in dreams, in acts of forgetfulness, in slips of the tongue and in omissions which Freud described under the general name of parapraxes in his *Psychopathology of Everyday Life* (1901).

Freud solved the dilemma between determinism and free will by showing how decisions which appear to be entirely spontaneous are nevertheless determined by unconscious motives. These facts made it possible to recognize how psychoanalysis could be applied to the 'normal' mental functioning and that it was not restricted to the 'neurotic mind'. The influence of the unconscious processes and their interference with conscious functioning was thus established: this led to the basic assumption of psychical determinism.

From the dynamic point of view, therefore, there are fundamental differences between conscious and unconscious mental functioning. Freud accordingly attempted to present a theoretical model of the psychic apparatus by dividing it into systems, the Conscious (Cs) and the Unconscious (Ucs). This *first topography* recognizes a mode of functioning peculiar to each of the systems.[1]

---

[1] Described by Freud in Chapter VII of *The Interpretation of Dreams* (1900). The first topographical model was followed by a second one, which introduces into mental functioning the play of the three agencies: the Id, the Ego and the Superego (see S. Freud, *The Ego and the Id*, 1923a).

In its passage from the unconscious to the conscious, the mental representation does not change its location but a displacement of energy is involved. According to whether the representation is invested with this energy or not, it passes from one state to the other. This division into two systems will give us a better understanding of the part played by repression.

IV. Repression

The concept of repression is closely linked to that of the unconscious. Certain instinctual drives and mental representations collide with resistances which prevent them from becoming conscious. Freud gave the name *repression* to the process which prevents certain emotions and their mental representation from becoming conscious.

Repression must, therefore, come into play whenever an instinctual gratification, *as a result of the attendant circumstances*, meets with an unpleasure which supersedes the pleasure of gratification, in other words, when this gratification conflicts with a prohibition coming from the ego.

Freud (1915b) emphasized that repression is concerned with the mental representation of the instinctual drive. These representations, inaccessible to the ego, are rejected from the conscious: this process is called by Freud *primal repression*. Subsequently, however, every experience, every emotion and idea linked with this mental representation will also be repressed. In this way, emotions and ideas coming from elsewhere but associated with this repressed drive-representative will be expelled from consciousness by a process called *secondary repression*. This is the repression that the analyst has to deal with in his practice.

> Repression does not hinder the instinctual representation from continuing to exist in the unconscious, from organising itself further, putting out derivatives and establishing connections. Repression in fact interferes only with the relation of the instinctual representation to *one* psychical system, namely, that of the conscious.[1]

The essential role of repression is not to suppress the representation resulting from the drive but to keep it unconscious. Furthermore, repression can have a bearing on certain affective states. Thus Freud speaks of emotion whose representation is unconscious:

[1] S. Freud, *Repression* (1915), Standard Edition, 14, p. 149.

An instinct can never become an object of consciousness—only the idea that represents the instinct can. Even in the unconscious, moreover, an instinct cannot be represented otherwise than by an idea. If the instinct does not attach itself to an idea or manifest itself as an affective state, we could know nothing about it. It is possible for an affective emotion to be perceived but misconstrued. Owing to the repression of its proper representative it has been forced to become connected with another idea and is now regarded by consciousness as the manifestation of that idea.[1]

It is important to emphasize that the unconscious character of mental representations and affective states in no way diminishes their psychic effectiveness and that they remain active without being conscious, perceived without being identified. Although repression may succeed in preventing the emotion to manifest itself through 'feelings', thus compelling it to remain unconscious, it does not however suppress its psychic efficiency.

Initially, an event creates an instinctual demand which asks to be satisfied. This satisfaction is refused by the ego either because of the magnitude of the demand or because it recognizes the demand as a potential danger. Faced with such a demand, the ego seeks to avoid it or, through repression, to expel it from consciousness. This, however, is an imperfect solution. If the drive has retained its energy or if it has been revived by a recent incident, it becomes active once more. Since repression has barred its way to normal satisfaction it seeks to find a substitute satisfaction which manifests itself as a symptom—and all this without the acknowledgment of the ego, but also without its understanding. All the phenomena of symptom formation may justly be described as the *return of the repressed* which is characterized, however, by the distortion to which the returning material has been subjected as compared with the original.[2]

There is a close relation between the concepts of the unconscious and of repression—a dynamic term which expresses the aspiration of all mental affects to become conscious but which have come up against an antagonistic force, an unconscious resistance.

The conscious and the unconscious are separated by a barrier which Freud called censorship. Functionally, this is not a mere obstacle but an active force which thrusts back into the unconscious the painful affects which the subject finds intolerable, in the same

[1] S. Freud, *The Unconscious* (1915c), Standard Edition, 14, pp. 177–8.
[2] S. Freud, *Moses and Monotheism* (1939).

way as it bars certain affects already repressed from coming into consciousness, thus maintaining the state of repression.

The mobile character of repression has already been emphasized. It is not to be regarded as a process which indeed has a lasting or definitive effect.

A persistent expenditure of force is indispensable to maintain the repression and if this were to cease, the success of the repression would be jeopardized so that a fresh act of repression would be necessary. We may suppose that the repressed exercises a continuous pressure in the direction of the conscious, so that this pressure must be balanced by an increasing counter-pressure. Thus the maintenance of the repression involves an uninterrupted expenditure of force. We recall the fact that the motive and purpose of repression is nothing else than the avoidance of unpleasure.[1]

From the point of view of the psychic economy, the lifting of this repression represents a considerable gain in energy which can then be used for other psychic functions.

V. Infantile amnesia

Linked to the concepts of the unconscious and of repression is that of infantile amnesia which veils for most people the first years of childhood. The unconscious content is inaccessible but active, and represents the basis of subsequent behaviour in the child and the adult. Exploration of a subject's past is fraught with considerable difficulty. When one questions a child about its early years one soon comes to a halt for want of material. An older person subjected to the same questioning will give a more or less coherent account starting from the fourth or fifth year of life, but he too is often not capable of reporting the events of early childhood in any organized way. The only things to emerge will be a few disconnected images, isolated from their context and relating to places where he lived or to some apparently trivial happening. One would be inclined to think that this paucity of information was due to some reluctance in front of a third party but the experience of personal introspection shows the same paucity of material even when the subject does not deliberately avoid the recall of unpleasant or distressing events.

This dearth of early childhood memories always struck Freud as

[1] S. Freud, *Repression* (1915b), Standard Edition, 14, p. 151.

somewhat paradoxical. Everything seemed to indicate that the child during those years has a rational behaviour and is participating in social activities, expresses pain or pleasure, utters remarks which prove that he possesses understanding and a budding power of judgment. Still the child knows nothing of all this when he becomes older. This blurring of memories could only be attributed to the fact that the child goes through painful moments of conflict in the very earliest period of life. Classical psychology attributes this difficulty in retaining memories either to the immaturity of the mnemic function or to the effects of fatigue or hazard.

Analytical practice has since shown that forgetting, like all parapraxis (inadequacies of psychic functioning), is not fortuitous but motivated by an underlying meaning which has been repressed.[1] Repression is also the basis of *infantile amnesia*. Thus, the psychic representatives of instinctual drives pass into the unconscious, either because fulfilment of those drives is forbidden to the child, or because the anxiety it would involve cannot be tolerated. This amnesia accordingly embraces all the component elements of early psychic conflict which are too painful to be faced or too difficult to be resolved because of the child's affective immaturity. Repression enables, not only the conflict itself, but all memories, even those which are remotely associated with it as well, to be removed from consciousness. Thus pleasant and painful memories alike disappear.[2] Entire stretches of the child's life succumb to amnesia, leaving only some incomprehensible 'screen-memories' devoid of all affect.[3] Only associative analysis of these screen-memories could reconstruct the past which they are trying to hide.

Are these memories the equivalent of true mnemic traces? Some authors are of the opinion that the impact of the earliest events in life, those occurring at the pre-verbal stage, can only engender an experience which could not be verbalized and which therefore could not become conscious in the sense of reflective consciousness. Such experience cannot therefore be repressed and, *a fortiori*, recalled. Nevertheless, analytical experience teaches us that the pre-verbal stage can certainly leave *unconscious traces* and these may have considerable influence. Kinaesthetic, proprioceptive, visual, auditory and olfactory sensations do contribute to the

---

[1] S. Freud, *Psychopathology of Everyday Life* (1901).
[2] S. Freud, *Three Essays on the Theory of Sexuality* (1905).
[3] S. Freud, *Screen-memories* (1899). They are seemingly trivial childhood memories which are vividly remembered all through life; they often represent a condensation of various scenes and allude to conflictual elements of the child's early life. (*See also* Kris, 1956; Smirnoff, 1967.)

formation of a certain unconscious pattern of early experience. Among the most striking are the first experiences of breast-feeding to which the subject is linked by particular images: the *Gestalt* of the nursing mother as described by Spitz in the work 'The Primal Cavity' (1955), where visual memory, kinaesthetic sensation and proprioceptive traces are intimately mingled. The unconscious character of these traces is found in the Isakower phenomenon and in the white dream-screen described by Lewin,[1] both of which refer to unconscious traces of these early experiences.

VI. Pleasure principle and reality principle

To explain the functioning of the mental apparatus Freud formulated a certain number of principles.

The *pleasure principle* is the tendency of the mental apparatus to maintain the amount of excitation at as low or as constant a level as possible. A tendency towards excessive excitation induces behaviour which allows it to be reduced, so as to diminish the unpleasure which that involves and thus to seek satisfaction. When the psychic apparatus functions according to this principle, it tends to ensure immediate satisfaction by a reduction of tension.[2] The pleasure principle governs the behaviour of the very young infant, who seeks immediate gratification of his needs and instinctual drives and wards off any change tending towards a state of unbalance, and, hence, tension.

Thus the sensation of hunger in the newborn provokes a state of painful tension. The infant seeks to reduce this tension: the cries and motor manifestations are at first only a sign of this attempt and not a signal intended for the mother. The solution is ineffective but nevertheless tends to diminish the state of need. As far as the sexual drive is concerned (in the wider sense as understood by psychoanalysts), it is obvious that they obey the pleasure principle and that they maintain this function throughout their development.

[1] Isakower (1938) refers to hypnagogic experience in which the subject imagines soft, doughy masses moving towards his face, and he interprets this as a revival of the infant's breast-feeding experience. Lewin's (1946) description of the *dream-screen* postulates that the visual content of the dream is projected on to a 'screen'; this screen is interpreted 'as a symbol of the breast with which sleep is unconsciously equated, i.e. the screen represents the wish to sleep and the visual imagery represents the wishes disturbing sleep'. However, a somewhat different interpretation is given by Rycroft (1951).
[2] The pleasure principle is an idea borrowed by Freud from the German physiologist G. Fechner, who had described a *constancy principle*, the function of which is to spare the mental apparatus any change and to maintain the flow of excitation at as low a level as possible.

The pleasure principle is soon hindered by the intrusion of reality into the life of the subject. Reality is an obstacle to immediate satisfaction and the subject has to adjust to the situation—he has to abandon his search for gratification in the interest of a more adequate behaviour. The ego finds that it is essential to renounce immediate satisfaction, to postpone the feeling of pleasure, to put up with certain difficulties and in general to abandon certain pleasures. The ego, thus educated, has become reasonable; it no longer allows itself to be dominated by the pleasure principle but conforms to the *reality principle*, which, at bottom, also has pleasure as its goal but a pleasure which, though delayed or attenuated, has the advantage of offering that certainty obtained through contact with reality and conformity to its requirements.[1]

The reality principle thus seeks a means of gratification which is more effective and more favourable than that sought by the pleasure principle without, however, displacing it, and taking into account the limitations imposed. The qualities which characterize the *secondary processes* according to which the reality principle functions are effectiveness, judgment, choice and decision.

The idea of *primary process* rests on the disposition to confuse the mnemic image with the perception of the real object. Thus the primary process attempts to satisfy a libidinal drive by a hallucinatory wish fulfilment. This mode of functioning is to be found, for example, in the dream which seeks to fulfil a wish by evoking it in a dream. Certain gratifications may therefore be delayed. The same applies to 'magical or wishful thinking' which attempts to substitute a wish fulfilment for the real satisfaction. Since the primary process is incapable in the long run of satisfying a need or fulfilling a wish, it is finally replaced by the secondary process.

The primary process is controlled by a psychic agency (the id) which only recognizes a subjective reality where the only things that matter are the attainment of pleasure and the avoidance of unpleasure, and which seeks immediate gratification whether by dream, hallucination or wishful thinking. The *secondary process* marks the advent of a second psychic agency (the ego) and introduces the reality principle into the subject's economy. In the child's life, certain activities remain subordinate to the pleasure

[1] In an article written in 1911, 'Formulations on the Two Principles of Mental Functioning', Freud quotes Bernard Shaw to illustrate the final priority of the reality principle over the pleasure principle: 'To be capable of choosing the line of the greater advantage instead of yielding in the direction of least resistance.'

principle (primary process), such as, for example, games and day-dreams.

This secondary process is regulating the functioning of the ego which will restrain the urge towards immediate discharge through the use of conscious functions of adjustment to reality—attention, memory, judgment—and by substituting them for repression or denial. It could thus be said that the unconscious functions according to the pleasure principle and that the reality principle intervenes in order to make the expression of those tendencies compatible with the demands of the conscious ego.

VII. The ego and the id

When the search for immediate gratification collides with the limitations imposed by reality, a conflict appears between instinctual drives and a *regulating system* which seeks to contain them. A second topographical (structural) model is superimposed on the conscious-unconscious duality in which Freud distinguishes two psychic agencies: the ego and the id.

The id may be defined as the original form of the mental apparatus governed from birth by innate instincts which originate from the somatic organization and which find a first psychical expression in the id.[1] The functioning of the id observes the pleasure principle, that is to say, the id ignores space and time as well as causal or logical relations. The forces governing the id are conceived as striving to bring about satisfaction of the sexual and aggressive drives. In this second topographical system the id is essentially in the area of the unconscious; in addition to the instincts, it embraces everything which is the product of repression. From a dynamic point of view we may say that the function of the id is entirely outside consciousness and that it represents the raw material of subsequent differentiations.

The forces of the id have to come to terms with a system of motivation or action, the ego, which becomes differentiated in the mental apparatus by direct influence on the external world. Its

[1] The expression *das Es* (the id) was borrowed by Freud from Groddeck, who, in his book, *The Book of the It* (1923), defines *das Es* as the representative of the instinctive forces which imprint their own dynamic on the unconscious.
Although Groddeck's *It* and Freud's *id* have in common the idea of an impersonal force, they differ in that the id is a psychological concept, as part of the psychic apparatus, while the *It* is a *psychosomatic* concept: 'a power by which we are lived while we think we live. Just as the symptomatic activity of the It in hysteria and neurosis calls for psychoanalytical treatment, so does heart trouble and cancer' (see Rycroft, 1968).

functioning is regulated by the secondary process; its regulation is determined by the reality principle. In the description given by Freud,[1] the ego controls the voluntary motility and has a task of self-preservation; it perceives stimuli, records memories, adapts to excitations and sensations, avoids excessive tensions, processes the information which comes to it and seeks to modify the environment by making it more and more ready to respond to its need and satisfy its wishes.

The ego thus appears to be an agency mediating the relations of the subject with the outer world. It has also, however, to confront the inner drives by setting up control of instinctual demands. It has to decide in what conditions and at what moment gratification may be given; it must delay satisfaction till the most favourable moment, and it must even suppress completely a demand which may involve harmful consequences. The ego has the task of confronting both the demands of external reality and the drives coming from within: the ego thus has a synthesizing or problem-solving task.[2]

However, the ego cannot be reduced to a simple regulating system. Controlling, as it does, access to consciousness of perceptions, affects and drives, it plays a part in the resolution of psychic conflicts, that is, it determines the relation of the subject with itself. Federn speaks of the 'feelings of the ego' which represent the subject's sensations of himself in his bodily and affective experience and which is a subjective, permanent experience not connoted by the terms 'consciousness' or 'knowledge of self'.[3]

It would be a mistake to think that the division into conscious and unconscious coincides with the distinction between the ego

[1] S. Freud, *An Outline of Psychoanalysis* (1938).
[2] R. Waelder (1960) justly remarks that the ego has been described as *a problem-solving agent.* It is a teleological concept. The ego is being defined in relation to the goal (adaptation, learning, control, etc.) while disregarding the internal functioning of the system. Nowadays 'the reduction of teleological to casual explanations is brought about by describing goal-directed behaviour with the help of models which are equipped with feed-back mechanisms. . . . Information about outside events is continuously fed back into the apparatus and the apparatus is regulated on the basis of this information' (*see also* N. Wiener, 1954).
In psychoanalysis, teleological concepts are only used as a description, and are not meant to be explanatory. Thus notions like the 'strength' or the 'weakness' of the ego do not explain inability to tolerate frustration.
[3] Federn, 'Ego Feelings in Dreams' (1932), in *Ego Psychology and the Psychoses* (1952). He is perfectly justified, as is emphasized by R. Waelder (1960), in considering the ego both as a means of integration and resolution of conflict and as a system which explores the feelings between the different parts of the mental apparatus. From the clinical standpoint, however, it has not been shown that there are, in fact, either clinically of theoretically, two modes of functioning of one and the same system rather than two different systems.

and the id. For although everything taking place in the id in fact remains unconscious, the processes going on in the ego *may* become conscious but are not all, or necessarily, so. The elements of the id may be said to remain unconscious. Its content can only be confronted by reality through the intermediary of the ego. Elements coming from the id may penetrate the ego and remain there in a 'pre-conscious' state.[1] One of the functions of this unconscious part of the ego is to keep repressed certain unconscious elements deemed by it to be inadmissible.

VIII. Defence mechanisms

Freud recognized that the ego has to defend itself against external dangers from which it can escape either by flight, or, if it were possible, by modifying the circumstances to make them harmless or tolerable. But flight or modification of the environment are ineffective against dangers coming from the id, that is, those arising from instinctual drives. Only psychological mechanisms can inhibit or keep them at bay or modify them. When a wish is accompanied by the anticipation of a danger and hence arouses anxiety, the ego summons defences directed both against the desires themselves and against the painful emotions which they arouse.

Freud had already used the word *defence* in his early writings. He later replaced it by repression (*Verdrängung*). In his work, *Inhibition, Symptom and Anxiety* (1925a), Freud reserved for the word *repression* its specific sense and designated under the word *defence* (*Abwehr*) all those techniques employed by the ego to protect itself against instinctual demands. He thus acknowledged that repression is dominant in hysteria whereas other defences, like isolation and reaction formation, are peculiar to obsessional and similar neuroses. Only some of the defence mechanisms will be described here.

Repression was described by Freud as the most fundamental of these defence mechanisms. Its main role is to thrust painful affects back into the unconscious, to keep them there and, by so doing, to modify the conscious manifest content. Freud compares this

[1] Freud emphasized many times that his 'topography' which distinguishes 'deep' and 'superficial' levels is intended to express a spatial relationship only in order to make clear the way functions fit with one another. These images belong to the speculative superstructure of psychoanalysis and each part can, without damage or regret, be replaced by another as soon as its inadequacy becomes plain.

repression with the *censorship* of a text where the words which it is intended to suppress are either erased or replaced by others in order to distort the original meaning and make it acceptable to the conscious mind.

Denial is the counterpart of the hallucinatory wish-fulfilment by which the subject seeks an imaginary gratification. Faced with reality, this attempt at imaginary satisfaction is bound to fail and the ego resorts to a defence mechanism which tries to maintain as long as possible a *status quo* by denial of external reality. Everything happens *as though* this reality did not exist for the child, who has therefore no need to face it. With increasing development and a progressively growing grip of the reality principle, denial becomes more difficult. It does nevertheless maintain itself in the games and phantasies through which it finds expression. Denial has to be distinguished from *negation*: 'A repressed image or idea can clear a way for itself to consciousness on condition that it may be negated. Negation is a way of taking cognizance of the repressed; it is, in a way, the removal of the repression without signifying that the repressed content is accepted by the subject' (Freud, 1925b).[1]

The subject who, at the unconscious level, may admit a particular painful fact or intuition, cannot do so at the conscious level except in the form of negation. The example quoted by Freud of the sentence, 'You must think I want to say something unpleasant but I have no such intention', may be interpreted thus: 'I had in fact (*unconsciously*) thought of something annoying to say but I have not admitted it to consciousness'. Such a negation allows the child to keep himself in a state of ignorance, particularly as far as sexual reality is concerned—of which he may have an unconscious 'intuition' but cannot admit it consciously. By denying the sexual difference between male and female or the reality of parental sexual relations, the child may for a time avoid psychic conflict. The pesistence or even the extension of this denial may pervade all cognitive functions and culminate in a 'refusal' to learn or understand, in so far as intellectual acquisition may be equated with acknowledgment of certain facts or thoughts, and might thus endanger a certain instinctual balance.

By *projection* the subject may deal with the anxiety caused by feelings he is trying to deny if they seem unacceptable to the ego. In this way, he may project the hostility he feels: 'I hate him' may be converted to 'He hates me'. Accordingly, instead of being the

---

[1] S. Freud, *Negation* (1925b). See also the commentary on this by J. Lacan and Hyppolite in J. Lacan's *Ecrits* (1966).

one who hates, he becomes the object of his hatred projected on to the hated object. And then, freed from any guilt or anxiety, the subject may accept his own hostile feelings which will be felt only as a justified reaction to the feelings of hatred considered to be directed against himself. Thus, through projection, specific wishes are imagined to be located in some object external to oneself.

Melanie Klein has made extensive use of this defence mechanism as well as its indispensable complement, *introjection*, in which she recognizes the means by which the child is capable of operating the successive modifications of its libidinal economy.[1] Projection and introjection of parental images are expressed in phantasies concerning feelings of love and hate, fears and libidinal demands, possessive and destructive drives, and are directed towards the object of their phantasy relations. One's own aggressiveness may thus be masked behind a fear of the imagined aggressiveness of another. As defence mechanisms, projection and introjection are of particular importance in the child because of its situation *vis-à-vis* the outer world. At a stage when the distinction between self and non-self does not allow a clear differentiation between what is properly the child's and what is external to him, the confusion of feelings is particularly easy.

Furthermore, Melanie Klein assigns to projection and introjection an essential role in ego formation and the structuring of the limits of the ego, which gradually takes shape as it grows out of phantasies of incorporation and destruction. Thus certain effects linked to external images are introjected into the child's body image and others are projected and attributed to objects of the outer world. This influences the building up of affective experience and shapes the child's relations with the outer world from its earliest months—a world, as it were, split into 'good' and 'bad' objects. Projection and introjection, although they still ward off primitive anxiety, participate, according to Melanie Klein, in the 'normal' process of establishing object relations.

Reaction formation is a defence by which an unacceptable tendency is controlled by exaggerating the opposing tendency. Thus a behaviour pattern dictated by an earlier drive may be replaced by opposing forms of behaviour. Compulsive behaviour may thus replace destructive drives: meticulous cleanliness may take the place of coprophilic tendencies; disgust may displace forbidden sexual drives; and lack of interest may disguise scopophilic urges.

[1] Paula Heimann, 'Certain Functions of Introjection and Projection in Early Infancy', in M. Klein *et al.*, *Developments in Psychoanalysis* (1952).

Undoing is another mechanism by which a subject 'pretends' that prior thought or action has not occurred (Rycroft, 1968). It aims at 'blowing away' not merely the consequences of some event but the event itself. From this standpoint, certain compulsions such as tics or certain obsessional rituals, seek to efface symbolically in the present, an earlier thought or desire (Freud, 1925a).

The invasion of the child's mind with a *constant flood of phantasies* has been considered as a pathological defence of the ego (Lebovici, 1950). It is characterized by the large number of phantasies which break out spontaneously, though the child shows no particular anxiety. The presence of a large number of pregenital, oral-sadistic and anal-sadistic phantasies may be indicative of a pre-psychotic state.

Certain characteristics are common to all defence mechanisms (Waelder, 1960):
(a)   They tend to withdraw consciousness from all affects which are painful or difficult to satisfy.
(b)   Out of a considerable array of defence mechanisms every individual uses but a very few, which he automatically applies in inner danger.
(c)   Defence mechanisms will bring about substitute gratifications not intended as their original goal, but, in the form of neurotic symptoms, they replace a forbidden or impossible gratification.

IX. Fixation and regression

The idea of developmental phases[1] has dynamic consequences for psychoanalytic theory. If, for example, a particular event or experience has left its mark too vividly in one phase, thereby inhibiting the passage to the next phase, or making it too difficult, the result will be fixation at a certain level. A fixation may focus both on the choice of the libidinal object and on the mode of gratification or defences employed for averting anxiety. In normal development no phase is entirely left behind without bequeathing to the next characteristics which give it its particular quality. The subject may regress to a previous phase when he is confronted by unmanageable obstacles, and what is left over, as it were, from the previous phase may be of decisive importance in this connection.

To illustrate this notion of fixation and affective residues, Freud used the metaphor of migration:[2]

[1] See Chapters four and five.
[2] S. Freud, *Introductory Lectures* (1916–17), Standard Edition, 14, p. 341.

Consider that if a people which is in a movement has left strong detachments behind at the stopping-places of its migration, it is likely that the more advanced parties will be inclined to retreat to these stopping-places if they have been defeated or have come up against a superior enemy. But they will also be in a greater danger of being defeated the more of their number they have left behind on their migration.

Certain factors favour this fixation and predispose to regression. Among these are:

(a)   The magnitude of excessive gratification at a given phase, investing it with a special energy which makes it difficult to abandon this kind of gratification.

(b)   Obstacles, encountered during the resolution of conflicts of the next phase, will largely condition the intensity of frustration and favour a return to earlier modes of gratification.

X. The superego

The superego, conceived by Freud when he formulated his second topography, is presented as a differentiated portion of the ego. The superego corresponds to the repressive forces which the subject has met in the course of development and which have stood in the way of unconditional gratification of his instinctual drives. But the principal property of these forces, initially outside the subject, is that they are internalized and are accordingly no longer perceived as exterior impositions but felt as an inner force.

The ego, before putting to work the instinctual satisfactions demanded by the id, has to take into account not merely the dangers of the external world but also the objections of the superego, and it will have all the more grounds for abstaining from satisfying the instincts. But whereas instinctual renunciation, when it is for external reasons, is *only* unpleasurable, when it is for internal reason, in obedience to the superego it has a different economic effect. In addition to the inevitable unpleasurable consequences, it also brings the ego a yield of pleasure—substitutive satisfaction, as it were. The ego feels elevated; it is proud of the instinctual renunciation, as though it were a valuable achievement.[1]

---

[1] S. Freud, *Moses and Monotheism* (1939), Standard Edition, 23, p. 116.

E

The superego is thus an internalized agency and functions independently of the outer world and is in the position of producing new intrapsychic conflicts either by opposing the demand for instinctual gratifications coming from the id or by opposing the defences which the ego puts up against these demands.

One may recognize in the superego the successor and representative of the parents who in the first years of life have imposed their views on the child. The superego may continue to exert the same control by keeping the ego under its thumb, as it were, and keeping up a constant pressure upon it. It nevertheless needs to be emphasized, as Freud did (1932), that the principles by which parents bring up their children conform to the prescriptions of their own superego. The child's superego is not formed on the model of its parents' image but on the image of the *parental superego*.

The superego may be said to be the heir to the oedipal conflict in the sense that around this conflict the repressive forces of a *third person*, representing the obstacle, the prohibition, standing between the subject's wishes and the object of his desire, appear for the first time. The father becomes the natural support of this symbolic prohibition of the oedipal wish and hence the support of every moral pressure whose original prohibition any 'commandment' takes as model.

Through identification with the father—and, by extension, with every idealized parental image—law and authority, which he represents, become internalized. The constitution of the superego and its mode of functioning will largely depend on the way the oedipal conflict is resolved. In the course of evolution the superego of the subject must, according to Freud, have become 'sufficiently impersonal'; but in neurosis this superego retains the original character of the inexorable severity of the paternal imago.

Thus it is possible to consider the superego as a topographical system whose activity appears in conflict with the ego in forms of emotion 'which are linked to the moral consciousness, mainly feelings of guilt' (Lagache, 1955).[1] These conflicts are found in depressive forms of psychosis, in the form of self-criticism or self-deprecation, and also in self-denial of libidinal gratification, all of which make the subject's life unbearable by the anxiety they arouse. This morbid feeling of guilt, however, may also form part

[1] In order to avoid a major confusion it must be stated that the *superego* differs from the concept of *conscience* in that: (a) it belongs to a different frame of reference, i.e. metapsychology, not ethics; (b) it includes unconscious elements; and (c) injunctions and inhibitions emanating from it derive from the subject's past and may be in conflict with his present values (Rycroft, 1968).

of character structures marked by masochism which shows itself in neurotic failures or in self-punishing behaviour.

Although it has always been classically linked with the resolution of the oedipal conflict, the superego is not exclusively formed from the introjection of feeling arising out of this conflict. Some authors, Melanie Klein for example, consider the superego to be formed much earlier, not in the structured form of a moral consciousness but as the unconscious and distorted phantasy of the introjected parental image. Melanie Klein sees the manifestation of the early precursor of the superego in the phantasies of young children: phantasies of fragmentation and destruction which appear to play a preponderant role in the building up of bonds uniting the child with the parental object.[1]

Be that as it may, the infantile superego is in the process of steady development and does not yet appear with the rigid, definitive, even inexorable character which it may acquire in the adult. It is not for that matter less active, even in its earliest form. The prerational form of the superego has been emphasized in so far as it represents an unconscious motivation of behaviour. Its affinity with the id is clearly recognizable for, as Lagache says (1955), it rests on 'the child's identification with the first objects of its sexual and aggressive drives; both represent an influence from the past: the id—of heredity; the superego—of parental and social influences; whereas the ego is mainly determined by the individual's own experience'. But the broader concept of the superego, as stated by Melanie Klein, also covers those aspects where the protection and the encouragement provided by the parents are introjected by the child.

XI. Psychoanalytical psychology and metapsychology

Psychoanalytical psychology cannot provide an unidimensional explanation of psychic processes. To achieve a satisfactory conceptualization, the stratification of phenomena requires the use of a referential framework which Freud called *metapsychology*.[2]

The expression is confusing if only because of its very form,

[1] See Paula Heimann (1943), 'Certain Functions of Introjection and Projection'.
[2] According to Lagache, Freudian metapsychology may be said to be the opposite of what is called 'academic', non-analytical psychology. But even within psychoanalysis itself, it may be said to be opposed to the so-called clinical approach—both technical and applied—since it covers all the theoretical aspects.

which suggests something metaphysical or metapsychic. But it has nothing to do with either of these. It is not concerned with some 'beyond', outside the sphere of psychology, but with what Freud called 'the theoretical equipment of psychoanalysis'. 'Metapsychology elaborates a theoretical conceptualization, basing its arguments on models and aiming at causal explanation and the formation of hypotheses' (Lagache, 1955). Theories of mental functioning, the theory of the unconscious and the theory of instinctual drives, could therefore fall into the category of metapsychology since topographical, dynamic and economic formulations need to be introduced to provide an explanation.

The dynamic point of view expresses mental events in terms of conflict: antagonism between instinctual drives and the socialized defence of the ego, that is, in terms of the interaction of the processes involved. All motivation of human behaviour involves conflict, and the replacement of the pleasure principle by the reality principle is one of the aspects of adaptation whose dynamics oscillate between the immediate satisfaction of the drive and the sense of security in delayed gratification, or, in other words, between the dominance of the id, the ego and the superego.

The economic point of view refers to mental phenomena from the quantitative aspect of distribution of energy. The problems are posed in terms of instinctual energy, libido or of cathexes.[1] Thus we talk of the strength of needs, the strength or weakness of the ego, of the energetic charge of traumas and conflicts, of the strength of external factors or drives, of the energy of defence mechanisms.

The topographical point of view deals with the problems posed by the structure of the psychic apparatus. This standpoint deals with problems of opposition between conscious and unconscious, or in relation to the agencies of the personality (the ego, the id and the superego). The topographical aspect has often been called the spatial viewpoint, since it has sometimes been represented through diagrams, as for instance Freud's 'model' of the psychic agencies. Each part is assigned a particular function in a topographical relationship with the others.

This multi-referential approach characterizes metapsychology which Freud called the 'speculative superstructure of psychoanalysis', and which constitutes the most complete description of the psychic facts which we can at the moment hope to achieve.

[1] *Cathexis* is the English translation of a German word (*Besetzung*: investment) which Freud used to designate the quantity of psychic energy attached to any object-representative (Rycroft, 1968). A cathexis is a mobile charge of energy which can be 'bound' to one representation or may shift accordingly to mental development or conflicts from one representative to another.

4   Infantile sexuality

One of the first psychoanalytic discoveries concerning psychological development, such as it could be reconstructed from the material gathered by analysis of adult patients, was that of infantile sexuality. Others, before Freud, had vaguely referred to the 'love life of the child'. Psychoanalytic research did not only broach the question but explored it systematically, establishing the part it plays in the psychic development of any human being.

I. Definition of infantile sexuality

The desire to preserve at all costs the myth of childhood innocence and the sheer inability to recognize the manifestations of infantile sexuality were the reasons why the subject was for so long ignored. Also infantile amnesia played an important part in the failure to recognize the early manifestations of the sexual drive.

The concept of infantile sexuality is justified by the fact that certain patterns of behaviour, from birth onwards, can rightly be considered as the precursors of all subsequent sexual evolution. Infantile sexuality does not refer only to early sexual manifestations or needs, but also to various behaviour patterns which have been described as sexual perversions in the adult: by this we mean sexual behaviour involving 'erotogenic zones' of the body, which are not only the genital areas but connected with other activities and body functions (oral, anal, etc.). By establishing a parallel between sexual perversions in adults and infantile behaviour, Freud (1905) was able to recognize the 'sexual' significance of this behaviour, and to put into the category of infantile sexuality all the activities of early childhood which aim at obtaining local pleasures (*Organlust*) which any particular organ (erotogenic zone) is capable of achieving. *Sexuality is a much broader concept than genitality:* the mode of sexual satisfaction is not limited to the functions of procreation or to the genital apparatus but includes a whole series of manifestations linked in their ultimate aim to sexual pleasure and desire.

II. Theory of instincts

The notion of infantile sexuality must be set within a wider frame of reference, viz. the theory of 'instincts'[1].

Over a long period of time psychoanalytic theory was concerned

[1] Throughout this book we have generally used the term *instinctual drive*. However, the words 'instinct', as well as sexual or aggressive 'drive' do appear

mainly with instincts. However, Freud uses the German *Trieb*, which is only partly covered by the word 'instinct'. *Trieb* indicates in fact an irresistible *drive*, biologically determined and closely related to the somatic sources which give rise to it. It comes from within the organism (and thus differs from psychic excitation caused by external stimuli), and is characterized by a sense of tension which has to be relieved. However, the concept of *Trieb*, although it postulates the finality of the drive, does not imply a rigidly predetermined specific object and does not connote the same fixedness as 'instinct'. The pliability of the drive thus contrasts with the rigid determinism of instinct.

The various instinctual drives are not equal in their constancy and in the character which they imprint on the forms of behaviour intended to gratify them. The plasticity of behaviour is greater when the corresponding drive is less essential to self-preservation. This is particularly true in the case of the sexual drive, which shows the greatest variety in the patterns of behaviour designed to satisfy it.

The sexual drives, whose maturation comes later, are, over a long period, actuated by the pleasure principle. During childhood they are in the grip of phantasies, more susceptible than the others of receiving a 'hallucinatory' satisfaction and capable of auto-erotic gratification. Because of this they are more easily repressed, at any rate for a large part of the child's development. Lagache (1955) emphasizes that the sexual drives are a 'weak point' in the psychic organization and for this reason they play a major role in the 'choice of the neurosis'.

The instinctual drive is an *economic* concept and is defined (a) by its *source*, related to an endosomatic process: the 'instinct' is to be understood as the *psychical representative* of a continuously *flowing source of stimulation*; (b) by its *aim*, which determines the gratification of the instinctual drive by suppressing the state of inner tension which gives rise to it; (c) and by its *object*, in relation to which the aim can be achieved. The concept of instinctual drive thus lies on the frontier between the mental and the somatic and represents the flow of stimulations coming from within the body.

---

in several instances carrying the same meaning. Although J. Strachey, the translator of the Standard Edition, has chosen 'instinct' rather than 'drive', we have kept a compromise translation by using *instinctual drive*, in order to connote the specific meaning of the Freudian concept. [In the French original, the French word *pulsion* stands for the German *Trieb*. Cf. Strachey's discussion in the Standard Edition, Vol. I; also Laplanche and Pontalis (1967)].

The sexual drive, however, is the one that presents the greatest plasticity or flexibility, mainly because the *objects* which can satisfy it may be very variable or even interchangeable (as in the case of sexual aberrations). Because of this the sexual drive may sometimes appear in unrecognizable form.[1]

Freud was a proponent of a *dual-instinct theory*, holding that instincts could be categorized in two antagonistic groups and that conflicts between these opposing instincts were responsible for neurosis. Until 1920 he thus described *ego-instincts* (aimed at self-preservation) and the *sexual instinct* (whose psychic energy is called libido). In *Beyond the Pleasure-Principle* (1920b) Freud outlined a new theory where the *life instinct* or sexual instinct was opposed to the *death instinct* (*Todestrieb*). The death instinct, in Freud's views, seeks to lead what is living back to its inorganic state; primary masochism and repetition compulsion were considered by Freud to be clinical manifestations of such a drive. The death instinct, which is still one of Freud's most controversial concepts, has been sometimes identified with an aggressive drive, but it should actually be strongly differentiated, since the death instinct postulates a drive to self-destruction.

III. The development of the libido

The intensity, the object and the goal of the sexual drive evolves with the maturational process. Various phases of libidinal development have been described. This was one of the first attempts at systematization of psychoanalytic theory. Infantile sexuality may, of course, be defined in terms of manifestation of 'sexual' activity or the expression of any interest in childbirth, anatomical differences between the sexes, etc., but infantile sexuality does not start within the genital sphere and any search of instinctual gratification should thus be considered as being part of infantile sexuality.

[1] Instincts, as described by ethology, are innate and determine fixed and immutable behaviour patterns. They remain unchanged throughout the species and are identical in all individuals. But nowadays ethologists recognize that instincts may not be as rigidly predetermined and rigid and that, under certain conditions, learning and group-effects may lead to more flexible and better adapted behaviour. The concept of a 'blind instinctual force' which seems to be generally true in lower animals, has been abandoned to a certain extent. Environmental influence has been stressed by many ethologists (Chauvin, Lorenz). Malson (1964) observes that instinct 'still continues to appear as *a priori* the sort whose controlling force each creature expresses fairly clearly, even in the case of early isolation. In this sense animal behaviour would suggest something not unlike a nature.' In man, on the other hand, the instinctual equipment is under constant pressure from cultural circumstances.

Freud has pointed out that *sexuality* is defined in a broader sense than the usual use of this word seems to imply, since it is not restricted to the genital activity and pleasure. He thus talks about 'organ pleasure' (*Organlust*), pregenital organization of the libido. But he clearly indicates that libido has to do with pleasures derived from bodily activities, and we might add bodily activities not connected with biological need but pleasurable sensations. 'The sexual aim of the infantile instinct consists in obtaining satisfaction by means of an appropriate stimulation of the erotogenic zone. . . . This satisfaction must have been previously experienced in order to have left behind a need for its repetition.'

Freud (1905), has pointed out several important characteristics of infantile sexuality.

(a)   One essential characteristic is that sexual components are attached to vital somatic functions; that they have as yet no sexual object and hence are auto-erotic and that their sexual aim is dominated by an *erotogenic zone*, which are represented by some parts of the body (generally part of the skin or the mucous membrane) in which stimuli evoke a *specific* quality of pleasure. The sexual aim consists in obtaining satisfaction by an appropriate rhythmic stimulation of the erotogenic zone.

(b)   He stresses the *polymorphous perverse disposition*, i.e. that infantile sexual wishes are not firmly canalized in any one direction, and that the various sexual impulses belonging to various erotogenic zones do co-exist throughout the child's development. Thus oral and anal elements play an important part far beyond the duration of the oral or anal phase. These early instincts do persist even in adult sexuality.

(c)   Freud also noticed that in spite of the preponderating dominance of erotogenic zones 'infantile sexual life exhibits components which from the very first involve other people as sexual objects'. Thus exhibitionism, scopophilia and cruelty, which appear to be independent of sexual zones, are to be observed in childhood as independent impulses (component instincts). These dispositions can become later on an integrated part of the adult's sexual life, but they can be clearly observed in childhood.

The various components of sexual life do not evolve along parallel lines, and one component instinct may have an earlier development than others and may well be in the final stage of its evolution while another may be just beginning. The systematization of the libidinal phases was gradually completed by different workers in this field. Freud laid the basis in his *Three Essays on the*

Theory of Sexuality.[1] Abraham (1924b) continued this work, which culminated in his 'Short Study of the Development of the Libido'.[2] Finally, Melanie Klein attempted to clarify the phantasy themes corresponding to the various phases.[3]

1 *The oral phase*

Birth puts an end to the state of maternal parasitism. The biological separation from the vital source on which the child depended until then sets up a new relationship between mother and child. The new symbiotic relationship linking the infant to the maternal breast introduces the first phase of affective life, focused on the nutritional function.

The taking of nourishment fulfils a double role right from the very start. The *nutritional* function corresponds to a physiological need but the relief of tension created by this need is experienced as a satisfaction. *Libidinal satisfaction* must thus be distinguished from the purely nutritional aspect. One of the most obvious libidinal components of the oral phase is expressed in the infant's thumb-sucking *away* from the nipple. The satisfaction derives from an activity originally linked with the warm flow of milk but it soon becomes a separate search for pleasure, independent of the need for nourishment. Freud (1905) recognized this satisfaction as having a sexual meaning:[4]

> Sensual sucking involves a complete absorption of the attention, and leads either to sleep or even to a motor reaction in the nature of an orgasm. . . . No one who has seen a baby satiated from the breast and falling asleep with flushed cheeks and a blissful smile can escape the reflection that this picture persists as a prototype of the expression of sexual satisfaction in later life. The need for repeating the sexual satisfaction now becomes detached from the need for taking nourishment.

A number of characteristics defining the oral phase correspond to the mother-child symbiosis which continues throughout the

[1] The first text of this appeared in 1905 and underwent several revisions right up to 1915. The definitive text contains theoretical formulations belonging to widely differing periods of conceptualization (see Standard Edition, 7).
[2] *Selected Papers* (1924b).
[3] Melanie Klein, *The Psychoanalysis of Children* (1932). The author's essential thesis, contained in that volume, should be completed by the works of Melanie Klein et al., in *Developments in Psycho-analysis* (Hogarth Press, 1952).
[4] S. Freud, *Three Essays on Sexuality*, Standard Edition, 7, pp. 180–2.

first year. During this phase, a specific zone, the lips, tongue and mouth, constitutes the erotogenic zone. The sucking is accompanied by movements of the hand groping for the breast; it is in this sense that Spitz (1955) refers to a perceptual unity constituted by the infant's mouth and hands which he calls the 'primal cavity'. At this phase of libidinal development there is a corresponding mode of object relationship, the *anaclitic* relation, which is based on the attachment to early infantile prototypes (Freud, 1905).

The lips and mouth constitute the first *erotogenic zone*, in which stimuli of a certain sort evoke a feeling of 'pleasure' or, at any rate, an effect associated with pleasure to the extent that it corresponds to the inherent qualification of a need. There is no doubt that these stimuli are governed by certain conditions; a rhythmic character must play a part among them.

The oral phase corresponds to the child's first year and usually comes to an end when weaning starts. It has been subdivided into two secondary phases.

(a)   The primary level of this phase, called *preambivalent*, is linked exclusively with sucking. It corresponds to the incorporation, in phantasy, of an 'object', but not with the intention of destroying it. The child is not yet capable of differentiating the external object from its own body and so no distinction is being made between the sucking child and the suckling mother. As far as one can say, the child feels no love or hatred, and the psyche is therefore free of any affective ambivalence. This phase corresponds to Spitz's objectless stage.

(b)   The secondary level of this phase begins with the first teething, around six months. The sucking is gradually brought to completion by biting, teeth, being the first 'tool' the child has to attack the external world. Oral grasping is no longer simple sucking: it becomes a nibble, even a bite. In this phase the 'cannibalistic' organization predominates and this *oral-sadistic phase* runs parallel with the setting up of contradictory ambivalent feelings with regard to the object, which becomes both the object of satisfaction (love) and the object of hostility (hate).

It should be noted that it is the primacy of the erotogenic zone which provides the unity of the oral phase. The subdivision into two levels indicates an evolution in object relations which marks the passage from a preambivalent attitude—when the subject does not perceive any external object—to the appearance of a first conflict in relation to an external object in which the hostile component predominates.

To this oral-sadistic phase there are corresponding phantasies involving the incorporation and oral destruction of the mother's body.[1] The incorporated object is attacked, absorbed, destroyed or expelled in the course of phantasies closely linked both to the need for food and its concomitant libidinal drive.

A specific conflict is associated with the resolution of the oral phase—the *weaning*, which makes it possible for the subject to establish the primordial form of the maternal 'imago' (Lacan, 1938) on which are based the earliest feelings which link the individual with his family and hence with the social milieu in its widest sense.

The weaning crisis at first sight appears to be based on a biological, hence instinctual, fact of the species. Weaning, in fact, is inseparable from the cultural aspect of mothering.[2]

'In fact weaning is often a psychic trauma.' But whether it is or not, 'weaning does leave in the human psyche a permanent trace of the interrupted biological relationship. This vital crisis is coupled with a mental crisis, the first, probably, which has a solution with a dialectic structure' (Lacan, 1938).

Refusal to be weaned tends to re-establish the image of the nursing relation, an image which can be conceived only in terms of the psychic (sensory) content of the first months of life and hence prior to any conscious representation of the object.

This maternal image is an exteroceptive one—the human face—the *Gestalt* of which is recognized and later identified. The specificity of the infant's reactions *vis-à-vis* the human presence and its importance in the setting up of relations with the maternal object was clearly shown by Spitz (1946b) in his investigation of the smiling response.

Associated with this visual form, a proprioceptive satisfaction of sucking and oral grasping is evidence of an *oral fusion* which is neither auto-erotic (the ego not being as yet constituted) nor narcissistic, nor even oral erotic, since, as Lacan observes, the 'craving for the breast is only part of the weaning complex because of its revival by the Oedipus complex'. Lacan sees in this oral fusion a medley of cannibalistic elements, for which supporting evidence can be seen in the wealth of phantasies of incorporation, oral destruction, taking possession and rejection, phantasies which

[1] See Melanie Klein, *The Psychoanalysis of Children* (1932), for an account of children's phantasies during analysis.
[2] In this connection the reader is referred to the relevant works on anthropology and the studies relating to the cultural factors on modes of feeding and weaning. The work of S. Brody (1956) on patterns of mothering, with special reference to the cultural setting, is revealing in this respect.

survive in play and symbolic verbalization later on, as has been shown by Melanie Klein.

What the child feels and experiences in his first weeks and months is the basis of the primal relationship which is brought to its close by weaning. The imago of the mother's breast dominates the subject's life; for the woman, this imago often attains its ultimate completion in adult life when she is nursing her baby. During the nursing phase, when the first object-relations are established, the resolution of the mother's own 'weaning complex' is of no mean importance. If the mother's behaviour protects her child from the consequences of his own helplessness, the effects of this 'complex' will clearly be seen in various maternal attitudes, as has been shown by Hélène Deutsch (1946), Sylvia Brody (1956), D. W. Winnicott (1965) and others.

2 *The anal phase*

This phase only begins with the child's bowel control, that is when defecation or the retention of the faeces becomes an act which the child can control at will. This bowel control is dependent on neuro-biological maturation and appears about the end of the first year when the child takes his first steps; thus bowel control and mastery of walking are both invested with a similar meaning, that of a growing independence.

The *sphincter ani*, during this phase, represents the erotogenic zone, which is stimulated, in the first instance, by the passage of the faeces. Defecation is a stimulant of the anal erotogenic zone, and 'children who are making use of the susceptibility to erotogenic stimulation of the anal zone betray themselves by holding back their stool till its accumulation brings about violent muscular contractions and, as it passes the anus, is able to produce powerful stimulation of the mucous membrane. It must no doubt cause not only painful but also highly pleasurable sensations' (Freud, 1905).

This control by the child over its own body and the external world is accompanied by an infantile sexual satisfaction: this is obvious when the baby on the pot refuses obstinately to empty his bowels and disobeys his mother's orders and only performs when *he* chooses to *do* so. 'He is only anxious not to miss the subsidiary pleasure attached to defecating' (Freud, 1905).

The intestinal content which acts as stimulation has also another significance. The child obviously treats it as part of its own body; for him it represents a gift which, if he offers it, he can use to prove his love or compliance with his environment, and, if he withholds it, to show his obstinacy or even hostility. This 'possession' which becomes a symbolic object of exchange and expression, engenders a special relationship, characteristic of the anal phase.

The importance of anal eroticism in its bearing on character formation in the adult was discovered by Freud in his analysis of obsessional neuroses.[1] Under certain conditions, the anal phase can indeed leave important traces because it is at the basis of certain mother-child relations which will subsequently be repeated in the relation with others. This phase has been called the *anal-sadistic* phase to indicate this relational component. The pleasure of controlling is complemented by the desire to master, to exercise power, not only over the body but over the environment as well. Freud observed that the anal-sadistic phase introduces the distinction between *active* and *passive* and is accompanied by a very rich phantasy life (rediscovered by Freud, vestigially, in adult neuroses and by Melanie Klein in analyses of the very young child when these phantasies are expressed *in statu nascendi*).

With the anal stage, eroticism is linked with sadistic forms of behaviour which express, in the form of hostile feelings, the wish to destroy the object. Abraham (1924) has shown that anal-erotic and anal-sadistic components are associated with different functions. If the evacuation of the bowel can be accompanied by pleasurable sensations through the stimulation of the anal mucous membrane, the voluntary retention of the faeces may also give the child pleasure.

In this phase the child's relation to the object is in terms of possession: every object of the infant's desire is something over which he exercises a right and every object is comparable with his most primitive possession, i.e. his faeces. The link which structures his relation with the object has therefore an ambivalent character. He can, on the one hand, attempt to keep the object for himself, 'to retain it'; or he can refuse it by rejecting or expelling it. In the sadistic component, such as it exists in the infantile libido, there are two opposing tendencies, both gratifying. One is to destroy the

[1] Freud has described certain character traits which are preponderant in persons whose anal phase has played a major role in their libidinal development: frugality, orderliness, obstinacy, stubbornness and 'moral' superiority.
Frugality is a continuation of the anal habits of retention; orderliness is an elaboration of obedience to requirements, while obstinacy represents a rebellion against them. Stubbornness is a compromise between aggressiveness and passivity (the 'power of the powerless'). Moral superiority can find its expression either through the feeling of being unfairly treated, or through making the 'unfair' adult feel sorry afterwards, which should enforce affection from him (S. Freud, *Character and Anal Eroticism*, 1908c).

object, the other to retain it and to exercise control over it. Thus the anal-erotic and -sadistic components are to be found in both phases: the first, when the subject retains and controls the object; the second when he expels and destroys it.

3 *The phallic phase*

When the child abandons the libidinally cathected anal zone, a new erotogenic zone takes over. The solution of the affective conflicts centred on anality—which in normal development takes place about the age of two—is replaced by new preoccupations which show the child's interest in the genital zone and all the functions connected with it. An unprejudiced observation will not fail to discover that these preoccupations occur in every child at that age.

(a)   INFANTILE MASTURBATION   shows that the genitals have become an erotogenic zone. After the sucking and biting which characterize oral eroticism, after the functions controlling retention and expulsion marking the anal phase, the child's interests are centred on the genital area.

> Given the anatomical situation of this region, the secretions in which it is bathed, the washing and rubbing to which it is subjected in the course of a child's toilet, make it inevitable that the pleasurable feeling which this part of the body is capable of producing should be noticed by children even during their earliest infancy and should give rise to a need for its repetition (Freud, 1905).

This masturbation, which consists of a rubbing movement with the hand or of bringing the thighs together, represents what Freud calls the second phase of infantile masturbation. It leaves behind the deepest unconscious impressions and seems to be one of the main causes of infantile amnesia which is associated with the sexual activity and phantasies of this age.

This second phase is to be distinguished from primary masturbatory activity which belongs to early infancy and which is manifested by erections and may cause an 'orgasmic equivalent' well known to mothers. This manifestation is short-lived. Its reappearance round about the fourth year corresponds to the masturbation accompanying the phallic phase and continues until the latency period. After this it will not reappear until the onset of puberty.

The phallic phase is organized round the activity of the erotogenic genital zone. The mental life of the child, his curiosity, his games, his interests and object relations will be focused on genital sexuality.

(b)   THE SEXUAL RESEARCHES OF CHILDHOOD   During this period there is an awakening curiosity about sexuality: differences between the sexes, procreation, pregnancy, childbirth and parents' sexual relations. This curiosity does not come about spontaneously, from some search for causality. Every discovery is subordinated to instinctual forces. But the child's experiences cannot simply be considered as a concrete manifestation of an innate biological drive—for at all stages the relational component is closely involved. The instinctual drive becomes a significant element through the dialectics of the conflicts which sets the child face to face with the psychic representatives of the external world.

To understand the child's relations with his environment, one must bear in mind that between mother and child a symbolic, mediating, term is going to appear. In the oral phase, this mediating third term is represented by gushing milk between the infant's mouth and the mother's breast; at the anal stage this term is concretized by the faecal mass, abandoned or retained. In the genital, or phallic, phase, the child's unconscious reference becomes the phallus. The quest for the phallus will polarize the manifestations of his sexual curiosity, lead him to discover where it is to be found and to whom it belongs and tell him what its function is.

Where babies come from and the puzzle of procreation and pregnancy are questions which intrigue children at this age. The usual explanations offered by parents—the stork, cabbage-leaves, rose-bushes, etc.—are received with a certain mistrust, often with total incredulity. Such explanations are a confession of the adult's embarrassment, a sure sign that one is treading on forbidden ground. The child is not slow to notice the changes in his mother's shape during pregnancy and suspects mysterious goings-on between the parents, from which he is excluded. He thus acquires a 'subconscious knowledge', which he gains as much from 'stray or discreet signs which the child's sensibility is quick to pick up as an indication that something is "happening" between his parents, as from the revealing chance remark or act' (Lacan, 1938).[1]

---

[1] It is difficult to say what the child really 'sees' when watching the 'primal scene'; whether visual or auditory elements are retained. But the imaginary components certainly play a major part. And so Freud speaks of an *Urphantasie*, a primal phantasy, a notion which Laplanche and Pontalis have discussed (1968).

(c)   THE SEXUAL THEORIES OF CHILDREN   Failing to receive satis-factory explanations, the child interprets the facts in his own way and builds his own theories to fit in with his libidinal experience.

(i)   *The difference between the sexes and the primacy of the phallus*
Freud (1923b) observed that in this phase, when component instincts are under the influence of the genital zone, the male genitals alone mattered, both for girl and boy: it is specifically a question of the primacy of the phallus. As far as the boy is con-cerned, he undoubtedly perceives the distinction between men and women, but has no reason to think there is any difference between the male and female genitals. Only gradually do doubts begin to creep in. But even if his own experience brings him up against the real facts, there is always an initial failure to recognize or appreciate the true meaning of reality. In the earlier period the child tries to disavow reality, keep up the belief that they *do* see a penis and come slowly to the conclusion that the penis had at least been there before and taken away afterwards. The lack of a penis is regarded as a result of castration, and by wishful thinking the child conjures up some reparation which will subsequently allow the girl (woman) to acquire a penis. But even when the child does perceive and accept the difference between the sexes—that is, in the case of girls, the lack of a penis—it will attribute this lack, not to some fundamental disposition, but to a mutilation: the castration phantasy—the penis destroyed, lost or cut off—centres on an imagined punishment inflicted by the parents. The child lives out this phantasy by projecting his own sadistic impulses on to his parents, whom he holds responsible for the destruction of the penis.

The child, however, does not extend this lack of a penis to all women, only to those which he considers guilty of inadmissible impulses similar to his own. Over a long period the child keeps up his belief in an *idealized phallic mother* who has not suffered castration. In the child's eye she still retains the imaginary phallus, symbol and prerogative of adult power. The sequence of the child's attitudes concerning sexual differences can thus be sum-marized: (a) the phallic primacy; (b) the perception of sexual differences and disavowal; (c) the acceptance of the sexual differ-ences and (d) castration anxiety.

Only later does the idea of femininity become equated with the lack of a penis (when the child takes up the problems of birth), though the child does not discover the existence of female genitals. The difference between the sexes is envisaged only from the standpoint of the phallic primacy, that is, as one of two alternatives—to possess a penis or to be castrated.

(ii) *Theories about pregnancy* Just as the child knows nothing about the vagina, his ignorance regarding the existence of sperm leads him to build phantasies about the origin of babies. These phantasies are related to his libidinal experiences of the oral, anal or ureteral phase. The belief that impregnation takes place orally, by swallowing or through kissing, is linked with the erotic cathexis of the oral zone. Those beliefs are more widespread among girls, in whom they sometimes persist till puberty. Other phantasies are associated with urination, though here the role of the two partners is not very clearly conceived (simultaneous urination, urination in the woman, etc.); sometimes the cause is believed to be the 'exhibition' of the genital organs. All these phantasies indicate a *regressive* conception of sexual relations and are the reflection of phantasies corresponding to pre-genital instinctual components.

(iii) *The sadistic conception of coitus* corresponds to an interpretation of sexual intercourse, as something that the stronger participant imposes on the weaker one. Even when the 'primal scene' has actually been witnessed by children, their recollection of it often expresses aggressive or sadistic phantasies. It is probably true that marital difficulties or the disturbance of the sexual life of the parents (e.g. a frigid mother) may well have provided grounds for this; but the sadistic components depends much more on vestigial phantasies of the anal phase than on any actual scene which the child might have witnessed.

(iv) *The phantasy of anal birth* Once the child has accepted that the baby is carried in the mother's body, the actual act of childbirth still remains a puzzle. Belief that the child is evacuated through the anus, like a piece of excrement, fits in with phantasies of the anal phase.

These ideas are soon replaced by much more elaborate ones. Birth is thought to take place through the navel or by forced and bloody extraction from the mother's abdomen. The anal interpretation then undergoes repression: not so very long ago (in the child's life) defecation was something one could talk about without fear, shame or embarrassment: the child was not yet far away from his coprophilic tendencies. The fact of coming into the world in the same way as a heap of faeces was nothing degrading, because

F

they were not yet looked upon with disgust. The cloacal theory of birth was the only one which might seem probable to the child (Freud, 1908b). It will be seen that the repression of component instincts is at the basis of those phantasies which seek to come to grips with sexuality.

(d)   SEXUAL ENLIGHTENMENT OF CHILDREN   This phantasy activity brings us to the question of sexual education. The real problem is not, as A. Berge (1952) has pointed out, whether to instruct children in these matters, but whether enlightenment ought to be based on truth or made up of lies and fanciful stories. It would seem that we should be concerned less with the revelation of secret information than with making available in adequate words what the child has already perceived by a sort of 'unconscious knowledge'. For the child it is a question of reconciling this latent knowledge with the mixture of reservation and prohibition he can sense in his parents' attitudes. In the event, a straightforward explanation is not enough, for the child is not capable of assimilating all the facts presented to him. An over-informative explanation does not take into account his inner needs and his level of libidinal experience. The more elaborate explanation sometimes has the opposite effect and the child's reaction will be one of total incredulity. Because of the gap between his libidinal development and the level of his experience, he is incapable of assimilating the information given to him. He will forget what he has been told, simply because of his emotional immaturity to integrate this information. To quote A. Berge: 'all experience must be *affectively grounded* before it can be genuinely integrated.' The child will reject that part of the explanation which he cannot transcribe into the emotional language of the moment: the child interprets the explanation in his own way, according to the predominance of oral, anal or genital components—and to whether he has resolved, or not yet come up against, the oedipal problem. But there is yet another obstacle standing in the way of his acceptance of sexuality. Prior to the oedipal phase, the child's feeling towards his parents make him reluctant to admit that they have sexual relations. The little boy cannot entertain the idea of his mother's welcoming his father's advances, while the girl cannot accept that her father is giving to her mother something that she herself desires. Hence the reinforcement of a sado-masochistic conception of coitus and, by extension, of love. 'If sexual intercourse is often conceived as an act of aggression against the woman, many boys think it just as dangerous for the man, for they may be—at the oral and cannibalistic level—under the unconscious and imaginary threat of being devoured' (A. Berge, 1952).

S. Ferenczi (1927) contributes an additional argument concerning the resistance to information on sexual matters. In his view, any purely physiological explanation, however elaborate, ignores the erotic or sensual dimension of sexual intercourse. The child does not want scientific information, merely a confirmation that the genitals serve a libidinal function. His own sensation have already made him aware of this in respect of his own genitals and this enables him to suspect the pleasure his parents experience in their relations. But above all the child wants to make certain that his parents are capable of accepting the pleasure that sexuality can provide. As long as parents bring up children in a spirit of denial (conscious or otherwise) of sexual pleasure, they are bound to feel guilty about their own gratification. Parents who, out of guilt, rule out all sexual enjoyment from their lives are fostering in the child a 'pure and immaculate' parental image and this often suits their purpose very well. But they are at the same time hiding the truth about their own physical and psychic experience while demanding unconditional confidence. Sexual enlightenment thus becomes part of 'education' as such: one of its tasks consists of providing the child with a possibility of identifying with an adult parental imago, and thus paving the way for *individuation.*

The parents' sexual life and their sexual experience—using the term in its widest sense—play a crucial role in the outcome of the child's emotional life: their attitudes and their own satisfactions will determine to a greater extent the child's possibilities to solve the basic emotional conflict which he encounters on his way to independence—the Oedipus complex.

4 *The Oedipus complex*

As long as the child is biologically and functionally dependent on his mother he remains subjected to her whims and her wishes. To become the object of his mother's desire and to identify himself with this desire are ways by which the child ensures his relationship with her. This means that he must maintain the possibility of satisfying his needs, which always closely fit in with the mother's desire. Being his mother's object, the child cannot himself become a subject as long as this imaginary interdependence remains unbroken and this dual relation (ultimately alienating in its consequences) persists.

The child becomes aware that in his parents' relationship the object of his mother's wishes is his father. Possession of the phallus will be at stake in the mother-child relationship. As the one who possesses the phallus, the father comes to embody authority, power, law; but the phallus is also identified as the object of maternal desire.

(a)   Freud (1921) attempted to clarify the process of the development of the Oedipus complex in terms of *identification*. This is how he described it:[1]

A little boy will exhibit a special interest in his father; he would like to grow like him, and be like him and take his place everywhere . . . he takes his father as his ideal. . . . At the same time as the identification with his father, or a little later, the boy has begun to develop a true object-cathexis towards his mother according to the attachment (anaclitic) type. He then exhibits, therefore, two psychologically distinct ties: a straightforward sexual object-cathexis towards his mother and an identification with his father which takes him as his model. The two subsist side by side for a time without any mutual influence or interference. In consequence of the irresistible advance towards a unification of mental life, they come together at last; and the normal Oedipus complex originates from their confluence. The little boy notices that his father stands in his way with his mother. His identification with his father then takes on a hostile colouring and becomes identical with the wish to replace his father in regard to his mother as well. Identification, in fact, is ambivalent from the very first; it can turn into an expression of tenderness as easily as into a wish for someone's removal. It behaves like a derivative of the first, *oral* phase of the organization of the libido, in which the object that we long for and prize is assimilated by eating and is in that way annihilated as such.

Freud further emphasized that it is this ambivalence *vis-à-vis* the father and the altogether tender feelings for the libidinal object represented by his mother which constitute for the little boy the elements of the Oedipus complex.

(b)   CASTRATION ANXIETY   The Oedipus complex may be regarded as paradigmatic of psychic conflict. Since its prevalent imaginary content is focused on the place and the function of the phallus, castration is at the centre of the Oedipus complex.

[1] S. Freud, Chapter VII of *Group Psychology and the Analysis of the Ego* (1921).

The ease with which the child breaks away from the satisfactions of the anal phase is closely related to the discovery of the pleasure obtained from genital stimulation and masturbation. Parents usually attempt to suppress infantile masturbation entirely. Françoise Dolto uses the term '*castrating interdiction*' to describe every prohibition which initially aims to put an end to all genital activity on the part of the child. Subsequently the 'castrating' is extended to all prohibitions which seek to suppress activities having libidinal content, or, in other words, all attempts to check curiosity, the spirit of initiative and enterprise, the aggressive tendencies of the boy and the coquetry of the girl. Every intervention on the part of adults gratuitously meddling in the imaginative play-activities of children and their phantasy world (which invariably conceal sexual phantasies) in order, as it were, to bring them back to reason, must be called a castrating intervention. Its only effect will be to increase the usual and inevitable amount of anxiety (F. Dolto, 1936). Thus castration anxiety, the normal anxiety which exists without any external intervention, will be intensified and will become more sensitive because of it. By defending itself against this conscious and pre-oedipal anxiety the child makes its entry into the oedipal world.[1]

In the course of the oedipal conflict the boy will be induced to modify his attitudes to both parents. He is aware of possessing a penis, which is lacking in girls, and the penis will be libidinally cathected as a locus of sexual satisfaction. The penis, however, represents also a narcissistic confirmation of the self. To conquer the maternal object, the child will resort to attitudes of inveigling and of displaying aggression to affirm his phallic position, by expressing the sadistic components in his games and phantasies. These activities may be regarded as a first attempt at an identification with his father because they represent all those virile qualities which the child would like to possess. These activities also aim at getting hold of or retaining his mother, who remains the central figure both as the love object and as an agency who has the power to grant or deny permission. From this age, however, contact with reality causes the crude instinctual aggressiveness to become

[1] F. Dolto draws a line between *castration anxiety* and *castration complex*. The anxiety awakened by a realization of the differences between the sexes is a *conscious or pre-conscious* anxiety set up when the child notices the absence of a penis in himself or anyone else; its starting point is a false representation of reality (castration-mutilation phantasy): it is an interpretation which no child can escape, for the danger he invents is motivated, on the one hand, by the magical powers he attributed to grown-ups and, on the other hand, by his real inferiority in relation to them. In this conflict, the child is aware of his malaise and tries to throw it off.

sublimated and to manifest itself either in play activity, whose symbolic content is associated with unconscious conflict, or in his school performance. Dolto states that the primitive hedonistic goal is itself transformed into a sentimental one, 'enabling the child to gain recognition and increase his self-confidence, namely, to please others by his behaviour and not to conquer by phantasies of magic power'.

In the course of this attempt to win the maternal object, the boy meets a rival, his father, whom he envies because of his real superiority and whom he overrates because of his symbolic significance. The oedipal phantasies which are all bent towards the exclusive possession of the mother and the suppression of the dreaded rival, only reinforce the phantasy themes of castration. Lacan has called it 'the double affective movement of the subject': the child directs his aggression against the rival and simultaneously fears a retaliatory aggression from the rival. The child projects his feelings of jealousy onto his father and may even provoke punishment through his aggressive behaviour. The oedipal phantasies come up against reality. If the father feels threatened and actually reacts to this situation, it will become one of an overt conflict for the child. But even if the father remains unprovoked by the oedipal claims of his son, the child's guilt feelings will continue to grow, for the *presence*, real and symbolic, of the paternal image is sufficient to carry the meaning of law and authority against which the child is rebelling.

If the father's image is strong enough to withstand the unconscious aggressiveness of the boy, the child can attempt, with his help, to resolve the Oedipus complex without resorting to self-punishing behaviour which is determined by his unconscious guilt.

The mother represents a love image but the father is not only a rival to be supplanted but also a model to be imitated. He must be able to sustain the child's cathexis on both levels. The father has a function to perform in preventing incest because, as Dolto observes, 'incest is libidinally castrating'.

The oedipal competition, however, which pits the child against the father is not a 'fair' contest because the mother has already chosen the father and can only offer the boy maternal love and comfort free of the erotic genital component. When the child realizes the futility of his efforts he becomes able to overcome his anxiety and he can then bend his efforts to winning surrogate objects. The boy sublimates his genital libido by renouncing his seductive erotic activities and his competition with his father in the oedipal struggle.

Although giving up the erotic fixation on his mother is an essential condition of the dissolution of the Oedipus complex, the boy must also be able to give up every attitude of seduction towards the paternal rival.[1]

The complete solution of the oedipal conflict is accompanied by a detachment which, although not destroying the previous cathected objects, enables the boy to go through the process of mourning and sets free, consciously or unconsciously, the libidinal energy which is now available for new cathexis.

(c) THE OEDIPUS COMPLEX IN THE GIRL arises in conditions very different from that in the boy. With the discovery of the lack of a penis and after a period of denial and despair, the girl feels obliged to accept the situation, for it does not represent the threat of imaginary castration but is a physiological fact. In the boy's case, the castration anxiety appears during the dissolution of the oedipal conflict but the girl becomes aware of the absence of the penis long before the conflict begins.

The first feature of this is the girl's claim to a penis: she knows that she is without it and wants to have it. No amount of denial can remove this real anatomical lack. At first the lack is experienced as a narcissistic wound bringing with it a feeling of physical and genital inferiority. This realization also involves a loosening of the bond of tenderness with the mother whom the girl holds responsible for this. Also, at this stage, she often abandons clitorial masturbation, feeling incapable of competing with the boy, and

the recognition of that anatomical difference between the sexes forces her away from masculinity and masculine masturbation. . . . The girl's libido slips into a new position along the line of the equation: 'penis-child'. She gives up her wish for a penis and puts in place of it a wish for a child: and *with that purpose in view* she takes her father as the love-object. Her mother becomes the object of her jealousy.

[1] Dolto calls this 'the renunciation of passive homosexual satisfactions'. She observes that the latency period is marked by a physiological retreat of the erotic libido or by a 'uniform discharge of the libidinal flow' which is now used in the activities which the superego puts at the body's disposal. If this period supervenes before the child has completed his affective detachment from the father, all his activities in this period will be aimed at *pleasing the father* and not in attempting to compete with him. Dolto sees in this the beginning of passive, unconscious homosexual attitudes which inhibit aggressiveness and which may militate against sexual success with women or against any cultural and intellectual achievement; such are the effects of an (unconscious) castration complex indicating a non-resolution of the Oedipus complex.

Thus the little girl abandons her first love object, her mother, and shifts her wishes onto the father. This significant change precedes, in the case of the girl, the oedipal conflict.

In girls the Oedipus complex is a secondary formation. The operations of the castration complex precede it and prepare for it. As regards the relation between the Oedipus and castration complexes there is a fundamental contrast between the two sexes. *Whereas in boys the Oedipus complex is destroyed by the castration complex, in girls it is made possible and led up to by the castration complex.* This contradiction is cleared up if we reflect that the castration complex always operates in the sense implied by its subject matter; it inhibits and limits masculinity and encourages femininity (Freud, 1925c).

Dolto also has pointed out that from this absence of a penis comes a sense of security, the girl being able without danger to identify with the one who does not possess it: the threat of castration does not hold. In the case of the girl, castration anxiety is detrimental to the normal course of the Oedipus complex, *if the anxiety appears before the oedipal conflict sets in.* It is through penis envy that the girl relates to any masculine figure, not in an attitude of one demanding virility but to win the admiration of those whom her mother had chosen as love objects. The withdrawal of cathexis from the mother brings about, in the case of the girl, a shift leading to the resolution of her infantile dependence.

The young girl's difficulties lie in the attempts to identify with the mother. She does indeed succeed in renouncing the oedipal competition with her mother before the latency period with less anxiety and hostility than does the boy. However, the identification with the mother may well be at the root of subsequent difficulties. If a mother's life is represented as a succession of painful incidents, and marital life as a train of obligations without any compensating pleasures, the girl may be prevented from investing the erotogenic vaginal zone and her feminine aspirations will not become cathected with sufficient libidinal satisfactions.

If the phallic inferiority is not accepted by the girl and she is unable to abandon her penis envy, she will remain fixated at that point, unfit to cope with the oedipal conflict or to establish a cathexis of the vaginal erotogenic zone. It may also happen that the girl may be unable to establish a secondary cathexis of this zone if she has to identify with a depreciated maternal image.

(d) EFFECTS OF THE OEDIPUS COMPLEX The differences in the significance of the Oedipus complex enabled Freud to grasp the specific character of the sexual development of males and females.

> In boys the Oedipus complex is not simply repressed but literally smashed to pieces by the shock of threatened castration. Its libidinal cathexes are abandoned, desexualized, and in part sublimated; its objects are incorporated into the ego where they form the nucleus of the superego. . . . In ideal cases the Oedipus complex exists no longer even in the unconscious, the superego has become its heir (S. Freud, 1925c).

Since the penis owes its narcissistic cathexis to its organic significance for the propagation of the species, one may consider that the effects of the Oedipus complex—namely, the prohibition of incest and the institution of conscience and of a moral code—may be regarded as a victory of society over the individual.

In the case of the girl, since castration has already forced her into the situation of the Oedipus complex, it can be slowly abandoned or dealt with by repression: the consequences will be quite different. The feminine superego is never as inexorable, as impersonal, as independent of its emotional origins as we require it to be in man. Freud sees in the particular building up of the feminine superego the origin of certain feminine character traits: 'they show less sense of justice than men, they are less ready to submit to the great exigencies of life, they are more often influenced in their judgements by feelings of affection or hostility'. Freud does, however, readily acknowledge that these are general character traits liable to considerable variation. But beyond this Freud sees in the Oedipus complex the moment when the human being is brought face to face with the group at the level of its most elementary social unit: the family.

The Oedipus complex may be regarded as the crucial phenomenon in the foundation of psychic life as well as the nodal point around which the family is structured. J. Lacan (1938) has shown that 'if sexual drives provide the basis for this complex it is their frustration which forms its node'. The child is bound by his wish to the nearest love-object, the parent of the opposite sex; the frustration of this wish is attributed by the child to the *third person* of the triangle, the one whose presence marks him (or her) as the obstacle on the way to satisfaction. This prohibition is often aggravated by repressive upbringing which prevents any possibility of drive-gratification and prohibits any mastubatory outlet, that is, any manifestation of infantile genitality. 'The parent thus appears to him both as an instrument of sexual prohibition and an example of its transgression.'[1]

For Freud (1912), the Oedipus complex is a universal feature, one of the fundamental events which supports the social structures. This conception has been criticized particularly by anthropologists. B. Malinowski[2] emphasized the *cultural relativism* of this fundamental conflict and based his conclusions on the study of the Melanesian population of the Trobriand Islands. He maintains that the Oedipus complex exists only in patriarchal societies whereas in the Trobriand Islands, where the family structure is matrilinear and where the *couvade* still exists, the paternal authority is shifted on to the maternal uncle. In point of fact a displacement such as this only goes to confirm the essential point of the Freudian theory which emphasizes the importance of family structure in the establishment of a *system of symbolic values*, thus ensuring the transmission of fundamental laws regulating social relations in any given culture.

5 *The dissolution of the Oedipus complex and the latency period*

The working through of the Oedipus complex and its final resolution bring with them certain changes in the psychic economy of the subject and introduce a new phase in his development called the *latency period.* The way this period progresses depends entirely on the manner in which the Oedipus complex has been resolved, that is, it reflects the vicissitudes of the subject's instinctual drives when faced with anxiety.[3]

(a)   THE DISSOLUTION OF THE OEDIPUS COMPLEX   The resolution of this conflict may come about because the child's maturation abandons some of its libidinal positions which no longer obey the reality principle. The absence of satisfaction hoped for must turn the child away from his hopeless longing. Freud spoke of the destruction of the Oedipus complex from 'the effects of its internal impossibility'. But even if such a process takes place, the major reason for the dissolution, as clinical experience has taught

[1] J. Lacan, 'La Famille' (1938).
[2] Bronislaw Malinowski, *The Sexual Life of Savages of North-West Melanesia* (1930).
[3] There has been a tendency to see in the latency period a phenomenon akin to puberty and to look for a *biological* (hormonal) interpretation for this quiescent break in the sexual development which would fit in with man's physiological maturation. Apart from a lack of arguments to support this thesis, anthropological research tends to confirm that this latency period is subject to the influence of cultural, i.e. relational, factors.

us, is due to the destruction of the child's phallic genital organization which is contemporaneous with the Oedipus complex and is brought about by the repression of libidinal drives caused by the threat of castration. 'If the satisfaction of love in the field of the Oedipus complex is to cost the child his penis, a conflict is bound to arise between his narcissistic interest in that part of the body and the libidinal cathexis of his parental objects. . . . The child's ego turns away from the Oedipus complex.'[1] However, Freud does insist that it is *more than repression*, rather a genuine destruction or abolition (*Aufhebung*) of the Oedipus complex, leaving no repressed residue which might embarrass subsequent evolution, and its dissolution is thus accompanied by a considerable liberation of energy which may be used for other tasks. This is why during the latency period, when the psychic conflict is resolved, energies are freed which can be invested in the acquisition of intellectual resources.

The latency period is of interest from the standpoint of the child's fitting into the cultural pattern and also because of the structural reshufflings which the instinctual drives undergo during this period.

(b) FUNCTION OF THE OEDIPUS COMPLEX It is possible to recognize in the Oedipus complex the focal point around which infantile sexuality evolves and reality is structured. J. Lacan (1938) has shown the interrelations of those events.

The sexuality which conditions the Oedipus complex here reaches its peak: sexuality which was primarily expressed through auto-erotism, is now directed to objects. But the sexual drive in the boy follows a different path from that in the girl. The boy has to abandon the object of his desire (the mother) while reactivating thereby the tendencies awakened by weaning and which predispose him to sexual regression.[2] In the case of the girl, on the other hand, the maternal object, which remains a love object, diverts a part of the oedipal desire for the father and thus mitigates the severe psychic conflict. The Oedipus complex which marks the peak of infantile sexuality also heralds the temporary lull which characterizes the relative instinctual quiescence of the latency period. The oedipal conflict also has its share in establishing the reality status of the object cathected by the subject's desire. The object is

[1] S. Freud, *The Dissolution of the Oedipus Complex* (1924b).
[2] Freud emphasizes that the child perceives a narcissistic bodily damage in the first deprivations he suffers when weaned or when he is forced to abandon his faeces, or even in the separation from his mother at birth. The term *castration complex* is only valid, however, when the 'loss' concerns the male genitals.

established as a whole object, and replaces the part-object of the pre-genital instinctual impulses. This sexual object will only exist for a relatively short period, at any rate in this oedipal form, for it will soon be abandoned. It will be revived not in the form of the parental image but by the displacement of that image on to other objects. The parental object, on the other hand, is not lost but kept alive through the process of identification and contributes to the formation of the superego and the ego-ideal. 'The object of the identification is not, however, the object of desire but the one opposite to it in the oedipal triangle' (Lacan, 1938). It is thus that the oedipal reality may be sublimated.

(c) MODIFICATIONS OF THE INSTINCTUAL DRIVE   When the Oedipus complex is resolved, the sexual drives are transformed in such a way as to make possible the free disposal of the instinctual energy, which is then cathected on to other objects and used in the pursuit of other goals.

We have seen that when the satisfaction of an instinctual drive becomes impossible because of external circumstances, the growing tension must be satisfied in some substitute way. Such a displacement of the libido takes place at the time of weaning through the gradual detachment from the breast and the withdrawal of cathexis. The libidinal drive itself is not transformed by this but is assigned another aim, involving thereby a re-orientation of instinctual activity. This is akin to the mechanism which operates at the period of the resolution of the Oedipus complex, when the first libidinal object has to be given up in favour of substitute ones.

When, on the other hand, the subject is struggling against his instinctual drives, feelings or phantasies expressing an opposite tendency may appear. Thus disgust, shame, pity or moral judgment may appear as *reaction formation*, i.e. a defensive process by which an unacceptable instinctual impulse is mastered by exaggerating the opposite tendency (e.g. exaggerated concern for cleanliness may be a reaction formation against the pleasure to soil; rigid moral standards a reaction formation against aggressive or libidinal tendencies). The feeling expressed by this reaction formation has become as intense as the instinctual need from which it gets the necessary energy, which is then used to fight the original wish. Reaction formation is particularly marked during the anal-sadistic phase when, pressed by external demands, especially from the mother, the child gradually abandons his affective pleasurable valuation of his faeces and now views them with disgust; everything connected with them (and what they stand for symbolically) is marked by shame or depreciation. Likewise, sadistic or aggressive impulses are changed to pity or kindness. Thus the progression from the pleasure in feeling dirty to the compulsion to feel clean, just as the wish to be 'nice' replaces the aggressive feelings of 'being bad'; this is achieved by a mental process in which love for the mother and the wish to satisfy her becomes mitigated with fear of her and with rebellion against authority. A similar mechanism takes place in the Oedipus complex where castration anxiety and the identification with the parent of the same sex is going to give a new twist to the orientation of infantile sexuality.

In fact, reaction formation requires considerable investment of energy to keep the instinctual drive under control. Freud (1905), on the other hand, refers to

mental forces which are later to impede the course of sexual instinct and, like dams, restrict its flow—disgust, feelings of shame and claims of aesthetic and moral ideals. . . . These constructions probably emerge at the cost of the infantile sexual impulses themselves. Thus the activity of those impulses does not cease even during the period of latency, though it is diverted from their sexual use and directed to other ends.

This time it is not the object that is being modified but the instinctual aim; this is known as *sublimation*. The basic instinctual drives are transformed, the need to possess the primary love object is replaced by the acquisition of knowledge, sexual curiosity changed to intellectual inquisitiveness and cultural or social ambitions replace the oedipal competition. In Freud's view, this diversion of sexual instinctual forces from sexual aims and their direction to new ones is 'one of the most important factors in the development of civilization'. All authors in this field have emphasized the importance of sublimation from the standpoint of the individual's social integration, the establishment of ethical standards and artistic creativity or scientific research. The relative suppression of the sexual drives during the latency period makes sublimation possible and instinctual energy is thus cathected with social activity, acquisition of knowledge and enjoyment of leisure.

It should be added, moreover, that the libidinal impulses which have been desexualized and sublimated are prevented from reaching their aim and are transformed into tender emotions (*Zärtlichkeit*). When they lose the passionate character of their original state they also avert the possible danger of a castration which would inhibit the genital function. This is why Freud viewed the latency period as a redistribution of instinctual energy and not as a suppression of the libido.

The latency period is a particularly receptive period for acquiring and improving new skills and knowledge, the redistribution of the libidinal energy having liberated, as it were, a 'neutral', 'non-conflictual' area for this purpose. To the extent that the Oedipus complex remains active, there will be difficulties in all these areas, for the cognitive processes will not be cathected.

(d)   THE FORMATION OF THE SUPEREGO   The redistribution plays an important part in the structural organisation: at this stage a further prohibition is added to all the others, i.e. the child is forbidden to satisfy his sexual drive. This internalized prohibition completes the formation of the mental agency called the *superego*. 'The authority of the father or the parents is introjected into the ego and there it forms the nucleus of the superego which takes over the severity of the father and perpetuates his prohibition against incest, and so secures the ego from the return of the libidinal object-cathexes' (Freud, 1924b). In this sense the superego may be said to be *the heir of the Oedipus complex.*

The superego is dependent on internalization of parental images, and takes over the demands which are attributed to them. When the parental imago can be given up as a libidinal object it is introjected as a 'moral' agency and from then on the prohibiting or inhibiting presence of the adult is of lesser importance than the subject's guilt which is supported by internalized images. The superego may prove to be more stern than the real parents because the child's own aggressiveness which he projects on to them is superimposed on their image.

When belief in parental omnipotence is progressively weakened and the loosening of libidinal ties puts the child in a position of relative independence, the superego takes over as an autonomous system which becomes the support for moral conscience.

This parental internalization, however, does not take place solely by virtue of the authority of the superego. The Oedipus complex has to be resolved by the sublimation of the internalized parental image to which the child will subsequently address itself when it has to adopt towards the love object an attitude compatible with his own instinctual drives and psychic images. This sublimated parental image represents the first model of an agency called the *ego-ideal.*

6 *Puberty and adolescence: childhood's end*

Adolescence can be approached from two different angles: one approach emphasizes the adolescent's individual problems; the other envisages the adolescent's dealing with his social environment. Actually these two aspects can be said to be interdependent. The process of adaptation, ego-development and the impact of 'biological' demands are the basic element in producing the changes which are taking place during adolescence. The influx of biologically predetermined sexual forces at puberty is accompanied by a revival of instinctual drives which brings the latency period to an end and gives sexual life its final normal shape. Latency had enabled the child to organize himself, to acquire motor and intellectual equipment, to consolidate his ego-defences and to adapt himself to the reality principle. When the libidinal drives are reactivated, the conflicts of the oedipal phase, dormant during the latency period, may re-emerge. How they will manifest themselves will largely depend on the solution of the oedipal conflict. But new problems also do arise due to what has been called the conflict between generations.

(a) THE CONFLICT BETWEEN GENERATIONS has often been considered a necessary development stage and has been stated in terms of the adolescent's adjustment. But whatever the changing manifestations of this conflict may be—greatly intensified over the last ten years due to economic and political contradictions—a common psychological basis for this conflict exists and has been clearly defined by Hélène Deutsch (1968). She states that many adolescents are troubled by the fact that the image of the 'mature' generation has become somewhat indistinct, 'once they discover that their parents are often involved in their own unresolved adolescent problems'. Such a protest against the 'cultural standards', the 'establishment', the 'system' is of course based on some valid reasons[1] but its expression varies according to cultural background, specific problems and socio-political structure of the environment. As a result adolescents find their allegiance in small minority groups whose goals are in opposition to those of authority, and which will fulfil their wishes: essentially a protest against the established social order. Psycho-social research (Marcuse, 1955; Mitscherlich, 1965), has tried to approach this problem. But it

[1] This revolt has been voiced by many authors. The constant and rapid change of cultural references over the last ten or fifteen years has to a large extent modified the adolescent's outlook on life and society. A lucid and articulate account has been written by Jeff Nuttall (1968) in *Bomb Culture*.

has also been said that effectiveness of socio-cultural factors and attitudes of adolescents as a social group are to a great extent determined by individual psychological processes. Thus H. Deutsch (1968) states that all adolescents undergo common development processes: the devaluation of accepted values; the projection of their own shortcomings and failures on to the outside world; ourbursts of aggressiveness and the overcompensation for inertia and passivity by acts of overt rebellion or brutality. 'The goals of the grown-ups are distrusted or rejected by them, and contemporary socio-political aims do not seem to them to present ideas that are capable of fulfilling their emotional and intellectual needs.' It would be wrong to blame the massive dissatisfaction on psychological factors alone. These socio-political problems must be taken into consideration. However we are only going to deal with individual psychological factors which might explain why adolescents are sensitized to global refusal of, or opposition to, the adult world.

(b)   REACTIONS TO SEXUAL MATURITY   Against the intensification of sexual impulses the adolescent has to maintain some of his early defences, but he also must create new ones. Sexual maturation, as a purely physiological fact, may become an event that provokes severe anxiety: even though it is biologically determined its psychological impact is, as Hélène Deutsch puts it, 'immense and paradoxical'.

One of the most striking manifestations of the sexual reactivation is masturbation which, because of the social stigma attached to it, often carries feelings of guilt and frustration. Although masturbation at this period is a normal sexual outlet, since it generally represents the only possible expression for the pre-adolescent's sexual needs, it is a guilt-ridden affair. Frightening stories about its harmful consequences, such as madness, impotence or sterility, foster a constant fear and lead to resolutions which can never be fulfilled. It is possible, too, that the feelings of guilt are connected with a revival of unresolved oedipal conflicts or of castration anxiety as indicated by phantasies underlying the oedipal situation. It is not, however, masturbation as such which is harmful, but its psychological determinants.

The struggle is directed both against the content of phantasy and the bodily act. If the ego, under the influence of castration anxiety, inhibits even the occasional masturbatory relief, the libidinal and regressive energy of the masturbatory phantasy, being deprived of all normal bodily outlet, is neither totally dammed up nor deplaced on ego-activities. Thus masturbation should be considered as an indispensable activity during adolescence and fulfils several functions: (a) sexual feelings and phantasies can be experienced within the context of possessing mature genitals; (b) perverse phantasies can either be repressed or used as a vehicle of masturbatory satisfaction; (c) masturbatory phantasies contribute to reorganize ego-functions (M. Laufer, 1968).

The underlying psychological problems are of great importance, since they include not only the reactivation of oedipal conflicts, but impinge on the adolescent's body image and identity as a sexually mature person. Masturbation should enable the adolescent to establish the primacy of genitality and to include his genitals as functioning organs in his body image. Masturbation phantasies play an important part, particularly in helping the ego to reorganize itself. These phantasies are sometimes very regressive and in such cases adolescents may become aware that something is 'badly wrong' with them, i.e. that they are aware of being unable to use masturbation phantasies as a 'trial action' for adult sexuality. There is a close link between this gradual apprenticeship of adult sexuality and the adolescent's relationship to his own body. When certain pre-oedipal experiences have distorted the oedipal situation in a way that genitality would be disrupted, the question of the adolescent's 'ownership of his body' would arise.

One crucial factor seems to be whether the adolescent can affectively experience his mature body as belonging to himself or whether he reacts to it as if it still belonged to his mother who first cared for it. . . . These adolescents felt that in masturbation and in the accompanying fantasies they were reliving a real experience, and that this included the satisfaction of regressive wishes. They felt that they had no control over their bodies. They regarded their bodies as their enemies or as something separate of the rest of themselves. . . . In the need to create the feeling that their bodies were either nonexistent or free of danger, they resorted to various means—suicide attempts, taking drugs, overeating. The adolescents experienced masturbation (referred to by Freud as the 'primal addiction') or masturbation fantasies as something equivalent to a failure in repression or as the vehicle for the satisfaction of something perverse and shameful.[1]

---

[1] M. Laufer (1968), pp. 115–16.

G

Adolescents may be unable to use masturbation as a constructive step toward adulthood, such as establishing heterosexual object relationships or the primacy of the genitals. In such conditions adolescents experience masturbation either as a confirmation of their abnormality or as a threat to their whole ego functioning. Masturbation phantasies may thus express the hatred of the body which is experienced as forcing this activity upon the subject; or he might feel helpless in face of abnormal phantasies. In some of Laufer's cases the hatred for the body was equivalent to hatred of an internalized parent. These phantasies can be viewed as defensive efforts against oedipal wishes: the mother who was a protector of the child's body is now regarded as a persecutor.

These irrational factors, which represent traces of oedipal anxiety, may be partly dispelled by suitable discussion. However, as Kate Friendlander has pointed out (1947), 'although the adolescent knows that masturbation is quite common at his age, his emotional problems will not come to an end for all that, although he may well overcome his former conflicts with less difficulty'. Normally masturbation will continue until full sexual relations are established, but psychic conflicts should become less acute. Compulsive masturbation could be a sign of unresolved oedipal conflict and its consequences will subsequently appear in the subject's sexual behaviour as well as in his social relations.

(c) IDENTIFICATION AND NARCISSISM   The need to give up the parental love objects will express itself in the adolescent's overt conflict with his parents. The rebellion will be directed more particularly against the parent's authority, but also against everything invested with that authority. This rebellion will be all the more spectacular if there has been a strong parental fixation and hence a more compelling parental image: whether a forceful one or, on the contrary, an image of inconsistent or over-conforming parents against which the adolescent has to affirm himself.

The devaluation of the paternal image, which is criticized and rejected by the adolescent, serves as the rationalization for unconscious processes. This devaluation is not the consequence of increased intellectual capacities, but of the revival of grandiose phantasies, dreams of glory and omnipotence which are related to an over-idealized father image.

This struggle against the early cathexes may culminate either in total rejection of the parents or a breaking away from them, orientating the child towards an entirely different way of life, or in the re-establishment of harmony and mutual tolerance and affection. Although the parents' attitude often turns the evolution of this phase in one direction rather than another, it must be emphasized that the final outcome is largely dependent on the oedipal situation existing at the onset of the latency period and on the solution of the conflicts at the same time as the dissolution of the Oedipus complex. Puberty is the adolescent's last opportunity to find a *spontaneous* solution of the oedipal conflict.

One of the crucial problems of adolescence is the increase of narcissism which is due to regressive tendencies, and related to the fact that the old objects are lost before new ones have taken their place. This is being reinforced by the shattering of the ego-ideal which is critically injured by masturbatory guilt and increased superego demands: in order to restore an acceptable self-image, narcissism is being enforced as a defence against self-devaluation. Increased narcissism plays an important role: it enables the adolescent to use his energy for creative work; hence the usual artistic or scientific interests which can manifest themselves in a somewhat erratic but highly original way. On the other hand narcissism prevents premature emotional involvements.

Anna Freud (1958) points out that it is 'normal' for an adolescent to behave in an inconsistent and unpredictable manner:

to revolt against his parents and to be dependent on them;
to love them and to hate them; to be more idealistic,
artistic, generous and unselfish than he will ever be again,
but also the opposite: self-centred, egoistic, calculating.
Such fluctuations between extreme opposites would be
deemed highly abnormal at any other time of life. At this time
they may signify no more than that an adult structure of
personality takes a long time to emerge. . . .

She insists also on the fact that such adolescents should be given time and scope to work out their own solutions and that parents often need help and support so as to be able to accept their difficulties and cope with the adolescent's attempts to liberate himself.

In these attempts at a solution, the choice of new libidinal objects plays an important part. A consequence of parental identification may be that the first object-choice in puberty will turn out to be homosexual, although only rarely will there be overt homosexuality. This first choice will not determine subsequent sexual activity; it often only indicates the strength of the parental identification from which the adolescent is trying to break away. A heterosexual choice at this stage will facilitate the breakaway from the parental object.

The emotional conflicts at puberty will be less intense and of shorter duration if infantile sexual conflicts have received a satisfactory solution.

(d)   CHARACTER FORMATION   Peter Blos (1968) has emphasized the importance of character formation during adolescence. Although 'character' originates in psychic conflict its main function can be defined as harmonizing the tasks presented by internal demands and by the external world. Character can thus be considered as an ego function. The economic gain frees psychic energy (by automatization of dealing with threatening situations) which can be used for adaptive inventiveness and the actualization of the individual's potentialities.

Character performs a regulatory function by stabilizing ego-identity and by containing emotional fluctuations within a tolerable range. Character formation takes place during adolescence and takes over homeostatic function from other regulatory agencies.

According to Blos, four developmental preconditions must be met before character formation can take its course:

(i)   the loosening of infantile object ties, which Blos (1967) calls the *second individuation process*, makes it possible to disengage libidinal and aggressive cathexes from the infantile love and hate objects;

(ii)   trauma, as a universal condition during childhood, leaves a permanent residue. To integrate residual trauma as part of the ego is another condition for character formation: 'character then is identical with patterned responses to signal anxiety and with it continuance within an adaptive formation'. Failing to internalize the danger situation leads either to belated character formation or to a pathological outcome, the adolescent *moratorium*;

(iii)   the establishment of a historical continuity of the adolescent's life and family history is another condition for ego maturation: 'one cannot have a future without having a past'. It brings with it the subjective feeling of wholeness which is the necessary complementation of the body image.

(iv)   Blos also stresses the importance of sexual identity. While gender identity is established at an early age, sexual identity with definite boundaries appears only at the onset of puberty. 'Puberty represents the demarcation line, beyond which bisexual admixture to gender identity becomes incompatible with further development'. This becomes obvious in the adolescent's growing capacity to make heterosexual object choices and in the decline of masturbation.

Character formation can only proceed if those problems are solved; the autonomous or defensive nature of character structure will be determined by the extent to which these conditions have been fulfilled.

A higher level of integration is thereby reached which contains new homoeostatic possibilities. In this sense we can say that the utter dependence of the human infant on environment, protective stability has achieved in character formation its contraposition, namely the internalization of a stable protective environment. While contents and patterns of character are socially determined, it is only internalization that renders the psychic organism greatly independent from those forces that brought it into existence (Blos, 1968).

(e)   SOCIAL ADJUSTMENT   From the psychoanalytical standpoint adjustment to social life depends on three factors. (a) First, on the quality of the child's object-relations, traces of which are found in the adolescent and which will determine relations with others (particularly with images of authority and love). The adolescent's capacity to cathect new images and to establish a relation which is neither perverted nor neurotic in its demands on others will depend on the way the oedipal conflict has been experienced and resolved. (b) Furthermore, social adjustment will depend on the activity of the psychic agencies, the superego and the ego-ideal, which, when freed from the tutelage of the parents and/or their surrogates, will shape the individual's personality and his attitudes towards society. (c) Finally, the severity of the oedipal conflict also has repercussions on ego-functions and the defence mechanisms of the ego-tolerance of frustration, identification with the aggressor, the use of denial or reaction formations—all these will have an influence on what we call 'character', that is, the sum of all the behaviour patterns of the individual. The adolescent is thus confronted with society, not merely as a child facing the outer world, but with all the complexities of his still undefined and unresolved status, neither child nor adult. In all societies, both primitive and advanced, initiation rites do enable children to leave their families and take their place in the community. Breaking the link which made them dependent on their parents, recognizing their sexual potentialities, taking on responsibilities of fatherhood or motherhood—all these go hand in hand with the self-awareness of one's potential capacities.

5   Object-relations

Under the heading of object-relations theory, psychoanalytical psychology approaches the relation of the subject to *his* object (and *not* the relation between the subject and the object which is an interpersonal relationship). Through the successive phases of his development, the subject gradually establishes links with his objects, which may be either an external or an internal one. In other words, object-relations theory describes the transition from the physiological to the psychological, from uterine parasitism to the setting up of hierarchical social relationships. In the psycho-analytical sense,

> the object of an instinct is the thing in regard to which or through which the instinct is able to achieve its aims. It is what is most variable about an instinct and is not originally connected with it, but becomes assigned to it only in consequence of being peculiarly fitted to make satisfaction possible. The object is not necessarily extraneous: it may equally well be part of the subject's own body
> (Freud, 1915a).

According to this description, the libidinal object may change during development, depending on instinctual maturation and progressive differentiation. The word 'object' is used in a very different way from an academic psychology where an object may be described permanently by its co-ordinates in space and time. As viewed by the psychoanalysts, the libidinal object does not remain identical with itself. Only its *function* remains permanent whatever changes it might undergo during its evolution. The libidinal object is characterized by, and can be described in terms of, the structure and vicissitudes of instinctual drives and partial drives directed towards it (Spitz, 1965).

I. Psychoanalytic research and genetic propositions

The advent of psychoanalytic theories showed the inadequacy of methods based on introspection which were trying to identify mental phenomena through intuition, as well as the limitations of an experimental or psychophysiological approach which also failed to get to the core of psychological facts. Later, more importance was attached to the observation and description of behaviour, and it was from this that psychoanalysis took its cue when it had to create a new conceptual framework.

The concept of object-relations provided psychoanalysis with a privileged field from which it could check its hypotheses. The study of concrete factors and their influence on personality formation seemed particularly adequate for this investigation.

Other psychological theories had tried to deal with these aspects but they did not go beyond the scrutiny of social behaviour or of the individual's interaction with his environment, ignoring such things as intrapsychic and intrasubjective conflict with which psychoanalytic psychology is concerned.

Several factors favoured this kind of investigation. The elaboration, around 1920, of *structural* or *topographical concepts* and the exploration of *genetic propositions* (Hartmann and Kris, 1945), helped to determine the way in which conflicts are set up and to relate them with the structure and behaviour of the subject, and this provided new hypotheses for this work. The ideas of D. Lagache (1949, 1956) and E. Kris (1950) helped to clarify the principles and methodology of 'psychoanalytic research'.

The *genetic* point of view, as opposed to the *dynamic* point of view, was defined by Hartmann and Kris (1945). The dynamic point of view explains the interaction of forces arrayed in the psychic conflict, whereas the genetic viewpoint seeks to clarify how a certain nexus of forces or a certain conflict has grown out of the individual's past and why they have persisted throughout his life. While the dynamic viewpoint determines the causes and modes of behaviour under given circumstances, the genetic approach seeks out their explanation with reference to their 'historical' origin or to anamnestic data. It is concerned with finding out when a specific behaviour pattern was adopted, and why one rather than another; and what causal relation there is between these different expressions of behaviour and their later developments.

These genetic propositions lend themselves more readily to objective verification; they have, in fact, been explored, particularly by psychologists attempting to reconcile psychoanlytic propositions and learning theory with a view to formulating ideas concerning frustration, regression and aggression in terms of experimental psychology.[1]

These writers were well aware of the difficulty of their undertaking, and Sears (1944) pointed out the gap between frustration experienced and experimental frustration. When the analyst probes the origins of anxiety he links it partly to the child's experience and partly to its relation with the mother, whose own

[1] Among the better known texts on this, see J. Dollard et al., *Frustration and Aggression* (1939), O. H. Mowrer, *Learning Theory and Personality Dynamics* (1950), R. Sears, 'Experimental Analysis of Psychoanalytic Phenomena' (1944).

anxiety is determined by past experiences. In adults, anxiety may be caused by conditions originating long ago but still active. It should be emphasized that like conditions do not necessarily produce identical situations and that for the adult it is not a matter of a mere persistence or revival of former infantile situations but of a significant and symbolic transposition.

The genetic viewpoint introduces an additional distinction which separates the consequences of libidinal development from the processes determined by environmental influences. It emphasizes developmental factors as we have just defined them and tends to assign a special importance either to *events* or to the *individual predisposition to cathect certain situations with a specific meaning*. Be that as it may, the emphasis is on the subject's predisposition to perceive and deal with situations and tensions to which he may be subjected. The whole position thus centres on the ego's ability to adjust to external circumstances and this involves a twofold theoretical orientation. On the one hand, Hartmann, Kris and Loewenstein (1946) conceive of the ego as a psychic agency specially designed to control the subject's perception and activities and to solve the problems he comes up against. Some of these problems are, in their view, outside the field of mental conflict and form the *non-conflictual ego*. They distinguish two functions in the ego, according to whether the ego has to solve the problems posed by the instincts or to face difficulties arising out of the environment.

On the other hand—and to the extent that the importance of the experience and the lines along which the experience make their impression on the child's life depend on his particular phase of development—the *event* is re-valued as an effective and formative factor *in crucial situations*. Essentially, there is a conflict: either between two opposing instincts or between an instinctual demand and the ego, caused both by a maturational effect and by the appearance of new exigencies of the environment. The genetic viewpoint, which holds that every mental phenomenon is subject to causal laws which must be tracked down to their origins, has stimulated observational methods.

In psychoanalysis the object to be observed is not the child in isolation. In this it is different from genetic epistemology as it appears, for example, in the work of J. Piaget. Psychoanalytical observation is interested in the child as a subject in his environment, and this is why Hartmann and Kris (1945) consider psychoanalysis as an 'applied social science'.

Psychoanalysts who have been following this 'genetic' orientation, have tried to give a more precise definition to the child-mother relationship, in order to clarify the nature of object-relations and to examine more specifically how certain kinds of maternal behaviour or certain social and cultural patterns might influence the experience and personality of the child. When 'we proceed to establish the aetiological relevance of experiences in the child's life to show how various phases of the past were inter-related, to see the life history as a whole as it is organized by the personality and in turn has organized it', we come up against difficulties common to all research in the field of the social sciences (Kris, 1951). Here, more than elsewhere, the difference between *pure research*, which tends to establish general laws, and *action research*, which aims to lay down laws which are more effective functionally, is not easy to apply. Psychoanalysis, however, in its scientific approach, comes closer to *action research*.

Psychoanalytic research infers its theoretical basic concepts from therapeutic experience with adults and from clinical material gathered through the practice of psychotherapy on children. Its aim is to verify its principles and to extend the field of its scientific speculation by *observing* the child in its environment. This environment may be:

(a) a 'natural' one, restricted to the family or extending to the social surroundings;

(b) one modified by various factors which may be disruptive of its structure (family neurosis; social change; war; etc.);

(c) an artificial one arising from special circumstances (separation of mother from child, hospitalization, illness, etc.).

It contributes an interpretation of these facts with regard to external factors and intrapsychic conflicts. It attempts to integrate these findings into a general theory concerning the psychosocial development and neurophysiological maturation of the individual.

Finally, it has to validate its findings by examining the variations which result from cultural differences.

However, psychoanalysis cannot resort to experimentation and research can proceed only under *semi-experimental* conditions, since the number of variables and the interaction of the different factors cannot be eliminated or reduced. Psychoanalytic research cannot make any arbitrary changes into the actual conditions of the research (psychotherapy, observation) without risk of distorting its meaning.

The complexity of the problem and the variety of possible approaches are to be seen most obviously in the investigation of object-relations. It also shows up the difficulty inherent in any research where observation extends over several months or even years (longitudinal studies). A genuine validation of the data of direct observation may not be possible till after a lapse of time when a psychoanalysis of the subject will make it possible to see how the infantile experiences have been integrated and structured by him.

II. The genesis of object-relations

One of the most urgent tasks was to establish and classify those facts which punctuate the progression of the child's relation to its reality. From a genetic viewpoint, the study of object-relations confers a meaning on historic continuity and demonstrates the structuring role of external reality with regard to the integration of the neurobiological functions during development (Lebovici, 1961).

René Spitz has accomplished the most systematic work in this field. He has attempted to clarify the organisation of the relations which the child establishes with the libidinal object and to highlight the productive moments in these relations. From the appearance of the 'smiling response' which signals the first 'conscious' relation to the *recognized mother*, to the eighth-month anxiety, which marks his link with the *identified mother* and to the acquisition of the semantic use of 'no'—which is the inception of the social exchange of messages, the advent of semantic symbols— Spitz (1965) has traced the genesis of object-relations through the first years of life.

Spitz starts with a number of *basic principles*. He ascertains the fact that the neonate cannot provide for his survival by his own means. Development will enable him to free himself from this total dependence.

On the other hand, Spitz postulates that the newborn child is in a *phase of non-differentiation*. At birth he possesses no faculty of perception, representation or volition; thought, as such, does not exist. 'All these functions, including the instincts, will subsequently be differentiated by a process originating either in maturation or in development.' He considers that no psychic agencies exist at birth and therefore does not find it possible to speak of the ego, or, *a fortiori*, of the superego in the newborn. 'Likewise symbolism is non-existent and hence all symbolic interpretation. Symbols are bound up with the acquisition of language.'

The originality of this work lies in the fact that it focused not on the development or acquisition of any particular faculty (as in Piaget's researches in genetic epistemology), but on the mode of *mother-child relation* as the primal and major (not to say exclusive) relational object.

1 *Primary narcissism (Freud); 'objectless stage' (Spitz) or undifferentiated phase (Hartmann)*

Birth has been described as the child's first traumatic situation. It is the first experience of a separation which will forever after leave its frustrating effect. The concept of the birth trauma described by O. Rank (1924) and seen as the first experience of anxiety, was a bold and particularly striking extrapolation though not necessarily corresponding to any psychological reality. Subsequently, Margaret Ribble (1944), taking up a thesis expounded by Freud (1925a), saw in the reactions to anoxia at birth a prototype of the physiological manifestations of anxiety. Be that as it may, birth does inaugurate for the child a new mode of existence which brings the uterine parasitism to a close and in which he finds himself totally dependent on the outside world for his vital needs.

Nevertheless, at birth, this indispensable environment cannot appear as exterior to him because he is unable to distinguish his own body from his surroundings.

Only one manifestation of anything resembling emotion can be detected. This is a state of excitation, which appears to have negative quality. The negative excitation ensues when the newborn is exposed to stimulation strong enough to overcome his high perceptive threshold. For simplicity's sake, we will use the term unpleasure to describe negative excitation in the infant.

This should be considered as a process of discharge: it exemplifies the Nirvana (constancy) principle in which physiological needs and primary affects are fused, and according to which excitation is maintained at a constant level. Any tension rising above this level has to be discharged without delay. In the first hours and even days of life, unpleasure is the only observable effect; its counterpart is not pleasure but *quiescence* (Spitz, 1965).

In this phase, the interaction of the newborn child with the external world is determined by the play of neurobiological mechanisms in which signs of a cortical and sub-cortical integration may be discerned. The same applies to *rooting behaviour*, i.e. when stimulation in and around the mouth elicits rotation of the head towards the stimulation, followed by a snapping movement of the mouth. It is noteworthy that this 'response' may be attenuated or even disappear altogether after feeding, i.e. when satiety gets rid of the psychobiological phenomena of hunger. 'Up to the second month of life, the infant recognizes the signal for food only when he is hungry.' Spitz advances the proposition that this behaviour is predicated upon an innate releasing mechanism with survival value. It is the only *directed* behaviour of the infant at birth.

One could say that in this objectless phase, perceptions are still contact perceptions and thus basically different from distance perception, such as visual and auditory perception. But although the newborn child reacts to certain stimuli, he is still incapable of perceiving either their intrinsic or extrinsic character and hence unable to regard the object which relieves his tensions as a perceived object.

From this period, nevertheless, his reactions are interwoven in the network of communication with his mother. The infant trying to relieve a tension created by cold or hunger cries without any real intention of communication. It is the mother hearing these cries who interprets them and responds as though to a 'call'. Thus, what is only an *indicator*,[1] informing us of the infant's state of tension without any intention to communicate (a non-specific discharge), is interpreted by the mother as a *signal*[2] and thus achieves its goal. It is only *secondary* that this indicator will assume for the child—as a result of learning—the value of a significant symbol to be used intentionally.

In this phase the infant is still incapable of perceiving an object, but some of his (unintentional) manifestations of discharge produce a reaction from those around him and thereby introduce into his experience a meaning which he will soon be able to recognize.

This objectless phase corresponds to what Freud (1915a) described as *primary narcissism*.

When at the beginning of mental life the ego is cathected by its own instinctual drives, it is to some extent capable of satisfying them by himself. 'We call this condition "narcissism", and this way of obtaining satisfaction "auto-erotic".' For the neonate the outside world has no interest, for it is not yet identified as a possible source of satisfaction.

---

[1] Comparable with the buzzing sound heard when the telephone receiver is off the hook.
[2] Comparable with the *ringing* of the telephone informing us that a communication is to be expected at this moment.

We define loving as the relation of the ego to its sources of pleasure. The situation in which the ego loves itself only and is indifferent to the external world illustrates the first of the *opposites* which we found to 'loving'. In so far as the ego is auto-erotic, it has no need of the external world, but, in consequence of experiences undergone by the instinct of self-preservation, it acquires objects from that world, and, in spite of everything, it cannot avoid feeling internal instinctual stimuli for a time as unpleasurable. Under the dominance of the pleasure principle, a further development takes place in the ego. In so far as the objects which are presented to it are sources of pleasure, it takes them into itself, it introjects them; and on the other hand, it expels whatever within itself becomes a cause of unpleasure (mechanism of projection).[1]

Between the eighth and the twelfth week the external world begins to be perceived visually by the infant, thus paving the way for the next phase.

2 Anaclitic phase (Freud); the stage of the precursor of the object (Spitz)

This is the stage at which the infant turns from the *reception* of stimuli coming from the inside to the *perception* of stimuli coming from the outside. For the first time an element of organization is gradually introduced in the child's undifferentiated world which enables him to perceive certain signals.

Towards the end of the second month, the infant visually perceives the human being, though this specific reaction only occurs when he is in a state of physiological need—when he is hungry. When it is time for the feed and the mother approaches the whining infant, he will quieten down, turn his head towards the adult, open his mouth or perform sucking movements with his mouth.

'In other words he responds at this time to an external stimulus solely in terms of an *introceptive perception*, the perception of an unsatisfied instinctual drive' (Spitz). This behaviour pattern is to be distinguished from the one just described as the rooting behaviour, since the source of satisfaction has to be recognized by the child and the motor behaviour involved corresponds to a visual perception.

This appetitive behaviour, strictly related to the infant's needs,

[1] S. Freud, *Instincts and their Vicissitudes* (1915a).

improves and progresses; during the third month the child will be capable of following the adult's face with his eyes.

The hypothesis that the human face acquired preferential status in the infant's perceptual world because it is closely tied to his biological satisfactions was corroborated by Spitz, who noticed that during feeding and handling of the child, the child's eyes remain fixed on the mother's face, which is the most constant visual stimulus in the first six weeks. Spitz describes the human face as *the first sign* linked with the lessening of tensions in the child.

Indeed, from the third month onward and till the sixth month, a new pattern, the smiling response, makes its appearance. *The smiling response* is aroused by the adult's face when certain features are recognizable: the face must be presented straight on so that the child can clearly see both eyes, the nose and the line of the eyebrows, and it must be in motion (nodding, mouth movements).[1] The child responds to this sign *Gestalt* with a smile, whereas no reaction is elicited when a feeding-bottle is presented.[2] What the child recognizes in this *Gestalt* is a sign which is not determined by the essential, intrinsic qualities of the object but recognized by its superficial features.

For this reason Spitz prefers to speak of the precursor of the object, the *preobject*, which is related to the feeding situation and associates the mother's face with intra-oral contact and the satisfaction of a need. Thanks to the mother's face, recognized as a *Gestalt* signal, the baby manages to separate from the surrounding meaningless chaos of things one element which will become more and more meaningful. The author interprets this phenomenon as the transition from the primary narcissistic phase to the object phase by replacing the 'autistic' object of his own person by an external object.

The preobject which thus individualizes itself from the encircling chaos is a crucial point in the child's development. The appearance of the *social smile* means that the child has reached a certain level, called by Spitz an 'organizing point'.[3] The import-

---

[1] 'As soon as this *Gestalt* is altered, the so-called "object" is no longer recognized; it has lost its quality as an object' (Spitz). Experiments have shown that the profile does not elicit the smiling response, though a mask, presented front-wise, is recognized as a signal.

[2] Some children will try to extend their arms in the direction of the bottle, but they will not smile at the bottle.

[3] The idea of organizers of psychic development is borrowed by Spitz from the field of embryology, where it has long been known that 'the growth of cells is influenced by a particular environment in which they are placed at a particular phase of development. If transplanted before their critical phase, they will grow

ance of these 'organizers' lies in the fact that they represent crucial moments in the passage from one phase of development to the next. 'From this moment onwards a new way of being begins, fundamentally different from the preceding one.' The child, turning away from the inner perception of his experience, copes with the exterior perception of his surroundings and lays down the necessary premises for all subsequent social relations. This experience proves the existence of the subject's mnemic traces, and hence of a possible differentiation of the psychic apparatus into conscious and unconscious systems. This is what led Spitz to date the beginning of thought processes from the time of the appearance of the precursor of the object and to see in it the first signs of the formation of the ego as 'a central steering organization', mediating between the instinctual drives and voluntary activity.

3 Constitution of the part object

It is noteworthy that in this phase the breast is not perceived by the infant as an actual libidinal object. There can be no doubt, however, that the mother's breast represents the gratification of the need and is perceived as such through mouth and hand. Thus the oral cavity constitutes the cradle of perception. The modified and expanded memory traces of these perceptions will later be used in a symbolic form. A meaningful relation is established between the breast, which satisfies the physiological need, and the mother's face, by which the face becomes the symbolic representation of the satisfaction experienced. The breast becomes a 'part object' only because of the emotional cathexis invested in the instinctual drive.

It is in the imaginary reconstitution of this *part object*, as representing frustration or gratification, that the first object-relations are established.

Although in Spitz's sequence the part object apparently plays only a secondary role, this is because the genetic viewpoint seeks to clarify the constitution of a 'real' object. On the other hand, the part object, viewed as an unconscious phantasy, is a vital element in the building up of the outer and inner world.[1] In the part-

The English word 'phantasy' does not distinguish between conscious imaginary phenomena and the unconscious content of the phenomena. In an attempt to make a distinction between them, Anna Freud suggests that they have the same relation as the manifest and latent content of a dream.

in a way appropriate to their new environment.' If these cells are transplanted after this phase, they will continue their growth as they would have done in their original environment.

object phase, the infant does not conceive of himself as a unified being. This was expressed by J. Lacan (1938) when he described the 'fragmented body'. Fragmentation is also to be found in the concept of the *primal cavity* (Spitz, 1955), where the various elements—hand, mouth, breast, face—represent the fragmented dyadic image of mother and child: what belongs to the one being blurred with what belongs to the other. Because neither is as yet constituted as subject or as object, recognition of them is not yet possible. But Melanie Klein has elaborated still further this imaginary function in which the child's phantasy life is centred by the part object.

4 *Object phase*

The transition from part object to whole object marks another stage in the organization of object-relations. During the second six months the mother will be perceived as a whole object capable of being recognized by the child outside periods of need. The satisfaction shown by the child when it perceives the mother's face can be considered to be a continuation of the state of quiescence felt after the appeasement of hunger. One could speak of the oral cathexis of the maternal object. But when the mother is established as a whole object, the object-relation will no longer be conditioned by a biological fact and the child evinces satisfaction even when he feels no need: the 'pleasure' indicates that the gratification of the need is no longer the most important factor in the child's relationship with his mother.

5 *The eighth-month anxiety*

The way the child behaves when he encounters unpleasure resulting from feeling abandoned is regarded by Spitz as indicating that the mother has become established as the libidinal object over and above the specific feeding situation. Between six and eight months the child becomes capable of discriminating between different persons and the response of the *Gestalt* of the human face is replaced by a specific reaction to a 'stranger'. If a chance visitor approaches a baby actively, his behaviour will be characteristic:

> He may lower his eyes 'slyly', he may cover them with his hands, lift his dress to cover his face, throw himself prone on his cot and hide his face in the blankets, he may weep or scream. The common denominator is a refusal of contact, a turning away with a shading more or less pronounced of anxiety.

Spitz considers this refusal of contact with a stranger as the first sign of real anxiety.[1]

In his view, it arises from the infant's disappointment at finding himself confronting someone whom he does not recognize as his mother of whom he feels deprived. The stranger is perceived *as a face* with mnemic traces of the mother's face. This discriminatory function indicates that the infant has fixed his choice on a specific 'love' object, excluding all others, and that he has thus achieved a genuine object-relation. In other words, the mother has become an identifiable libidinal object who cannot be mistaken for any other. This important phenomenon in the development of object-relation shows the fusion of the libidinal and aggressive instincts on one and the same object.

The interplay of the instinctual drives plays a major role in the establishment of object-relations. At the phase of narcissistic non-differentiation, there is a fusion of libidinal and aggressive drives: they will become disentangled during the first months only when satisfaction or non-gratification are experienced in relation to the maternal object. As long as, in the anaclitic phase, the impulses are based on the child's oral needs (and their gratification), the mother remains the sole object of his instinctual drives. When more perceptual possibilities allow for a gradual integration of experience, the instinctual drives will become disentangled. The mother will be perceived not as a whole object but fragmented into 'good' objects, towards which the libidinal drives are directed, and 'bad' ones, which attract the aggressive drives.[2]

6 *The mother as object*

Thanks to the integrative functions of the ego, the child, by confronting his experiences and his growing awareness of his emotional world, localizes and identifies the maternal object as the only object of the instinctual drives. The mother is no longer split into part objects; she is *one* mother, one single object, on which

---

[1] According to Spitz, three distinct moments can be described during the first year in the ontogenesis of anxiety: (a) the *physiological prototype* of anxiety, which Freud and Ribble consider to coincide with the moment of delivery but which Spitz thinks is a simple state of tension; (b) during the neonatal period *avoidance and flight reactions* expressed in certain situations and before certain objects which are at the root of unpleasurable experiences and probably of fear; (c) *the eighth-month anxiety* in which he discerns a specific intrapsychic perception.
[2] As will be seen later, this splitting into 'good' and 'bad' part objects is due to the mechanisms of projection and introjection which are not only responsible for this direction towards part objects but also create them in the child's phantasies (see Melanie Klein).

opposing drives converge; she thus becomes the real libidinal object cathected at one and the same time by the child's love and aggressiveness.

Within the genetic frame of reference the fusion of the instincts on to one single object is to be attributed to the co-ordinating function of the ego:

> We realize that to deprive as well as to favour one or other of the two instinctual drives necessarily leads to a distortion of object-relations. As it is the mother who does the depriving or favouring, it is the mother's behaviour which will determine how the object relations will finally take shape (Spitz, 1954).

The infant's experience is therefore closely linked to the experience of the mother, who, by her behaviour, can reinforce the frustrating or gratifying meaning of each moment.[1] Thus the child gradually acquires the capacity to tolerate frustration and to adjust to the reality principle.

The postponement of immediate gratification in the interests of subsequent, more substantial pleasure makes it possible for the child to give up appetitive behaviour in favour of goal-directed activity by interposing, between the instinctual drive and its motor discharge, a mediating or regulating agency represented by the ego. Aggression will henceforth be discharged in controlled and exploitable form to exercise an ever-increasing mastery over the outside world. Spitz sees the establishment of this new type of relation with the environment as the *second organizer* in the child's development.

Spitz, however, recognizes a further importance in the setting up of this object-relation: the possibility for the child to gain access to a world structured by communication. The understanding of the social gestures as a means of communication becomes obvious in the child's understanding of commands and prohibitions. The consistency and reliability of signals which the child receives from his mother are a guarantee of the child's normal development. The signals themselves are determined by the

[1] Here, one of the differences between two psychoanalytic conceptions is clearly expressed. On the one hand there is the 'genetic school' which sees the mother's actual behaviour as the immediate source of the child's development, ascribes a determining force in the child's future wellbeing to the different methods of mothering and makes the real mother ultimately responsible for the formative processes. On the other hand there is the 'English school' (Melanie Klein) in whose view the reality of the mother's behaviour takes second place, the essential mainspring for the establishment of object relations being the child's primal phantasies and his intrapsychic experience, irrespective of parental behaviour patterns.

mother's own unconscious attitudes; her behaviour will manifest itself in a manner of which she herself is not necessarily aware.

Spitz emphasizes therefore the importance of the mother's presence and the security that it provides in creating an atmosphere that allows the introduction of do's and don'ts and opens the door to all the varieties of socialized activity in school and play and the acquisition of new motor, perceptual and cognitive functions. The mother is important not only for the security she provides but also because of the opportunities she offers for *identification* which, through the imitation of gestures, will gradually remodel the child's body-image. A certain *code* is thus established which goes far beyond the imitation of gesture and facial expression: this code becomes part of the body-experience and thus makes it possible for the child to identify with his libidinal object.

The genetic viewpoint emphasizes the importance of the 'dyadic universe', the relations established between *two* individuals. The emotional bonds established within the 'dyad' contain the whole development of subsequent social relations. These bonds set up patterns which cannot be explained by the mere learning process since the part played by unconscious identification is at least of equal importance. Maternal behaviour derives from the mother's unconscious attitudes; however, Spitz points out that one must also consider cultural determinants of the dyad, since 'cultural institutions provide the range of opportunity which delimits the expression of intrapsychic processes, in both mother and child'.

The child becomes aware of the object as and when he reaches the maturational point in a particular culture; but the ability to recognize the object as such contributes to the maturational process (Lebovici 1961).

7 The emergence of organizers

Thus, in the course of the first year and due to the development of the infant's own potentialities, he will gradually become independent. So far two nodal points (or critical phases) have been emphasized. These nodal points mark the integration of the various currents of development with the capacities resulting from the processes of maturation. This results in a restructuration of the psychic system on a higher level of efficiency. When successful, this integration leads to what Spitz calls an *organizer* of the psyche.

(a)   The visible sign, the indicator of the first organizer, is the *smiling response*. This integration marks the transition from the narcissistic stage to the stage of the preobject (in the third month of life), and indicates the child's perception of outside stimuli; the capacity to suspend the unconditional surrender to the pleasure principle and the onset of reality principle's functioning; the shift from passivity to directed activities; and, last but not least, the beginning of social relations.

(b)   The *eighth-month anxiety* indicates the emergence of the second organizer: the establishment of the libidinal object proper. This nodal point of the child's development marks the convergence of ego integration which becomes structured, delimited in regard to the id and the outer world, and of the progressive differentiation of aggression from libido. The culminating point of these processes is the establishment of the libidinal object, revealed by the appearance of the eighth-month anxiety.

The concept of *organizers* which, as it should be stressed again, are models constituted for the purpose of apprehending psychic development—and the various stages of object-relations, make it possible to establish certain orientation-points in order to get a better view of the infant's development. So far, we have envisaged this development from a topological and structural viewpoint. However, a different psychoanalytic approach has tried to shed some light on the child's unconscious phantasies during the early stages of development, as we shall see in examining Melanie Klein's contribution.

III. Unconscious phantasies and constitution of the object: the views of Melanie Klein

The establishment of object-relations must also be envisaged in the light of Melanie Klein's contribution. She approached this subject not through direct observation (in the sense understood by Spitz, i.e. with the observer remaining in the position of a 'neutral' investigator and as far removed as possible from any emotional participation) but by interpreting the phantasies produced during psychoanalytic sessions, in a situation where a strong emotional link is established between the child and the adult.

1 *The part object*

In Melanie Klein's view, the unconscious phantasy is the mental representative of the instinctual drive, and therefore exists, like the instinctual drive itself, at the very beginning of mental activity, that is, in the first weeks of life. What Freud described as 'hallucinatory wish-fulfilment' is an example of phantasy activity as conceived by Melanie Klein.

In these first months of life the child expresses oral needs and wishes. The mother's breast satisfies these needs electively. As a *part object* the breast may be hallucinated or phantasized and introjected. From then on the part object (the breast) is experienced by the child as part of his inner world. Introjection is easier at this stage because the external quality of objects is not yet clearly perceived.

Since the representation of this need is expressed through phantasies, the introjected phantasy object is experienced by the child as 'good' or 'bad': a good or bad breast, according to whether the (oral) need is satisfied or frustrated. These experiences of gratification or frustration are not yet felt as external events; they are part of the undifferentiated experience of the child. In this phase the oral gratifications and frustrations, whether real or imaginary, create the phantasy-images of a 'good' and a 'bad' breast.

The breast, however, is not the only introjected object. As we shall see, Melanie Klein considers that between six months and one year, the first elements of an early oedipal complex are already active and that the parental couple plays a role in the child's unconscious phantasies. Thus the mother becomes not only the repository of nourishment; she also has (by oral incorporation) appropriated the 'father's penis', a symbol of oedipal frustration.

The father's penis incorporated by the mother becomes an object both coveted and threatening and so it, too, becomes a 'good' or 'bad' penis. Although both breast and penis may therefore be invested with this gratifying or persecutory quality their functions are not comparable. Whereas the breast, good or bad, will remain for a time in the category of *need*, the penis already introduces the child to the world of *desire*.

Thus, in the view of Melanie Klein, all reality is introjected and plays the part of an internal, psychic reality, which is as compelling as the external one. The establishment of the object-relations, external or internal, is conditioned by the interplay of these phantasies. And the mental conflict does not oppose the instinctual drives to the repressive forces, since the conflict is waged in the introjected and imaginary confrontation of the psychic representatives of these instinctual drives.[1]

Melanie Klein takes one of her basic assumptions from the Freudian theory of two conflicting instinctual drives: the life instinct (or the libidinal drive) and the death instinct (which corresponds to the destructive drive.)[2]

The instinctual polarity is thus displayed in the phantasy life: among introjected objects, the good, gratifying ones represent the libidinal instincts while the bad, frustrating objects correspond to the destructive drives. If the mother's breast fulfils the child's need, it becomes the phantasized representative of the good object. However, in the oral-sadistic phase, the child suffers oral frustrations which are all the more painful because those needs are more intense and invested with aggression: the breast, closely related to frustration as such, becomes a 'bad' object, the focus of the destructive instincts and of the child's aggressive phantasies. In this way, through the mechanisms of introjection and projection, the child's relations with part objects are established.

To the extent that the child must be able to cope with the instinctual energy, Melanie Klein contends that he possesses an ego in the earliest months of infancy—different of course from the highly organized and well-integrated ego of a more advanced age. This immature ego allows him to experience anxiety, to protect himself against it, to deflect the death instinct and to establish primitive object-relations. The early ego is exposed to anxiety stirred up by the inborn polarity of instincts as well as by the impact of external reality.

[1] This conception raises the question of the status of the object: are we dealing with a *real* or *imaginary* object? Views diverge. For the 'genetic' analyst it is the real object which, by its presence or absence, by the gratifications or frustrations which it imposes, plays the structuring role. The 'English school', on the other hand, considers that these objects are not 'things' situated in the body or in the psyche; but are 'unconscious fantasies which people have about what they contain' (Segal, 1964). The child's development will be influenced, to some extent, by the real, favourable or unfavourable, experiences in his relation to the outside world. But the moulding of these experiences in terms of the child's—and later of the adult's—emotional life is determined by these unconscious phantasies and how they relate to external reality.

[2] 'Our hypothesis is that there are two essentially different classes of instincts: the sexual instincts, understood in the widest sense—Eros, if you prefer that name—and the aggressive instincts, whose aim is destruction. . . . We have argued in favour of a special aggressive and destructive instinct in men not on account of the teachings of history or of our experience in life but on the basis of general considerations to which we were led by examining the phenomena of sadism and masochism. . . . If for a moment we leave its (the masochism's) erotic components on one side, it affords us a guarantee of the existence of a trend that has self-destruction as its aim. If it is true of the destructive instinct as well (as of the libido) that the ego—but what we have in mind here is rather the id, the whole person—originally includes all the instinctual impulses, we are

When the child is faced with the anxiety produced by the death instinct, the ego deflects it. This deflection consists partly of a projection, partly of the conversion of the death instinct into aggression. The ego splits itself and projects that part of itself which contains the death instinct outward into the original external object—the breast. Thus the breast is felt to be bad and threatening to the ego, giving rise to a feeling of persecution. However, part of the death instinct remaining in the self is converted into aggression and directed against the persecutors (H. Segal, 1964). In the same way, the libido is projected on to an external object to create an ideal object: the good breast. As from this phase, the ego thus establishes a relation with two objects which result from the splitting of the primary object: the ideal breast and the persecutory breast. The phantasy of the ideal breast merges with gratifying experiences of love, whereas the persecutory phantasies merge with real experiences of deprivation and unpleasure attributed by the child to the bad object. The subject seeks to keep inside the ideal object and to identify with it, feeling it as a protection. But he attempts to keep out the bad object which represents a menace. The 'good', however, may be sometimes projected on to an external object so as to protect it from aggressive instincts, while the persecutors may be introjected so as to control its destructive power. However, 'the permanent feature is that in situations of anxiety the split is widened and projection and introjection are used to keep persecutory and ideal objects as far as possible from one another, while keeping both of them under control'.

---

led to the view that masochism is older than sadism, and that sadism is the destructive instinct directed outwards, thus acquiring the characteristic of aggressiveness. A certain amount of the original destructive instinct may still remain in the interior' (Freud, 1933, pp. 103–5).

It is this primal destructive instinct (*destrudo*) which Freud in the same text identifies as the *death instinct* and which is thus opposed to all libidinal instincts. 'If we recognize in this instinct the self-destructiveness of our hypothesis, we may regard the self-destructiveness as an expression of a "death instinct" which cannot fail to be present in every vital process. And now the instincts that we believe in, divide themselves into two groups—the erotic instincts, which seek to combine more and more living substance into ever greater unities, and the death instincts, which oppose this effort and lead what is living back into an inorganic state' (S. Freud, 1933, p. 107).

This theory of the death instinct is a very controversial one. Waelder (1960) observes that we must distinguish between the theory of a death instinct and the manifestations of a destructive instinct. The former belongs to the domain of biological theory, the second is a clinical or psychological theory. In Waelder's view (as in that of many others) the theory of the destructive instinct is valid even though the hypothesis of a primal death instinct (*thanatos*) cannot be validated.

2   *The paranoid-schizoid position*

These two mechanisms—persecutory anxiety and splitting of the ego and of its objects—have led Melanie Klein to describe this type of object-relations as the *paranoid-schizoid* (or *persecutory*) *position*.[1]

Certain defence mechanisms are linked with this position: introjection, which tries to keep the good object inside, and projection, which tries to exclude the persecutory object. These two are among the most primal of the mechanisms. Special importance is attached to the mechanism of *'splitting'* which is linked with the increasing idealization of the ideal object in order to protect it against the persecutory object. Splitting plays an important part in ego-organization, allowing it to discriminate between pleasant and unpleasant experiences and to distinguish the good from the bad. The extreme intensity of this splitting process during the early weeks will be useful later on when, in an attenuated form, it will be a basis for processes of discrimination and judgment, and will lay the foundation for later mechanisms like repression. Melanie Klein also identified another mechanism, *projective identification*: by projecting certain split-off parts of the ego on to external objects and identifying with them, the ego is able to identify with the feelings of these external objects. This has been described as the earliest form of empathy.

The paranoid-schizoid position must be seen in the context of the total infantile experience. In favourable circumstances, the child spends most of its time feeding, sleeping, experiencing real or hallucinatory pleasures. Through this he can assimilate his ideal objects and integrate his ego. But however favourable circumstances may be, all children must go through moments of anxiety which will form the nucleus of the paranoid-schizoid position, traces of which will remain throughout life even in the most normal individual. The paranoid position is a defence against anxiety and is an essential starting point for subsequent development.

The 'good' object is the first version, as it were, of the ideal

[1] In order to avoid any misinterpretation, we wish to emphasize that the paranoid-schizoid position is a normal one and *does not imply that the child is psychotic.* It refers to a description of a state where the leading anxiety is comparable to a paranoid one, while the state of the ego and of its object is characterized by the splitting and hence can be labelled schizoid. 'It must be remembered that a normal infant does not spend most of its time in a state of anxiety. . . . But all infants have periods of anxiety and the anxieties and defences which are the nucleus of the paranoid-schizoid position are a normal part of human development' (H. Segal, 1964).

object. The ideal and persecutory objects, when they have both been introjected, will form the rudimentary elements from which the superego will ultimately be built up.

The 'bad' devouring breast, the persecutory object, will be experienced as a dreaded legislator, the superego, source of all prohibitions. The introjected, good breast, on the other hand, is the ideal object and will be the basis of the ego-ideal which can be equally compelling by setting up an image of exemplary, unattainable perfection.

When circumstances are favourable and good experiences predominate over bad ones, the paranoid-schizoid position yields gradually to the next step in development, the depressive position. The ego will gradually acquire a belief in the prevalence of his ideal object and his libidinal instincts over the bad object and the death instinct.[1] The repeated identification of the ego with the ideal object protects it against persecutory anxiety and increases its capacity to cope with anxieties without resorting to the primitive mechanism of splitting. The ego is better fitted to tolerate its own aggressive drives and does not feel the need to project them on to other objects. A growing distinction between what belongs to the self and what to external objects thus begin to emerge. In other words, the ego is ready to differentiate its own body from the outside world.

3 *The depressive position*

In normal development when favourable conditions do predominate over bad ones, the persecutory position will be progressively abandoned and replaced by a process of integration, described by Melanie Klein as the *depressive position*. In this phase the child can recognize the *object as a whole*, this first object being the mother.

> When we speak of the infant recognizing his mother as a
> whole object, we contrast this with both part-object
> relationships and split-object relationships; the infant, that
> is to say, relates himself more and more, not only to the
> mother's breast, hands, face, eyes, as separate objects, but

[1] When Melanie Klein refers to favourable or unfavourable circumstances she takes account of both external and internal factors. She admits that deprivation or frustration, be they physical or psychological, stand in the way of gratifying experiences. But even when these 'environmental factors' are favourable, the gratification may be tempered or even cancelled out by the intervention of internal factors, most important of which she identifies as *envy*, which she considers the most fundamental emotion, to be sharply differentiated from jealousy or greed. See Melanie Klein, *Envy and Gratitude* (1957).

to herself as a whole person, who can be at times good, at times bad, present or absent, and who can be both loved and hated. He begins to see that his good and bad experiences do not proceed from a good and bad breast or mother, but from the same mother who is the source of good and bad alike (H. Segal, 1964).

Recognizing the mother as a whole person implies recognition of her as an individual and the discovery by the child of his own helplessness, his dependence on her and his jealousy of other people. This altered perception of the object suggests that the child's ego has undergone a fundamental change: it is no longer split but whole, like the object itself.[1]

This ego-integration runs parallel with a physiological and psychological maturation and the development of thought and memory processes, a development which brings with it the knowledge that he both loves and hates one and the same person—his mother.

During this phase, relations with the object are characterized by *ambivalence*. The persecution anxiety existing at the time of the paranoid position is replaced in the depressive situation by an anxiety centred wholly on the fear that his destructive instincts might have destroyed (or might destroy) the object he loves and on which he depends so completely.

The need to ensure possession of this object which he feels might escape him, intensifies the processes of introjection. By incorporating the object he protects it against his own destructive impulses. The depressive position sets in at the oral-sadistic phase where need and love are linked with the aggressive drive of biting and devouring. Introjection enables him to protect the good object against the destructive instincts represented by both the external and internalized bad object.

Thus, at the peak of his ambivalence, the child feels the depressive despair, the mourning for this lost or destroyed object and the guilt of having himself destroyed the internal object which, from then on, is felt by the child as a fragmented object. Because of identification with his love object the child might feel that he too is injured or destroyed.

The child's despair and his guilt of having destroyed his mother arouses the wish to restore and to recreate her in order to regain her as an object, alive and whole. The depressive conflict is a constant struggle between the destructive phantasies and the

---

[1] Although described in different words, the *depressive position corresponds* to what Spitz calls the *eighth-month anxiety*.

reparative wishes, both of which are part of the child's feeling of omnipotence. 'The wish and the ego's capacity for reparation of the good object is the basis of the ego's capacity to maintain love and relationships through conflicts and difficulties. . . . Reparative phantasies resolve the anxieties of the depressive position.'

The depressive position marks a crucial moment in the child's development. When he discovers his own psychic reality, he also becomes capable of distinguishing phantasy from reality. In favourable circumstances, when the child is confronted with the reality of his mother (that is, her reappearance after absence, her continued love and care) he gradually modifies his belief in the omnipotence of his destructive impulses and his magical reparations, and learns to estimate more reasonably the limits of both his love and his hate.

> The depressive position is never fully worked through. The anxieties pertaining to ambivalence and guilt, as well as situations of loss, which reawaken depressive experiences, are always with us. Good external objects in adult life always symbolize and contain aspects of the primary good object, so that any loss in later life reawakens all the anxieties experienced originally in the depressive position.

> If the child has established a good internal object in the depressive position he will be able to cope with depressive anxieties later in life. But when the depressive position has not been worked through to a sufficient extent the belief in the ego's capacity to regain good internal objects is not firmly established; hence 'the ego is dogged by constant anxiety of the total loss of good internal situations . . . its relation to reality may be tenuous and there is sometimes an actual threat of regression into psychosis' (H. Segal).

4 Early phases of the oedipal conflict

When the mother is perceived as a whole object, that is during the depressive position, the child has to recognize that an important link exists between her and the father. However, their relationship can only be perceived through anaclitic tendencies; the child phantasies his parents as being engaged in an almost uninterrupted succession of mutual gratifications which may be perceived as oral, anal or genital, according to the prevalence of his own impulses which he projects on his parents. This gives rise to feelings of intense jealousy and envy in the child because he feels excluded and deprived. The phantasy of the mother's oral incorporation of the father's penis is one of the most frequent themes in this connection.[1]

But during the anal-sadistic phase and the accompanying anal frustration, the child seeks to acquire in phantasy his mother's contents (breast, babies, penises, etc.), by destroying her so as to penetrate her body. By projecting his aggressive tendencies, the parental relations themselves will be identified with a mutual aggression.

It is not possible within a brief space to explore all the vagaries of the oedipal phantasies. What follows is an attempt to show what happens:

(a)   through the phantasy of the oral incorporation of the father's penis the mother carries it inside her body and wishes to keep it for herself; the mother appears to possess all the objects coveted by the child. Thus the mother with the hidden internal penis is the forerunner of the 'phallic woman';

(b)   by aggressive phantasies, the child wishes to break into the mother's body, robbing from her what she withholds: both the good breast and the good penis;

(c)   the child projects his own aggression on to part objects; these objects are cathected with aggression and in turn become persecutory objects;

(d)   by this projection the bad objects threaten the good introjected ones, and the child thus feels exposed to retaliatory destruction. He fights against these anxieties and his feelings of deprivation, envy and destructiveness with all the defences already described: denial, splitting, idealization, etc.

Melanie Klein attaches great importance to the phantasy of the *combined parents*: the mother appears as a whole object, but not yet fully differentiated from the father; the child phantasies the father—or his penis—as part of his mother. The child, by idealizing his mother, idealizes everything in her and the mother becomes the container of everything desirable. But by projecting his aggressive tendencies on the combined parents figure, it can be transformed into a dreaded persecutor.

In the course of the oedipal conflict, as understood by Melanie Klein, the parental couple, combined or divided, is seen as the frustrating object. To this the child reacts by an increase of

---

[1] This conception does, of course, presuppose, at a very early age, some awareness, even if intuitive, of sexual anatomy. Whatever the neurophysiological bases of this mental activity, it is true that all early analyses stumble on to the primal scene, a primitive phantasy (*Urphantasie*) which strongly indicates the existence of imaginative activity from earliest infancy (*see* Laplanche and Pontalis, 1968).

aggressive phantasies in which he attacks and destroys his parents. These destroyed parents are introjected and felt by the child as becoming part of his internal world. Thus during the depressive phase the child not only incorporates a destroyed breast but also a destroyed, and destructive, parental couple. The annihilation anxiety which existed at the persecutory phase is thereafter replaced by castration anxiety.

At this early phase of the oedipal conflict the child is faced with his desire to destroy his parents. To protect himself against the feelings of deprivation, envy and his destructive phantasies, which arouse anxiety and guilt, the child resorts to various forms of defences such as denial, splitting and idealization. Splitting tries to separate the good from the bad parent, idealizing the one while the other is felt as a persecutor. This relation thus appears as a prefiguration of the 'genital' oedipal conflict, 'except for the extreme idealization of the desired parent and extreme hatred experienced in relation to the rival parent'. The early stage of the oedipal conflict is characterized by the predominance of oral trends, ambivalence and the uncertain choice of the sexual object —for 'the role of the ideal object and the persecutor usually shifts rapidly from one parent to the other'.

The transition from the oral situation to the genital one is marked by constant fluctuation. If the first object of desire is the mother's breast, the father can only be perceived as a rival. In view of the persecutory and depressive anxieties experienced in relation to the mother and mother's breast, the father's penis becomes the alternative object of oral desire and therefore an object to be conquered, incorporated and destroyed. For the little boy this turning to the father's penis is a move towards homo-sexuality; but at the same time the incorporation of the father's penis helps the boy to identify with the father and thus reinforces his heterosexual position.

For the little girl, on the other hand, the turning to the penis represents the first heterosexual move—the wish to in-corporate the father's penis in her vagina. But at the same time the wish to possess a penis contributes to her homosexual ten-dencies.

Recognition of his own sex will enable the child to fix his object choice on the parent of the opposite sex and to renounce the parent of the same sex. In the course of subsequent development, the genital oedipal situation will always bear traces of the oral and anal tendencies in their symbolic representation, but also in the actual clinical features. 'The genital act may thus incorporate and symbolize all the earlier forms of relationships.' Every sexual object choice will, to a certain extent, be ambivalent.

With the progressive resolution of this early Oedipus complex and the possibility of identification with a parent, the superego will lose its initial terrifying aspect and become identified with the image of the introjected parental couple. By now, the early superego is not exclusively cathected with guilt feelings but must enable the child to overcome his destructive tendencies.

The pain of mourning experienced in the depressive position and the reparative tendencies which seek to restore the lost internal love object are at the root of all sublimation and creative activity. In Freud's view, sublimation is the culmination of a successful renunciation of an instinctual aim for a new, more advantageous one or one more acceptable to the superego and the demands of psychic economy. The reparative tendency leads to a wish to re-create, or restore, what has been destroyed or injured, but also to sublimate one's destructive instincts in order to protect and preserve the loved object. The wish to spare the object bends the instinctual drives in a new direction and inhibits the primary instinctual drives, especially when these are felt to be destructive or self-destructive.

Starting from this, Melanie Klein considers that the so-called psychotic defence mechanisms, e.g. splitting, are abandoned and replaced by neurotic defences—repression, displacement and inhibition.[1]

The genesis of symbol formation also belongs to the depressive position. The displacement of the instinctual aim involves the replacement of the original object by substitute ones. There is a close link between sublimation and symbol formation. Successful renunciation of a libidinal object, which is, in the last analysis, the mother's breast, is only possible through a process of mourning. The object, however, cannot be abandoned unless it finds its place within the subject's ego by becoming a symbol. The transition from the imaginary world to the symbolic order inaugurates the processes of abstract thinking.

In the Kleinian conception the object is not taken in a 'genetic' sense (as it appears in the work of Hartmann, Spitz and others) but

---

[1] She considers that the paranoid and depressive position represents the *fixation points of psychoses*. When the subject regresses to these early phases of his evolution, he loses his sense of reality and becomes psychotic. If he has been able to pass through these phases he will not regress to this level and may become neurotic. Melanie Klein sees the difference between psychosis and neurosis as one depending essentially on the depth of the regression, neurotic regression never reaching these first phases.

results from the progressive working through of phantasies. Melanie Klein does not deny the sensory experiences of the child. She obviously regards them as vital because she attaches a crucial importance to the predominance of favourable experiences over bad experiences, in the outcome of the psychic conflict. She does, however, limit the scope of these experiences, or rather, she sees them as having an effect only to the extent that they are submitted to a working through in the imaginary, and thus can take on a symbolic meaning.

5 *Critique of Melanie Klein's work*

The clinical data and accounts of early phantasies as described by the English school have been of major importance to psycho-analysis. Melanie Klein has shown their importance in the under-standing of the clinical investigation and treatment. The theoretical conceptions underlying her work have, nevertheless, aroused many criticisms.

Edward Glover's criticism (1945) concerns what he calls the 'new Kleinian metapsychology'. According to Glover, in the Kleinian system the difference between conscious and unconscious phantasy, thing-representation and memory traces, is lost, as is the topographical distinction between the various psychic agencies. What emerges is simply an oral-phallic ego, in opposition to a primitive superego. The disappearance of the process of repression and its replacement by projection and introjection as basic defence mechanisms does not appear to him as being based on the funda-mental distinction between the conscious and the unconscious systems. Neither is he willing to accept Melanie Klein's hypo-thetical reconstructions by which she infers the sequence of persecutory and depressive positions by interpreting the infant's behaviour or utterances. Glover stands by the conception that phantasy is the product of frustration and that it is deter-mined by three factors: (a) failure of the hallucinatory wish-fulfilment; (b) recognition of a libidinal object; (c) repression of instincts.

The main argument against the Kleinian conception of the establishment of object-relations has been stated by Lebovici and Diatkine (1954). While Melanie Klein allows a psychic structure in the very early months, involving a distinction between 'good' and 'bad' objects (and this independently of the nature of the object itself), these analysts take the view that the structuring process can only be secondary to the established object-relations, their concern being to demonstrate the working out of these relations.

Any differentiated object-relation takes shape the moment the maternal object is no longer an exclusively functional one, but only when it can be hallucinated. Until then, the pre-object-relation (first anaclitic, then gradually differentiated) was established only at moments of need (Lebovici, 1962).

The reality of the object itself thus becomes the chief point of the controversy and called for the introduction of a fundamental distinction by Lacan between the Real, the Imaginary and the Symbolic.

IV. Object-relations and communication

Within the mother-child dyad some forms of communication are established in the very first months of life. In the pre-object phase the mother reacts to the child's unintentional manifestations (signs) as though certain forms of his behaviour had some meaning (signals). This has been interpreted as a *pre-verbal communication* from infant to mother.

Research on the influence of the nursing situation on the child's behaviour has shown that from the very first months the child responds to certain maternal attitudes and to the emotional tone that goes with them. This exchange between mother and child (but chiefly in the direction from mother *to* child) has been termed *extra-verbal communication*. At this stage the mother takes over the functions of the child's ego. (Spitz has advanced the proposition that the mother is the child's *external ego*.) She controls the child's access to directed mobility, provides nourishment and protection: she acts as the representative of the child both in respect to the outer world and to the child's inner world.

It is not until the advent of the object phase, during the second year of life, with a whole object identified as such and unified into a whole bodily image, that symbolic communication can be established. When locomotion is acquired the vocal exchanges of the preverbal stage—the mother's running monologue and the child's babbling—is replaced by prohibition and the mother's use of the word 'No', shaking her head and preventing the child doing certain things: the child is thus pushed back from activity to passivity. The child understands these prohibitions through a process of identification and imitates the negative head-shaking, which becomes the symbol and the 'enduring vestige' of maternal frustration.[1] The giving of meaning to a negation—the negative shake of the head—shows that the child can henceforth indicate his refusal, not by flight, which is regarded as an affective discharge, but by a gesture which acquires a meaning independently of the initial motor pattern and assumes the sense of a *symbolic* (later, a verbal) gesture. This appears between the ages of fifteen and eighteen months, indicating that the subject is now able to exercise control over the outside world as a result of a system of symbolic communication replacing direct action. Spitz insists on the fact that the head-shaking gesture and the word 'No' are the first semantic symbols. 'Global' words such as 'mama', 'daddy', etc., represent wishes and needs. The negative headshake and the word 'No' represent *a concept*: 'It is not only a signal but also a sign of the child's attitude, conscious and unconscious.'

In his monograph *No and Yes* (1957) Spitz examines the origins of the first semantic sign which establishes the child as a subject with whom one can communicate. He found the neurophysiological precursors to the negative head-shaking:

(a) ROOTING BEHAVIOUR, a motor pattern consisting of a series of rotatory head movement with open mouth which persist until the infant succeeds in snapping the nipple. As soon as he succeeds the rotating movement ceases and sucking begins. In this exploratory function of the mouth, seeking to grasp the breast, the movement has an appetitive, positive (hence affirmative) meaning, but it also *prefigures the motor pattern of negation* since the same movement reappears, after the sixth month of life, in a situation which is diametrically opposed to the original one.

(b) THE AVOIDANCE MOVEMENT, when the satiated infant turns away his head at the end of the feed, avoiding the nipple. Thus the rotary movement is transformed into a withdrawal behaviour and has acquired a negative meaning. At this stage it is nothing but a motor pattern which has a specific function, but even if this

---

[1] We wish to repeat the definitions of the terms used by R. Spitz:
(a) '*Sign*' is a percept which is *empirically* linked with the experience (e.g. Koplik's sign of red buccal maculae is evocative of measles in the prodromic stage).
(b) '*Signal*' is a *conventionally* accepted connection between a sign and experience (road signals are a good example of this). The signal is a specific usage of a sign.
(c) '*Symbol*' is a sign which stands for a situation or an idea: it has significance *beyond its formal aspect* (gestures, words, emblems are the most elementary symbols).

behaviour, seen from the outside, expresses a refusal, it remains objectless and is only a manifestation of a psychophysiological state.

(c) THE SEMANTIC GESTURE, the head-shaking 'No', can be interpreted as a message, addressed to another person. In this third stage, around fifteen months, 'the motor pattern has been placed into the service of an abstract concept of negation, and is integrated into a communication system'. The semantic gesture of negation thus has a twofold origin but is bound up with breast-feeding and the anaclitic situation.

One still has to establish the specific mechanism which allows the passage from the motor pattern (rooting) to the signal (avoidance movement) and to the semantic symbol (the negative head-shaking). The 'No' is a symbol, for it is a gesture intentionally communicating a meaning which originally was not included in it. Because rooting, which is an appetitive reflex and has the meaning of an affirmation, has changed its function, it can now act as a model for a gesture, subsequently cathected with an opposed meaning.

This change of function takes place as the result of identification. At the end of the first year the infant imitates some of its parents' gestures but these are simply imitations without semantic content. But even then the child uses those gestures—and later on the word 'No'—under specific circumstances, primarily when he refuses something: from then on it is certainly a question of identification: 'the child has incorporated into its ego's memory system those actions which it has observed in the libidinal object'. At about the same period, between nine and twelve months, while gesture identification is being established, the child becomes capable of understanding commands and prohibitions.

Any prohibition is invested with an affective significance, which carries the meaning of refusal, and hence of frustration. The same is true of the memory traces of this experience: this cathexis ensures the permanency of the memory trace. By the same token, prohibition tends to push the child back into passivity and he will not tolerate this without resistance. And finally a third factor is added, namely the unpleasure which accompanies frustration and which provokes an aggressive thrust: the memory trace of the prohibition will be invested with this aggressive cathexis.

The child is caught in a conflict between his love for the mother and his aggressive feelings, between his own wishes and the maternal prohibition, between the unpleasure of yielding to her commands and fear of losing her love. He will have recourse to a compromise solution: an autoplastic change provided by a defence mechanism, the 'identification with the aggressor'. (In Anna Freud's view (1937), identification with the aggressor—i.e. with the agent of the prohibition—represents the internalization of the conflict between the ego and the exterior object.)

The dynamics which lead to the acquisition of the semantic gesture of 'No' are the following: the negative head-shaking gesture and the word 'No' spoken by the libidinal object are incorporated into the ego of the infant as memory traces. The affective charge of unpleasure is separated from this presentation; this separation provokes an aggressive thrust, which will then be linked by way of association to the memory trace in the ego (Spitz, 1965).

Spitz regards the 'No' as a link of identification with the libidinal object which, by its prohibitions, has a frustrating effect. When this frustration is felt many times it invests the gesture with its affective quality of unpleasure. Subsequently, the 'No' becomes for the child a vehicle of aggression through which he can spontaneously express his refusal and turn against the libidinal object. The semantic 'No' shows that a new phase of autonomy has been achieved, when the child perceives *the other* and recognizes himself as *self*.

With the acquisition of the gesture of negation, action is replaced by messages, and distance communication is inaugurated. . . . Here begins the humanization of the species; here begins the *Zoon politikon*; here begins society. This is the reason why I consider the achievement of the sign of negation and of the word 'No' the tangible indicator of the formation of the third organizer (Spitz, 1965).

The *three organizers* of psychic development indicate the successive stages in the process of individualization.

(a) At about the age of three months the *smiling response* indicates that something is recognized by the infant as existing outside himself—termed by Spitz the non-I. It is a first cognitive organization of experience which enables the infant to distinguish the outside world from his personal experience and the 'I' gradually emerges as an identifiable bodily experience. It thus marks the point of transition from the narcissistic stage to the stage of the preobject.

(b) *The eighth-month anxiety*, which occurs at more or less the same time as weaning, shows that the child can identify a libidinal object from among all those around him: he has located in his surroundings a love object—the mother—whom he recognizes as distinct from himself.

(c)   Between twelve and fifteen months the *semantic gesture of negation* gives the child access to a new domain of social relations; he recognizes himself as *self*,[1] independent of the libidinal object. This new relation culminates in identification with the frustrator (or aggressor) which enables the subject to show his refusal, or even his aggressiveness, in the course of distance communication. Whereas the first two organizing moments were still part of the instinctual discharge (and hence of action), the 'No' is the beginning of a communication operating according to the reality principle. The communication changes from an egocentric one (as it was in the neonate) to an allocentric one with the introduction of semantic symbols and gestures.

The child's various experiences are involved in the establishment of this communication, both in external reality (his relation with the mother) and in the internal reality of his phantasy world.

If object-relations are to evolve in a normal fashion, the communication system between parent and child must remain constantly open. There must be a generous supply of sensory and affective elements, absence of which may cause frustration syndromes to appear.

According to Thérèse Benedek (1959), the image of the self is built up, essentially, from the image of the object (identification with the other). She refers to the 'transaction spiral' which structures the reciprocal relations from childhood to adolescence and which involves introjections of the mirror image. This would explain why development is more favourable when the child can identify with parental attitudes which are outside the non-conflictual areas of the ego.

Lidz (1964) emphasizes that linguistic communication enables man to transmit his experience and to institutionalize techniques. Predisposition to speech may be regarded as innate in man, an ontogenetic *Anlage*. Transcultural studies have shown that language influences the way a child experiences and perceives his environment.[2] It is obvious that the acquisition of meaning is not dependent on physical maturation alone but also upon the nature

[1] It is to be noted that the *I* and the *self* are two ways of apprehending the relation between the subject and the *other* during the process of working out object-relations. In analytic theory the concept of *ego* is entirely distinct from the *I* and the self and refers to a *psychic agency*, a functional locus where consciousness of self takes place.

[2] The example quoted by Lidz concerning the Indian languages of North America are mainly based on the linguistic studies of Edward Sapir and Benjamin Lee Whorf. The reader is referred to the excellent study (from the standpoint of psychoanalytical anthropology) by Eric Erikson (1963) on the meaning and learning of cultural values among the North American Indians.

and the breadth of the child's experience. The child learns to know words both as an expression of his own experience and as a part of the shared cultural meaning ('dictionary' meaning). The personal meaning, which varies according to individual experience, and the shared cultural meaning, which is provided by the family life, must be concordant. Any marked discrepancy between these two meanings—itself a result of parental neurotic conflict—will give rise, in the child, to a semantic confusion which can only aggravate emotional incoherence. Lidz's contention is that schizophrenic patients, during childhood, have been persistently exposed to distortion of meanings and paralogical reasoning: they have received a 'faulty grounding in learning the shared meanings of the culture within their families'.

If a mother does not perceive her child's emotional needs, if she remains impervious to the unspoken clues of these needs, she will be unable to communicate with him. This failure to communicate may, in fact, be the result of her own unsatisfied needs or be bound up with her neurotic defences, and she may sometimes treat the child as though he were no more than an extension of herself. She might, for example, feed or clothe the child according to her own feelings of hunger or cold without being aware of the child's real needs. Although some parents seem to devote themselves to their children, their constant intrusions, rigid control and regulation of the child's behaviour clearly betray their inability to establish ego-boundaries between themselves and the child. This attitude hardly helps the child to rely on his own physiological signals and creates despair over the usefulness of communication.

The same thing applies to the frequent use of denial by parents in order to maintain a certain image of themselves or to keep hidden some family situation which they do not want made public. Their words are then in contradiction to the facts, and although the child knows that something is amiss he does not dare mention it or ask for an explanation. The child may well lose confidence in his parents' words or mistrust his ability to understand what they mean. All in all, verbal communication will be impaired as far as the child is concerned and these intra-family distortions in communication will have their repercussions on ego-functioning.

Language permits the child to postpone or control the gratification of his instinctual drives, to internalize prohibitions, and to master reality. Thanks to categorization, which language makes possible, the child's world, his needs and the behaviour pattern of his environment become predictable.

The child should be able to rely on the consistency of verbal cues. Automatization of the linguistic tool releases energy for other purposes. If he is to resort to words to master reality, they must be a more efficient signal than non-verbal cues. If the words of adults belie their deeds, if their promises are not kept, *predictive value* of verbal communication can no longer be trusted by the child. This sort of contradiction can also be used by parents as a means of coercion, deliberate or otherwise, or it might represent verbalizations of the phantasies of a schizophrenic parent. Although the extent of the confusion or incoherence thus created may vary, it always creates utter confusion in the use of verbal tools. It should be clear how intimately the process of establishing and fostering verbal communication is related to parent-child transactions.

V. The body-image

The image of our self springs from two sources: (a) the awareness of body sensations and thought processes as an experience identified as our own; (b) the indirect perception of our bodily and mental self by process of identification, i.e. the constitution of one's own coherent self as a subject.

Thus Schilder (1935) considers that the body-image proceeds from a 'biological' basis which provides the necessary somatic and motor-sensory elements; it is structured by the libido which gives this image its meaning and is related to the environment which, in turn, co-ordinates the individual's experience and his social frame of reference.

Memory traces of pleasurable and unpleasurable sensations which are integrated by the infant under the influence of auto-erotic activities of investigations of one's own body are the kernel of the early body-image. Thus the visual and tactile explorations and the libidinal cathexis of bodily functions play a major part in the gradual building up of the whole body-image which (a) must become detached from the symbiotic, dyadic, mother-child conglomerate and experienced as an independent entity; (b) must be perceived as a whole and not as a composite of bits and pieces.

Winnicott (1960) also refers to the infant's psychosomatic existence, defined as 'the psyche indwelling in the soma'. He considers that this is the result of a linkage of motor and sensory experience. A 'limiting membrane' is perceived by the infant (which is to some extent equated with the surface of the skin) and the infant experiences himself as having an inside and an outside: this lays the foundation for the body scheme. 'In this way meaning comes to the function of intake and output; moreover, it gradually becomes meaningful to postulate a personal or inner psychic reality for the infant' (Winnicott, 1960).

The body-image is intimately related to the development of ego-function, in particular perception and reality testing. Freud (1923a) stated that the ego was foremost a 'body ego' and that 'the ego is ultimately derived from bodily sensations, chiefly those springing from the surface of the body. It may thus be regarded as a mental projection of the surface of the body.' At the root of the body-image formation, during the first months, oral and tactile sensations, supplemented by kinaesthetic responses, furnish the bulk of the sensory life of the infant. The role of libidinal cathexis of motility has been stressed by Freud (1905a, 1923a), Mittelmann (1957) and others. But we shall restrict the subject to visual and tactile sensations. Greenacre (1958) states that the relations of vision to touch and orality is the greatest moment in the establishment of the body image. But certain body-areas are more significant than others in establishing individual recognition of the body-self: these areas are the *face* and the *genitals*.

Vision is extremely important, not only because it is prehensile, but because of its increasing scope, its range and distance. Much more than touch or extensor motion, it can 'take in' the surroundings with extraordinary fineness. Our body image develops largely from endogenous sensations, from contacts with the world and from seeing our own bodies. However, not all of our bodies are actually visible to us; and in the case of those parts of the body which are not visible to the child himself, the endogenous and contact sensations are supplemented by visual impressions of the bodies of others. It is evident that the genital area and the face are the two most highly differentiated parts of the body which cannot be 'taken in' thoroughly through visual perception of the own body—the face even less than the genitals. We are indeed aware that although their own genitals may be partly seen by the male and very little seen by the female, they can never be quite so clearly observed in any event on the self as on others. It is probably this which makes them so peculiarly important in the sense of body self, the senses of reality and identity. The genital area is probably more important than the face because of the grosser differences between the sexes and the discrepancy therefore which may occur between that which is visually 'taken in' more strongly from another body than it can be from one's own.

This interplay between the infant's discovery of his own body and his visual introjection of the other's appearance—and primarily of the genitals 'of the other'—results in an 'exquisitely sensitive body-phallus identification'.

For the mother to be recognized as a whole object, the child must be able to conceive of himself as a whole person. To grasp an object in its totality, the subject must be capable of seeing himself, not as a fragmented body, but as an *in-dividual*.

This corporal unity is established gradually from the very beginning of life. It is due to the integration of various perceptive faculties, but most of all to an affective perception of his own body, which expresses the intero- and exteroceptive sensory experience of the subject as well as the unconscious representation of libidinal experience. This *body-image*, which is what Lacan calls the *'anatomie phantasmatique'*, is continuously changing, for at any given moment it is made up of images superimposed on the actual image, and is therefore determined by the specific libidinal cathexes of each libidinal phase. This conglomeration of images takes the child away from a body-image which he experiences as being 'in bits and pieces' (*corps morcelé*), and leads to a unified image of his body.

Wallon (1934) has already described the formation of this *consciousness of the body* (*conscience du corps propre*), which is akin to what analysts designate by *body-image*.[1] He described the gradual development of this body-consciousness as being unified by the child's reactions when confronted with his mirror image. He remarks that the various parts of the body are not integrated right away by the child as a complete perceptual unit of his body-image, for he does not grasp the connection of his own body with the reflection in the mirror. Even if he is capable of perceiving a resemblance or concomitance between the image and his body, he is unable to grasp their actual relationship.

In one of the examples quoted by Wallon, a child (thirty-five weeks) looks at his image in the mirror every time he is called by name: but the illusion of reality still persists, since the child reacts

---

[1] The analytic concept of *body-image* (*image du corps*) should be distinguished from the usage made by neurophysiologists who deal with cortical representations of somatognosis (*schéma corporel*). Analysts refer to body-image as the 'subject's phantasies about his body and his libidinal physiology'. The concept is thus related to unconscious phantasy rather than to conscious representations.

as if the image—at which he laughs and stretches forth his arms—is a live object. He does not, therefore, connect his name with his proprioceptive 'ego'[1] but with the exteroceptive image reflected in the mirror.

The child does not appear to be disturbed or confused at the sight of his exteroceptive 'ego' coming between his active, exterior 'ego' and himself. There is no conflict between the two real images and no need to eliminate either of them. What exteroceptive image of himself could he have other than the one which is necessarily exterior to the one perceiving it? He can have a direct visual perception of his own body, but he only sees certain parts of it and does not put them together. And this fragmented vision may coincide with some of his gestures and movements. It may even, by combining with his intero- and proprioceptive feelings, form perceptual patterns but it cannot give a coherent image of the whole body.

> Between the immediate experience and the representation some dissociation must necessarily take place, separating the specific qualities and specific existence of the object itself from the impressions and movements to which it is initially related, by conferring on it the essential quality of outwardness.

This would imply that the notion of existence is no longer linked with every sensory impression and that the data of immediate experience must necessarily be 'represented' in the psyche. Thus, the multiplicity of representations creates a nexus of resemblances and differences which is the prelude to symbolic activity.

Round about the first year of life the mirror image ceases to have any existence for its own sake; it has become a symbolic system of reference.

Lacan, in 1949, interpreted the child's *recognition* of his own image in the mirror as the first indispensable phase in the process of identification. This theory is the basis for the later distinctions between the Symbolic, the Imaginary and the Real.[2]

---

[1] Wallon uses the word *ego* in a broad sense, and does not refer to the specific psychoanalytic concept.

[2] Lacan has introduced into psychoanalysis the categories of the *Symbolic*, the *Imaginary* and the *Real*. The *Real* is not synonymous with external reality, but rather with what is real for the subject. The *Symbolic* is the primary order which represents and co-ordinates both of the others and stands for discursive and symbolic action. It designates an unconscious symbolic structure based on a linguistic model composed of chains of signifiers. And in the same way that Lévi-Strauss's concept of the *Symbolic function* in human society depends upon the law which founds society (the law of incest), Lacan's notion

This act, in effect, immediately comes back to the child in a series of gestures where he feels, as in play, the connection of the image's movements with his own reflected environment and the relation of the whole complex to the reality in which he doubles for the image, that is, for the reality of his own body, for persons, and even for objects lying at his side.

Through the perception of the image of another human being the child discovers a corporal unity which is lacking to him at this stage of his development. Lacan interprets the child's fascination with the other's image as an anticipation of his maturing to a future point of corporal unity by identifying himself with this image (Wilden, 1968). Lacan adds evidence from animal psychology, where experimentation has shown that a visual relationship to another of the same species is necessary in a normal process of maturation. Without this visual presence the maturational process may be delayed, although it can be restored by placing a mirror in the animal's cage.

This 'joyful assumption of his specular image by a being still in a state of utter helplessness and dependent on his mother to feed him' is, in Lacan's view, the symbolic matrix in which the ego takes shape in a primordial form, a *Gestalt*, where the total form of the body appears to the subject 'in statuary relief and in a symmetry which inverts it, which is in contrast to the welter of movements which he feels to be animating him'. But in Lacan's frame of reference it is important to notice that this 'form' situates the ego as an agency 'which will only asymptotically rejoin the becoming of the subject'.

The function of the 'mirror phase' turns out to be a special case of the function of the *imago*, which is to establish a relation of the organism to its reality or, as it is said, of the *Innerwelt* to the *Umwelt*.

This 'mirror phase'—the onset of which corresponds to the eight-month anxiety described by R. Spitz, but can also occur much later (from twelve to fifteen months)—enables the subject to discover a corporal unity. It is by identifying himself with this image that the child can recognize himself in it and, as emphasized

---

of the symbolic order depends on the law of the symbolic father (see Wilden, 1968).

The *Imaginary* can be roughly defined as the intersubjective relation of the ego to another; the capture of the ego by another in an erotic or aggressive relationship. For Lacan the Imaginary relation is a 'lure' where the subject is trapped into a dyadic, deceptive, fallacious relationship based on the narcissistic relation between ego and subject.

by J.-L. Lang (1958), this primordial experience is symptomatic of what makes the ego an Imaginary construct. 'By conceiving himself other than he is, by establishing a relationship between his body and this image, the child fills the gap between these two terms . . . and thus defines the ego.' In this way the child may outgrow the fascination of the subject with an image and the alienation revealed by the mirror phase and may grasp the distinction between himself and the other, identify himself as subject and recognize the other as object.

When a whole object appears in the field of experience, it modifies existing relations between the subject and his objects. Instead of the dyadic, imaginary relationship between the fragmented body and the part objects of his phantasy life, a new relationship is thus established between the body as a corporeal unit and the whole object. The connections of the preceding phase, which were regulated by the satisfaction of a biological need and intended to relieve a tension, are replaced by a search for pleasure in which the subject pursues the fulfilment of a desire. This becomes a dialectic process in so far as the desire is recognized as his by the subject, but also recognizable as such by the other.

The *stade du miroir* must be considered as a crucial moment of genetic development, closely related to narcissism and to the establishment of the self. The mirror phase enables the child to reach the Symbolic order where the dyadic mother-child relation comes to be replaced by a triangular relation as a result of the supervening of a 'third party', a prelude to the setting up of the oedipal conflict leading to the beginning of social activity. The mirror stage, as described by Lacan, has also been envisaged by D. W. Winnicott: however, his contention is that the 'precursor of the mirror is the mother's face'. He thus stresses another dimension of human development where the individual ego-development is related to the subjective childhood experience.

VI. Childhood experience and mother-child relationship

In recent years psychoanalysis has approached the problem of personality development in the light of environmental 'stimulation', provided not only by maternal behaviour but in terms of the interrelations between mother and child. This emotional experience has thus become the core of analytic research.

1 *Definition of childhood experience*

S. Escalona (1963) defines experience as 'a series of events ordered in a time-space continuum, unified by the virtue of the fact that they occur in a single organism'. Thus experience is something subjective. In trying to establish a relationship between factors that determine experience, and specific behaviour patterns that result, she points out that this must be based on the consistency of behavioural response. Throughout her clinical investigation she was able to show 'that very different actions on the part of the mother (or other environmental variations) may have very similar consequences in terms of their impact on the child's experience', and conversely that similar stimulations may have varying consequences. These experiences, however, make it possible for the child to recognize an environment that exists independently and to develop a selective tie to the mother. 'Ego functions necessarily emerge and differentiate in the course of these successive encounters and adaptations.' By emphasizing *experience* (rather than distinguishing between maturation and learning) S. Escalona does away with the futile controversy as to whether infantile pathology (e.g. autism) is due to inadequate mothering or to inborn deficit. She stresses the importance of *lack of experience* as the pathogenic factor: it may be because the mother does not provide the 'average expectable environment' or because the child cannot participate in the usual pattern of interaction. Whatever the cause, 'it is the absence of those vital experiences in early childhood, which we regard as the necessary conditions for ego synthesis', which are responsible for the developmental process.

2 *The mother as facilitating environment*

D. W. Winnicott in his work has defined the basic emotional setting provided by an adequate mother-child relationship. Winnicott's basic concept of *holding* denotes not only the physical holding of the infant by the mother, but also the total environmental provision. In the holding phase the infant is entirely dependent: this dependence is an absolute one when the infant has no means of knowing about maternal care and is only in a position to gain profit or suffer disturbance, but is not able to control what is well or what is badly done. Later on the infant gains awareness of details of maternal care. At the holding stage the environment meets the infant's physiological (and psychological) needs in a reliable way. Maternal care must be *good enough* to fulfil the infant's needs. Holding includes the physical holding of the infant which is perhaps 'the only way in which a mother can show the infant her love'. Here Winnicott refers to maternal qualities which cannot be acquired by mere instruction: 'there are those (mothers) who can hold an infant and those who cannot; the latter quickly produce in the infant a sense of insecurity, and distressed crying'. Adequate maternal care is essential for the mental health of the individual (freedom from psychosis or liability to psychosis).

It is in this sense that Winnicott refers to the *good enough mother*, who actively adapts to the infant's needs. This starts off with an almost complete adaptation and, as time proceeds, lessens according to the infant's growing ability to account for failure of adaptation and to tolerate frustration: this demands 'an easy and unresented preoccupation' with the one infant; success in infant care depends on what Winnicott calls devotion to empathy, not on intellectual enlightenment. This almost perfect adaptation affords the infant the opportunity for the illusion that the mother's breast is part of the infant.[1] Thus, if all goes well, the infant profits from the experience of frustration, since the gradual withdrawal of the mother's total care, i.e. the incompleteness of adaptation, confers on the object a status of reality: it can then be hated or loved. (If exact adaptation is continued too long, not allowed to decrease, the object cannot be perceived as real and the infant cannot develop a relationship to external reality.) 'The mother's eventual task is gradually to disillusion the infant' and by this process of disillusionment 'the stage is set for the frustrations which we gather together under the word weaning. . . . If illusion-disillusionment has gone astray the infant cannot attain to so normal a thing as weaning'. Here again we encounter the importance of the psychic conflict, but in terms of both a subjective *and* objective phenomenon, one being conditioned by the other. If weaning has to be accepted as a paradigmatic experience for all, it can only be in so far as the conflictual quality is not based on a gradual adaptation but on a sudden and unprepared-for event, i.e. separation and not weaning as a 'normal' experience. As Winnicott points out: *mere termination of breast feeding is not a weaning.*

[1] This internal object depends on the qualities of the external objects—breast, mother figure—and failure o the latter leads to the badness or persecutory quality of the internal object. Such a conception, although close enough to the Kleinian theory, differs from it since the actual *experience* is the necessary basis for unconscious phantasy and not merely the result of instinctual conflict.

D. W. Winnicott has given us an elaborate and coherent account of the caretaking role of the mother. He states that the 'primary maternal preoccupation' is the incentive for the mother's role whose libidinal investment goes far beyond the imperative biological needs. The infant's helplessness requires her constant care, but Winnicott points out that the mother's caretaking role goes far beyond the mere necessity of the infant's survival.

It is during this holding phase that essential developments take place in the infant. In this phase the ego acquires a structured integration which still depends on the continuation of reliable maternal care or on the infant's capacity to build up memories of maternal care. With the acquisition of the body-scheme, which enables the child to perceive an inside and an outside and to build up his own psychic reality, the infant becomes able to experience anxiety. At these early stages, anxiety relates to the *fear of annihilation* as an alternative to the *continuity of being*. Being and annihilation are the two alternatives at a time where death has no meaning.[1] At the time of holding there can be no 'object relationships'.

Thus, in Winnicott's conception of the infant's experience, *holding* is the basis for ego-integration and object relationships. Maternal care is not only an objective way of handling the infant, but the whole subjective experience of mothering. To the extent which this subjective experience provides the child with the necessary confidence in the environment, will the infant be able gradually to attain relative independence.

J. Robertson (1962) comes to the same conclusion in her study of mothering as an influence on infant development. By examining Well-Baby Clinic records she has been able to find that the outcome of the adaptive period is successful when the mother feels and experiences pleasure not only in *owning* a child, but in the *activities* of mothering; if she is aware of the infant's emotional states and when she is able to use the heightened anxiety—which is normal during this period—in the service of the baby. The author's conclusions corroborate Winnicott's description of the 'good-enough mother'. Thus the mother plays a dual role in the child's development: (a) she provides the opportunity for a gradual disillusionment, i.e. she makes it possible for the child to conceive of and deal with external reality; (b) she functions as a *protective shield*.

---

[1] According to Winnicott, '*death* has no meaning until the arrival of hate and the concept of the whole human person'.

3 *The mother as a protective shield*

The mother's function as a *protective shield* has already been discussed by Freud when talking about the necessary protection against powerful external (and internal) stimuli which he considered as a possible cause for trauma. M. Khan (1963) points out that the mother's role as a protective shield is a theoretical construct, and that 'it includes her role *vis-à-vis* the infant as well as her management of the nonhuman environment on which the infant is dependent for his total well-being'. But it must be remembered that 'the mother's role as a protective shield is a limited function in her total life experience, a special instance of her personality and emotional functioning'. This role becomes invaded by her personal needs and conflicts. Such an intrusion may result in failures in respect of this role and the child reacts to these failures. Such failures may be (a) due to the excessive intrusion of the mother's psychopathology; (b) in terms of loss or separation from the mother; (c) when the mother is faced with an 'impossible task', i.e. the child's severe physical illness, congenital defects, blindness, etc.

But under less dramatic circumstances the breaches of this protective field are not traumatic singly; they cumulate silently and get embedded in the specific traits of character structure. They are not traumatic at the time or in the context in which they happen and only achieve the value of trauma cumulatively and in retrospect (M. Khan, 1963). This should remind us of the Freudian concept of *Nachträglichkeit*, by which early and often forgotten events take on a new meaning through the activity of present psychic conflicts.

In favourable circumstances the maternal protective shield serves a number of purposes (M. Khan, 1963): (a) it enables the normal course of maturation and defends the child against the mother's unconscious hate; (b) it enables the child to project his unpleasant experiences on to her; (c) it protects the child against the awareness of his dependency; (d) it helps the infant's inner world to differentiate into ego and id and to build up supplies of primary narcissism and object cathexes.

Hence the shift from total dependency to relative dependence can take place and makes it possible for the child to experience separateness, which is the core of disillusionment (Winnicott, 1953).

However, it must be noticed that although environment has important effects it is not true that without a bad environment no aggressive phantasies would exist. The environmental fact should be evaluated in relation to what it means in terms of the infant's own instincts and phantasies.

When the infant has been under the sway of angry phantasies, attacking the breast, then an actual bad experience becomes all the more important, since it confirms, not only his feelings that the external world is bad, but also the sense of his own badness and the omnipotence of his malevolent phantasies. Good experiences, on the other hand, tend to lessen the anger, modify the persecutory experiences and mobilize the baby's love and gratitude and his belief in a good object (H. Segal, 1964).

As Masud Khan (1969) points out, little has been said about a fundamental issue in mother-child relationship, i.e. 'the mother's task as the provider of phase-adequate aggressive experiences, deriving from her capacity to tolerate aggression and hate in herself and in the child'. Whenever this is lacking it interferes with the mother's weaning *from* the child and leads to a failure to enable the child to distance itself from the mother. These children are, in later life, unable to neutralize or harness aggressive energy through ego-functions and their mood is one of diffuse aggressive apathy and inertia. The mixture of compelling and clinging has been designated by the author as 'symbolic omnipotence' which results from cumulative trauma in which the mother failed to provide a *protective shield* during the child's development.

4 *Individuation and frustration*

Thus the infant's biological and emotional unpreparedness and dependency is the basic fact underlying the mother-infant symbiosis. From this symbiotic phase proceeds the development of a new phase in mother-child relationship, namely the *separation-individuation phase* (Mahler, 1963). This separation phase is a normal process which takes place while the infant develops into a toddler and the symbiotic relationship is gradually transformed into object relationship. It is not a traumatic separation (as will be described later): it takes place in the mother's presence, and although it also confronts the child with minimal threats of object loss, the process is characterized by the child's pleasure in independent functioning because of the libidinal presence of the mother. This separation-individuation is seen as a crucial prerequisite for the development and maintenance of the sense of identity, through which the child attains the feeling of wholeness as an individual. The feeling of identity is defined by Mahler as 'a cohesive cathexis of the individuated and differentiated self-image . . . as the child gradually emerges, that is to say "hatches" from the symbiotic common membrane'. Thus the demarcation of the body-image from the image of the object (mother) is the core of the individuation process.

The mother plays an essential part in this process, since a balance must be found between the necessary and unavoidable frustrations evoked by normal mothering on one hand and, on the other hand, the mother's acceptance of the infant's individual rhythm of needs. Thus the process is either facilitated or hindered by the mother's conscious and, even more important, unconscious psychic conflicts.

The influence of early mother-child relationship on the child's predispositions have been extensively studied by the research group at the Yale University Child Study Centre. Thus Ritvo and Solnit (1958) compared the effects of maternal restraint and of maternal overstimulation on the child's early identification process. The mother's influence on promoting the process of differentiation of the infant's self from the object world has been formulated by E. Jacobson (1964).

Ritvo and Solnit make the point that the child's *equipment factors* are important in determining what is experienced as frustration and plays as significant a role as the maternal care. This can be clearly seen in two of the cases reported by Ritvo and Solnit: Evelyn, whose needs were easily gratified, was met by a sensitive, introspective mother, responding to the child's needs and able gradually to impose restrictions and substitute gratifications. The child's needs did not impinge on the mother's deep conflicts, but seemed to dovetail with the mother's defences. The mother-object lent itself readily to introjection in the forming of ego-identification. The other child, Margaret, a tense, hyperactive, crying infant who was difficult to comfort, collided with an insecure, apprehensive and rigid mother who had difficulties in recognizing the infant's needs. The disturbance of Margaret's early physical experience led to the establishment of a threatening mother image. Later on, persistent imitative identification with the mother served the purpose of defence and warded off the anxiety. Such defensive behaviour interfered with the child's identifications, which were used more for defence than for adaptation.

Early gratification-frustration experiences are intimately connected with ego-development and identification processes. The need-satisfying object is discovered by the child in its relationship

K

to the mother and this becomes the matrix out of which the psychic representations of the love object arise. These object-representations play an essential part in the process of identification.

Rubinfine (1962) points to the importance of maternal stimulation (including delay and frustration) which provides for (a) the turning of aggression towards the outer world, (b) the energizing of the perceptual apparatus leading to the destruction of self and nonself and of object-relations.[1] Experiences of frustration make the infant aware of the need-satisfying object's existence as an entity separate from himself and not under his control. This suggests the possibility that the infant forms representations of need-satisfaction and frustration, which leads to inner representation of need-satisfying and frustrating objects.

Mahler (1963) has shown how the first signs of individuation may be observed by the fourth month, and in the second half of the first year sensorimotor patterns unfold rapidly.

> As soon as free locomotion is mastered the normal toddler seems to need to return to the mother to seek proximal communication with her. . . . By the time the toddler has mastered the ability to move from and to the mother the balance dramatically shifts within the bipolar mother-toddler interaction from activity on the part of the mother to activity on the part of the child. Once the toddler has mastered locomotion and begins to learn manipulation, these functions, and every new skill, become elements of a language weighted with a steady accretion of secondary and largely unconscious meaning—a wordless appeal for love and praise from the mother, an expression of longing, a search for meanings, a wish for sharing and for expansion. The mother, as the catalyst of the individuation process, must be able to read the toddler's primary process language.

The mother must be able to adjust to the gradual growing independence of her child. Her reactions depend largely on the specific meaning which the child has for the mother and on the phantasies connected with each child. These emotional tasks of

---

[1] The necessity of frustration for development has also been corroborated by animal psychology. Thus rhesus infant monkeys raised with inanimate surrogate mothers—which are always available, never frustrating, rejecting or intrusive—grow up to be entirely antisocial; they present an unnerving picture of apathy and sit in contorted positions. They do not play, do not clean or groom themselves. Encounters between individuals are random and do not result in play. They do not mate (see H. F. Harlow, 'Love in Infant Monkeys', *Scient. American*, 1959). Whether this should be considered as the result of a *non-frustrating* cloth surrogate mother or the consequence of the absence of an active mothering object depends on the interpretation of these facts.

motherhood have been described by Bibring *et al.* (1961) and the mother's emotional availability seems the most important factor: she must be able to participate in the toddler's progresses.

Thus the individuation process appears to be an essential developmental phase, which is far from being a mere maturational fact but a developmental process which depends mainly on the mother-child relationship: the child's experience is predominantly conditioned by the mother's emotional maturity and the gratifications she finds in mothering procedures. As long as the child represents merely a cherished possession—an illusory phallus, as it is often the case in the mother's unconscious phantasies—and not an individual human being whose gradual independence the mother expects and furthers, individuation cannot take place in a normal fashion.[1]

VII. Early deprivation of emotional needs

The absence of the mother in the first year of life produces drastic changes in the child's environment. His physiological maturation will be affected, as will his psychological development, both being intimately linked together. Anything which hampers the fulfilment of the neonate's or the infant's needs is bound to produce a psychophysiological deprivation.

1 *The needs of early infancy*

The physiological prematurity in the human infant makes inevitable the neonate's complete dependence on his environment. The precarious state of his motility, the inadequacy of his vegetative controls, the frailty of his metabolic balance, his susceptibility to intercurrent diseases or infections, shows that he has to be protected against any variation in temperature, any nutritional deviation, etc. This prematurity which underlies the neonate's helplessness (*Hilfslosigkeit*) means that the basic *physiological needs* have to be provided for by adequate supplies of oxygen and feeding, the maintenance of an even temperature and by protection against infection. But behind the satisfaction of these basic needs, which are essential for survival, lie the less obvious but equally urgent *psychological needs*.

The need for sucking, which is independent of the alimentary

[1] See Mahler's description of symbiotic psychotic children ('Autism and Symbiosis', 1958).

function, is itself an important source of sensory stimulation; it influences the regulation of the digestive functions and appears to have an effect on growth. The need for sucking may be regarded as the libidinal side of feeding and is part of the instinctual behaviour with which the child is equipped at birth; the mother's behaviour and attitudes during the feeding situation do of course play a major role to ensure this kind of oral stimulation until it becomes the all-absorbing performance.[1]

The same applies to what Margaret Ribble has described under the heading of *stimulus hunger* concerning the needs of sensory stimulation (visual, auditory, kinaesthetic) and which are normally found to be satisfied by a mother who breast-feeds, bathes, rocks, sings and talks to her child. To be especially noted is the stimulation of the cutaneous erotogenic zone: considerable satisfaction for the child is involved in the course of fondling and caring for his bodily hygiene, and much physical tension is alleviated in this way.

The need for emotional stability has both a physiological and psychological aspect. But even more important than the setting up of feeding and sleeping schedules is the emotional climate which is the most important factor making for the child's security. The infant always reacts unfavourably to maternal anxiety. A mother who is needlessly rigid in keeping to feeding schedules, obsessionally preoccupied with hygiene, clumsy or insensitive to the non-verbal cues which indicate the child's discomforts, builds up a climate of tension which has its impact on the child. The lack of security will manifest itself in long and frequent bouts of crying, in sleep and feeding difficulties, and the psychosomatic consequences of all this will be reflected by gastro-intestinal symptoms ('colicky babies') and fluctuations in weight.

In psychoanalysis the notion of deprivation is defined in terms of fundamental needs: not only those needs which are necessary for survival, but also the ones which are bound up with emotional development. In this regard, as Racamier (1953–4) emphasizes, mothering is not only a gratifying activity but also a formative one, and it is in this connection that Margaret Ribble speaks of the 'rights of infants'. Everything included under the heading of early 'frustration' comes actually into the category of deprivation.

[1] Attempts have been made, in the field of animal psychology, to get at the objective facts of breast-feeding. Bottle-fed puppies have been compared with a control group fed from the mother bitch. The control group was found to develop more rapidly than the bottle-fed group (see D. Levy, 'Animal Psychology in Relation to Psychiatry', in Alexander and Ross, *Dynamic Psychiatry*, 1952).

One of the essential conditions for mental health is the establishment of secure, affectionate and consistent relations between mother and child. These are indispensable for keeping anxiety and guilt feelings within normal psychological bounds. When this kind of relationship is lacking in the life of an infant one is entitled to speak of an *early emotional deprivation* (Bowlby, 1951).

2 Consequences of early emotional deprivation

The earliest work in this field, and one which attempted to study the consequences of deprivation, was concerned with the effects of separation of mother and child. The researches of M. Ribble, Goldfarb, R. Spitz, based on direct observation, have shown the effects of hospitalization:[1] early and prolonged separation can lead to emotional retardation and, in extreme cases, may even be the cause of mental deficiency.[2]

In 1945–6 Spitz published his first articles about the consequences of emotional deprivation. In the course of a long-term study of infant behaviour in a nursery he observed infants who during their first six months had good relations with their mothers. When at some point between the sixth and eighth months these children were deprived of their mother for a period of three months they developed a syndrome which Spitz called *anaclitic depression*.[3] In marked contrast to their previous 'happy' behaviour, children became first weepy, then withdrawn, lying prone in their cots, faces averted; after two months they would lose weight and show an increased susceptibility to intercurrent infections. Their developmental quotient also declined. After some months the weepiness subsided and was replaced by a rigidity of expression and lack of interest in what was going on around them.

It should be noted that a necessary condition for the development of this syndrome is that prior to separation the infant should have experienced good and satisfying relations with his mother and that he remains deprived without being provided with an acceptable mother-substitute.

It is important to emphasize that in this phase of anaclitic depression which we have just described the recovery is prompt

[1] A survey will be found in J. Bowlby's work (1951).
[2] We cannot adequately discuss here the relation of mental deficiency to emotional retardation. It should be noted that some authors refuse to recognize mental deficiency as an innate condition and see it as a consequence of a distortion of the mother-child relation (see Mannoni, 1964).
[3] This has to be set off clearly from Melanie Klein's concept of the 'depressive position' and of what J. Bowlby described as 'mourning'.

if the mother returns within a period of three to five months.[1] But if the emotional starvation is prolonged beyond five months a state of somatic and mental deterioration will set in which has been described as 'hospitalism' and which may lead to marasmus or even death, but the effects of which, in any case, are irreversible.

The effects of this total emotional deprivation appear fairly rapidly and are manifested in an overall regression of the child's motility, eye co-ordination, etc., but primarily affect the most recent, and hence the least stable, acquisitions. The most affected aspect of development is what A. Gesell calls adaptivity, an impairment of communication with the environment, in play relations and in the beginnings of what might be considered as 'socialization'. If the deprivation continues, motor patterns such as rocking appear; others show bizarre finger movements reminiscent of athetosis. Ultimately, the vegetative functions (digestion and breathing) are impaired and the weakening of the physiological defences make the child more susceptible to stress and infection. Spitz has found a 'shockingly high mortality rate'. This regression predisposes the child to an infection liability which may, according to Racamier (1954), make him more susceptible to certain diseases later on.

However, even in the mildest cases, it is the psychological development which is most seriously affected. Emotional deprivation may involve retardation in development which should be distinguished from 'simple' mental deficiency. The deprivational retardation affects the entire psychological development, but more specifically the ability to abstract and to conceptualize.[2] The child's failure to integrate his experiences, the retardation (or regression) in speech, the passivity that replaces the initial eagerness for social contact, impair relationships and may be regarded as the main cause in subsequent maladjustment and antisocial behaviour (Bowlby, 1951). This *acquired 'immaturity'* is evidence of the ego's failure to function as a regulating agency between the child and his surroundings. Impoverishment of the ego, both in its narcissistic and its object cathexes—inability to love or be loved—has been described by Racamier (1954) under the term

[1] Spitz is doubtful whether the recovery is complete and assumes that the syndrome will leave 'scars'.
[2] Bowlby (1951) reports on the various assessments of the development quotient (D.Q.). The decline of D.Q. is constant, though of variable importance. Spitz has reported progressive declines which, by the end of the second year, reach 45 per cent of the normal. With few exceptions, those children cannot sit, walk or talk.

apersonalisation, which he attributes to the child's difficulty in identifying with a parental image.

The onset and development of the deprivation syndrome follow certain rules:

(a)   Some infants are more susceptible than others to emotional deprivation. Recamier relates this to the level of instinctual integration which he considers to be a constitutional factor: some infants have a particularly low threshold of tolerance to frustration.

(b)   The earlier in life emotional deprivation supervenes the more marked will be its effects. In this connection it has been noted that the maximum effects occur in the first six months of life and are more intense when the infant has originally been brought up in surroundings where he had a good relationship with his mother and where he felt happy.

(c)   The longer the period of emotional deprivation the more intense are its consequences. A recent research has pointed out that some children who have been placed in institutions for eight months during their first year, show a progressive decline of their development quotient reaching an average D.Q. of forty-five.

(d)   If the child is restored to some form of mothering (i.e. return of the mother or a mother-substitute), or to intensive 'mothering'-type psychotherapy, normal development can be resumed. But when a very early separation has continued beyond a certain period of time it produces irreversible effects, tantamount to a permanent deficiency, which become part of the very structure of the child's psychosomatic organization.

The realization of the importance of the mother's presence and the effects of early emotional deprivation have provided the theoretical grounds for the Rooming-In research project.[1] Nevertheless it still remains difficult to pinpoint precisely what it is that the child is being deprived of and exactly how it is expressed psychosomatically and, of course, what it is that the mother has to 'provide'.[2]

[1] A Rooming-In research project was set up at the Yale University School of Medicine in 1946 in order to evaluate two factors of parent-child relationship: (a) the importance of environmental factors on the child's personality development; (b) the predictability of the child's behaviour from the knowledge of maternal attitudes. Rooming-In and flexibility represent an ideology in infant care which diverged from the rigid schedules and coercive methods dominant from 1910 till 1940.

It had been hoped that such a revision of child-care methods would stimulate parental insight into the child's emotional needs and reduce the incidence and severity of behaviour disorders (Jackson, Klatskin et al., 1952).

[2] The reader is referred to the work of Liddel (1952) on twin goats suckled by their mother. One of the kids was separated from the mother for one hour each day. During the experimental period the lights were periodically put out

Maternal deprivation, however, is very far from resulting only from the separation of mother and child. Thus G. Heuyer (1952) felt justified in coining the term *family hospitalism* to designate those instances where, despite the mother's presence, the infant's needs remained unsatisfied. This led to the idea of a *family pathology*, the result of some overall impairment or some emotional deprivation in the parent-child relation. This could find expression in disorders affecting the family cohesion: broken homes, adverse home conditions, absence of father, etc., or it could develop surreptitiously when the real cause is the pattern of relationships in what looks like an apparently normal home. D. Levy speaks of emotionally starved children and G. Guex (1950) refers to 'separation neurosis' (*névrose d'abandon*) and to '*enfants abandonniques*'. Clinically, these children will, later in life, show a constant feeling of frustration (*emotional hunger*), a craving for affection or an apparent indifference, which may manifest itself in excessively clamorous attitudes or in more or less total dependence on society or on the spouse. These attitudes are an attempt to fill the void which has left its indelible imprint on the child's experience.[1]

Current research is concentrated on the investigation of the long-term consequences of these early deprivations. In serious instances it is sometimes impossible to fill the basic defect and this may be reflected in a somatic compliance or by an inability to establish social relations, to offer or to accept love. The gravity of these cases, where the subject is fixated, 'in a kind of tragic compulsion',

---

[1] Beres *et al.* (1950) remark that most studies have pointed up the similarities in the psychological consequences of deprivation. Their own studies seem to demonstrate a great variability, since they find that, by late adolescence, about half of their cases have made some degree of favourable social adjustment. They insist on the necessity to evaluate individual cases, to take into consideration the various factors (maturation, satisfactory placement, educational opportunities' psychotherapy, facilities provided by social agencies). The therapeutic nihilism is not warranted if our therapeutic aim is limited to increasing ego-functioning to the level of social adjustment. However, even this optimistic conclusion shows that at least half of the cases considered fall into the diagnostic category of psychosis, mental retardation and severe psychic immaturity.

(analogous to experiments of *sensory deprivation*) and this was found to produce very different behaviour in the twins. The kid which had not been separated from its mother was at ease and moved around freely; the isolated kid discontinued sucking and died. However, as Spitz (1965) points out, it should be realized that sensory deprivation and emotional deprivation are not interchangeable concepts. It is true that it is practically impossible to inflict the one without involving the other. Recent experiments show that the higher the place of the species on the evolutionary scale, the more severe the consequences. Spitz comes to the conclusion that the damage inflicted by sensory deprivation increases in direct ratio to the level of ego development and to the quantity of object relations (see Spitz, 1964).

on an urge to fill, at all costs, the basic void in his life, can be observed very clearly in the psychological aspects of delinquency.[1]

A few remarks may here be relevant concerning the use in psychoanalytic theory of the concept of deprivation.

Racamier (1954) makes a clear distinction between 'deprivational' pathology and neurosis. Deprivation creates in life a *basic defect* from which the subject never fully recovers. There is never any question of a 'conflictual frustration of desires' with a possible chance of solution that could turn out to be, as in the Oedipus complex, a formative experience.[2] In neurosis, frustration never has the authenticity of a genuine deprivation. Furthermore, relations with the parents, which are maintained in the case of neurosis, enable the subject to enter into an imaginary game of identification; the deprived child can never take part in this.

Finally, it must be pointed out that there is a danger in assigning a preponderant or exclusive role to deprivation in analytical psychopathology. This would be tantamount to a 'traumatic' conception of neurosis, whereas there are, of course, numerous other factors involved. The pathology of deprivation has been useful in highlighting the close psychosomatic interdependence in the child's evolution and the imperative necessity of a *maternal image*, whether this is provided by the real or a surrogate mother, if the child is to be capable of establishing object-relations. (There can be no doubt, however, that *qualitative* changes in this primordial relationship may cause deep disturbances, quite apart from any factors specifically related to deprivation.) M. Balint (1968) talks of the *basic fault*.

> There is a feeling that the cause of this fault is that someone has either failed the patient or defaulted on him. . . . The origin of the basic fault may be traced back to a considerable discrepancy in the early formative phases of the individual between his bio-psychological needs and the material and the psychological care, attention and affection available during the relevant times. This creates a state of deficiency whose consequences appear to be only partly reversible. The cause of this early discrepancy may be congenital, i.e. the infant's bio-psychological needs may have been too exacting, or may be environmental, such as care that is insufficient, deficient, haphazard, over-anxious, over-protective, harsh, rigid, grossly inconsistent, incorrectly

[1] *See* Bowlby (1951).
[2] In Racamier's view (1954) 'the wish emerges and is maintained only if the *need* is at first satisfied'.

timed, over-stimulating, or merely un-understanding or indifferent. As may be seen from my description, I put the emphasis on the lack of 'fit' between the child and *the people* who represent his environment.

VIII. Maternal behaviour and personality formation

The establishment of object-relations is not to be confused with the maturation of an inborn quality: it presupposes a link between subject and object; the behaviour of the libidinal object actively intervenes in this relationship and it has therefore been necessary to clarify the precise part played by the *maternal factor* in the mother-child relationship. Freud (1908a) had already mentioned that psychological conflicts in the mother were capable of orienting her relationship to her child.

He points out:[1]

A neurotic wife who is unsatisfied by her husband is, as a mother, over-tender and over-anxious towards her child, on to whom she transfers her need for love; and she awakens it to sexual precocity. The bad relations between his parents, moreover, excite its emotional life and cause it to feel love and hatred to an intense degree while it is still at a very tender age. Its strict upbringing, which tolerates no activity of the sexual life that has been aroused so early, lends support to the suppressing force and this conflict at such an age contains everything necessary for bringing about lifelong nervous illness.

Thus did Freud inaugurate research which aimed to elucidate the nature of the link between mother and child. Alice Balint (1938)[2] saw this link as one of *emotional interdependence*.

The child's love for the mother is an archaic, egotistic way of love, directed exclusively towards her but ignoring completely the true interests of the love object. This *pseudo-ambivalence* is not perceived by the child who, in his naïve egoism, confuses his and the object's interests: the child feels that his mother must not be ill, not so much out of concern for her as from fear that his own well-being might be endangered by the other's illness. Alice Balint also emphasized the difference between the child's love for the mother and his love towards the father. Although the father has

[1] S. Freud, *Civilised Sexual Morality and Modern Nervous Illness* (1908).
[2] Alice Balint, 'Love for the Mother and Mother-Love' (1938), in M. Balint, *Primary Love and Psychoanalytic Technique* (1952).

assumed many maternal traits, yet the archaic bond linking mother and child is missing. Relations with the father are more in accordance with the reality principle because the archaic link here has never been based on a natural identity of interests. The greater pedagogical effectiveness of the father is not to be accounted for solely on the grounds of paternal authority; rather it has to do with the feeling in the child that the mother could not want anything which might run contrary to the child's wishes. 'Hence, love for the mother is originally a love without a sense of reality, while love and hate for the father—including the oedipus situation—is under the sway of reality.'

Alice Balint emphasized that maternal love is intended only for the very young child, depending upon the mother's body. The fact that certain mothers continue to regard their children as 'babies' even until they are quite grown up is yet another proof of the remoteness of maternal love from reality: it is the 'almost perfect counterpart' of the child's love for the mother. In this sense the child is to the mother an object of libidinal gratification, an object whose needs and interests she regards as identical with her own. The relationship is thus based on an interdependence of reciprocal, instinctual aims. A. Balint calls this behaviour 'instinctive maternity' as opposed to 'civilized maternity', where biological interdependence, which makes the egoistic love-relation of childhood possible, is to be replaced later on by a new, adult interdependence. The gap between the infantile and adult period leads to a conflict which is resolved by the progressive strengthening of the power of reality. The first difficulty to be encountered is caused by the mother's turning away from her growing child, and the sexual significance of the child for the mother ceases to exist before the child reaches sexual maturity. The essential difference between maternal love and love for the mother lies in the fact that the mother is unique and irreplaceable, but the child can always be replaced by another.

The genetic viewpoint is that some situations are crucial in that they may be the starting point of neurosis or initiate a new level of maturation or be the basis of certain character traits. By tracing the beginnings of personality to as early a point as possible, i.e., back to the oral phase, psychoanalysis has attempted to pinpoint the maternal attitudes which have a formative or pathogenic role.[1]

---

[1] It has not been possible in this volume to discuss the psychological problems during pregnancy or the maternal attitudes arising from them; nor to examine the neurotic motivations of certain maternal attitudes (Hélène Deutsch, *The Psychology of Women*, 1946).

There have been a number of studies of the nursing situation, starting with the hypothesis that the mother's attitudes during this stage are representative of the general maternal attitude towards the child's instinctual demands. By observing the nursing situation we may learn something about her reactions in this specific context as well as in her attitudes concerning other needs of the child. The nursing situation represents the stage in which the first emotional conflict is acted out, namely, weaning.

This conflict, in its apparent simplicity, seems to be particularly accessible to the techniques of direct observation, and makes it possible to explore the mother's response to the child's instinctual demands, and to investigate the specific consequences of various attitudes in the formation of the personality.

Margaret Ribble (1944) has described two types of reaction in infants where the feeding pattern has been disorganized. One reaction is characterized by negative attitudes—refusal to be fed, anorexia, muscular rigidity, shallow breathing and periods of apnoea. The other, the depressive type, is marked by apathy, low muscle tone and gastro-intestinal disorders. All these disturbances are reversible and disappear when certain habits are modified and if the mother gives more time to fondling and feeding and generally devotes more time to the child.

The work of Sylvia Brody, *Patterns of Mothering* (1956), shows both the importance and limitations of this kind of research. She attempts to define the nursing situation in as minute a detail as possible. She considers the different methods of feeding: breast-feeding and bottle-feeding; rigid schedules or self-demand; number of feeds; postures to be adopted by mother and child; fondling and cooing accompanying the feeds, etc. In this way she has attempted to get an objective view and collect data of the feeding situation.

In addition to all this, interviews with the mother attempt to gauge her attitudes to feeding, her insight as to the child's satisfaction and gratification of need and her ideas on the manner and timing of weaning. Sylvia Brody concludes that the fact that a child is breast-fed, that he has flexible feeding schedules and that he is held in his mother's arms during feeds, are not sufficient to warrant a 'satisfying' feeding experience, either for the child or the mother. Although certain norms, generally considered proof of a 'good' mother-child relation, may well be respected, the mother may actually derive very little satisfaction and the child may be only imperfectly gratified. It would seem possible to appreciate the quality of the nursing situation only on the following indications: (a) the mother's sensitiveness to the infant's needs; (b) her capacity to establish a physical and verbal communication with her child during the feeds; (c) her unconscious motivation for the choice of feeding method which she has adopted.

The way the child will experience this situation depends ultimately on the mother's unconscious attitudes. Sylvia Brody has described various categories of maternal behaviour according to their approach and attitude, but she does not go as far as to attribute to them any precise prognostic values as regards the formation of the child's personality. Her thorough investigation illustrates the difficulty of judging, from direct observation only, the consequences and significance of any one attitude. Behind the *manifest* attitude of the mother it is necessary to explore its *latent* meaning if we wish to uncover the full significance of this inter-relation.

Similar work by Sears, Maccoby and Levin (1957) on methods of *child-rearing* look into the emotional repercussions of weaning. Although the 'breast-experience' is integrated by the child and assumes significance in the way he will establish object-relations, the authors take the view that what really matters is the specific way in which he experiences the situation, rather than any particular method of weaning. However, some conditions appear to be more favourable than others in reducing traumatic effects: (a) weaning should start somewhere between the fifth and the tenth month; (b) the transitional period should be as short as possible; and (c) the infant should be prepared for it by the gradual introduction of solid foods. These conditions in themselves, however, are not sufficient to establish any significant correlation between the attitudes and techniques of nursing and the psychological make-up of the infant.

All these studies come up against the difficulty of pinpointing so-called 'objective' reality. However exact the observation, reality cannot be reduced to purely statistical terms as long as the latent phantasy content has not been brought to light.

The influence of oral experiences on character formation has already been envisaged by Karl Abraham (1924a), who described an *oral character* by emphasizing that oral pleasure never disappears completely and that libidinal gratification connected with sucking continues to exist in adult life in various forms. The particular feeding method used and the weaning experience influence the individual's character formation by the gratification and frustration they impose. Extremes of personality, ranging from the optimistic, confident and friendly to the dependent, envious, hostile, impatient and excitable, all depend on the first oral experience. The mother's part in these experiences, obvious though it may seem, is not always easy to identify from among the multiplicity of factors involved.[1]

Others have emphasized the *qualitative* changes in maternal attitudes and their impact on the child's development. R. Spitz (1965), has described various types of *psychotoxic disturbances*. He has tried to relate certain kinds of maternal behaviour to specific psychosomatic syndromes in the child. Thus maternal over-permissiveness often leads to a syndrome called the *three-month colic*; maternal hostility in the guise of manifest anxiety may induce infantile eczema; cyclical mood swings of the mother may lead to fecal play and coprophagia in some infants. In all these cases a qualitative factor of the mother's personality structure is thought to be responsible for those psychotoxic diseases, whereas in the deficiency syndrome the factor is a quantitative one, i.e. deprivation of maternal care and of vital emotional supplies due to the mother's physical absence.

D. Levy (1943) examined the unconscious motives behind maternal over-protective attitudes. Rigidity, disquiet or constant demonstrations of affection may be due to anxiety, hostility or rejection, which attempt to compensate for the fundamental lack of satisfaction felt by the mother in her relations with her child.

If we consider that the development of the personality in the first year of life involves a constant reshaping of the child's behaviour (under the influence of maternal stimulation) then the child must learn to desire what must satisfy his own needs; but also he learns to desire according to the mother's needs or according to her desire.[2]

Any deprivation, deficiency or distortion cannot be considered only in relation to maternal reality, but as attributes of the maternal image as it gradually takes shape in the course of the child's development.

The first relations are characterized essentially by the physical contact between mother and infant. The infant's emotional life is closely bound up with the maternal care: feeding, skin stimulation,

[1] The reader is once again referred to Hélène Deutsch's *The Psychology of Women* (1946) and is invited to compare it, for contrasting viewpoints, with Simone de Beauvoir's *The Second Sex*.
[2] The ambiguity of the term *the mother's desire* conceals the differing modes of relationship between subject and object: to be the object of the mother's desire; to become the expression of her desire; to set up the mother as an object of the child's desire (Granoff, 1956). This ambiguity also illustrates the whole difficulty for the child in defining his own status of subject or object (see M. Mannoni, *L'Enfant, sa maladie et les autres*, Paris, Le Seuil, 1967).

muscular comfort, are all prototypes of instinctual drives whose gratification or frustration condition the sensations of pleasure or unpleasure (R. Mack Brunswick, 1940). The 'hallucinatory wish fulfilment' is the only inner resource for keeping at bay the pain of frustration. In this phase the libidinal object's role is to fulfil the infant's need and has primarily a utilitarian role. In a second phase the libidinal cathexis is shifted from the gratifying experience on to the object which affords the gratification. Henceforth the experiences of pleasure and unpleasure are linked with the representation of the mother, who is cathected with the power of granting or refusing the coveted satisfaction. Her image is split into a 'good' or bad' maternal image according to whether it represents either a refusal or a gift. This is a fundamental dichotomy in which part images or objects coexist or may be opposing one another in a relationship which is sometimes positive, sometimes negative, but essentially ambivalent.

As a result of identification with this image, the child himself takes up the role played by the mother, who is perceived as active. He thus passes from initial passivity to an active role and cuts himself loose from maternal dependence. He can abandon the hallucinated object of his satisfaction and perceive the real object: the concept of *self* will thus emerge. Through the painful experience of giving up his mother, the child gradually abandons the pleasure principle by learning to recognize his own image, its limits and limitations. But his dependence and archaic demands never completely disappear, so that vestigial traces may be discerned later on in all his object-relations.

When D. W. Winnicott talks about the 'good enough mother', he is not singling out any particular form of maternal behaviour or any particular image but a type of relation which enables the child to work out a first object which belongs to him alone and which is not a part of him (a 'not-me possession'). This object has a special status: it belongs wholly to the child although it is borrowed from objects lying around him (bits of cloth, or wool, etc.) and yet *this object has not been given to him*: it is the first to be felt as having been created as such by the child himself. This *transitional object* (Winnicott, 1953) prefigures and delimits the intermediary emotional area which properly belongs to the child and which he will be able to invest subsequently with his intellectual, artistic and creative activities.

The mother's devotion, however great, can never wholly satisfy these infantile demands. Anna Freud (1954) criticized the notion of 'maternal rejection' as being responsible for the onset of 'infantile neurosis which is often thought to be a result of an actual' frustration imposed on the child.

> . . . a mother may be experienced as rejecting by the infant for a multitude of different reasons, connected with either her conscious or unconscious attitudes, her bodily or mental defects, her physical presence, or absence, her unavoidable libidinal preoccupations, her aggressions, her anxieties, etc. The disappointments or frustrations . . . are inseparable from the mother-child relationship. . . . *The mother is merely the representative and symbol of inevitable frustration in the oral phase just as the father in the oedipal phase is the representative of inevitable phallic frustration which gives him his symbolic role of castrator.* The new concept of the rejecting mother has to be understood in the same sense as the familiar older concept of the castrating father. To put the blame for the infantile neurosis on the mother's shortcomings in the oral phase is no more than a facile and misleading generalization . . .

These lines emphasize that psychoanalysis has tried to go beyond the findings of genetic epistemology. A. Freud's remarks remind us that the area of childhood experience must and has been approached along different lines of research: the unfolding of the child's maturational gradients; the gradual establishment of his object relationships, the libidinal impulses of the various phases, the building up of the body image, the consequences of unavoidable trauma and frustration, the process of individuation must all be taken into consideration if we are to approach childhood experience as a multidimensional phenomenon.

Whatever attempts have been made to evaluate the part played by objective reality in the individual's personality formation, they always come up against subjective factors which cannot be quantified. Any behaviour transcends its objective effects and no parental attitude can be accepted at its face value. The imaginary matrix of the maternal object and the symbolic dimension introduced by the paternal imago modify and shape any childhood experience through the interplay of unconscious motivations and unconscious desires.

6 Analytic practice

In the methodology of therapeutics psychoanalysis holds an extreme position: its started out from clinical experience and its theories have been elaborated to explicate as well as learn from these experiences. Preconceived notions are rarely taken for granted, and the clinical findings of an analyst must be interpreted by him in frames of reference which are open to questioning and change. Hence analytic practice and theory are closely interwoven, and an analyst's clinical work is enriched further by the growing tradition of his own clinical experience. The theoretical framework is thus an essential part of practice, since without it psychoanalysis would be nothing but constant improvisation. Theory, however, can be helpful only if the analyst is free to evaluate its validity through clinical practice; this being his only check on the possible ossification of his preconceptions and theories into dogma.

This very problem of the relationship between theory and clinical experience is at the core of many problems raised by the analytic practice with children. One of the crucial points of debate was to define the specificity of child analysis in regard to 'adult' analysis and to verify whether the principles underlying the latter were valid in cases of analytic treatment with children. In its beginnings the psychoanalysis of children was simply a straightforward application of the method applied to adults. However, when Hermine von Hug-Hellmuth initiated the practice of child analysis around the year 1915, she introduced new techniques, including drawing and playing, which were to allow the child an easier way of expressing his phantasies.

Throughout the development of child analysis there has been this *search for a technique* which would allow the child to overcome the obstacles which blocked the path to analytic work, namely: his position of real dependency on his parents; his difficulty, even inability, in using the method of free association; the initial absence of motivation for committing himself to treatment and establishing a transference with the therapist. Over and above the question of techniques, however, there are important theoretical problems, viz., the formation of the superego, the maturation of the ego and the origin of anxiety.

The application of psychoanalysis to children came relatively late. Almost twenty years elapsed between Freud's case-report of Little Hans' analysis and the burgeoning of child psychoanalysis as a specialized discipline.[1]

---

[1] In this long case-history, *Analysis of a Phobia in a Five-Year-Old Boy* (1909b), Freud reports the development and resolution of Hans's phobia. The therapy was conducted by Little Hans's father, who reported, sometimes daily, his son's

L

A number of circumstances go some way to explaining this state of affairs which, in fact, indicated a change in the medical attitude towards child psychiatry. As we have already seen, the only problems which had so far been tackled by the 'straight' psychiatry were those of mental deficiency, epilepsy, cerebral palsy and juvenile delinquency, where neurological defects and organic symptoms were emphasized to the exclusion of 'psychological' factors. Behaviour disorders did not seem to attract the attention of the psychiatrists; the problem of childhood neurosis, like that of pre-psychotic states, was looked at from the angle of mis-behaviour, of learning difficulties and poor social adjustment, and were thought to require 'remedial teaching' or disciplining rather than psychological methods of treatment.

The child-guidance clinic movement focused the attention on the importance of psychological difficulties by extending the area of psychiatric help to problems which had hitherto been frankly regarded as 'minor' incidents in the development of the child, or as manifestations of some physical disorder. By stressing the specific value of psychological difficulties child psychiatry not only gained recognition as a medical speciality but also exerted a determining influence on the development of psychotherapy. Thus, the analysts came up against practical and theoretical problems due to the specific requirements of child analysis.

I. Specificity of psychoanalysis

Paradoxically enough, the conditions which had favoured the development of psychoanalysis of the child were also the cause of initial theoretical difficulties. With the development of the child-guidance movement the number and variety of psychotherapies increased. They ranged from the so-called 'supportive' techniques to classic psychoanalysis.

---

difficulties and the conversations with him to the 'Professor', who directed the father in his understanding and in the handling of this case. Freud only saw the boy twice. It should be mentioned that the parents were 'analytically enlightened' people. Freud's interest was obviously aroused by the possibility which was offered to him of verifying his ideas about infantile sexuality.

This, of course, is a rather unusual procedure. However in some cases, where no child analyst is available, a parent may be able to solve the child's neurotic problem with the help of an analyst (Geleerd, 1967). Some cases have been reported by Bonnard (1950), Furman (1957), and others. Bonnard reports a case of obsessional neurosis in a four-year-old boy where the mother was used as a therapeutic intermediary between the child and the analyst: she remarks that in this case 'the child received a twenty-four-hour service'.

It is important to distinguish the psychoanalytically inspired therapies from genuine psychoanalysis—not an easy distinction to draw in the case of child analysis.[1]

One may say that the 'analytic psychotherapies' are those which are based on psychoanalytic principles without any underlying reservations. From a practical point of view they differ from 'classical' analysis in that they generally avoid the individualization and elucidation of transference. These therapies are often of shorter duration and do not always aim at achieving a structural change but rather a re-evaluation of attitudes. The unconscious material, once it has been brought to light and interpreted, often remains at the level of oedipal problems and does not generally reach the pre-genital level. Although the principle behind this distinction appears clear-cut, it is, in the practice of child analysis, much less rigorous than it might appear in this statement. What adds to the confusion is that many analysts conduct therapies which are difficult to distinguish from psychoanalysis proper, because child analysis involves technical adjustments which make it suitable to the actual conditions of the practice.

II. The psychoanalytic treatment of children: the views of Anna Freud

The debate on the question of *adapting psychoanalysis to meet the requirements of the child* oscillates between two poles: the group represented by Anna Freud and that of Melanie Klein and her followers. Anna Freud published her first works in 1926 and 1927 and although she has since modified some of her opinions, her general principles concerning child analysis have not undergone any radical change.[2]

[1] The non-analytical techniques, such as so-called non-directive therapies, are not discussed here. Their theoretical assumptions diverge from those of Freud. We are not making a value judgment but merely emphasizing that their practice and basic concepts are quite distinct from the body of knowledge which it is the aim of this volume to survey. It remains nevertheless true that non-analytical psychotherapies are possible, though one cannot fail to note, in Carl Rogers's writings, the absence of any use of Freudian metapsychological concepts; he draws his inspiration chiefly from a 'dynamic' theory of personality. Any reference, in the present volume, to psychotherapy, is always, of course, to that practised by analysts. The dissident schools, associated with the names of Jung, Adler and Karen Horney, are not discussed here, their theories being too far removed from psychoanalysis. The reader is referred to the very useful volume by J. A. C. Brown, *Freud and the Post-Freudians* (1961).

[2] Anna Freud's *Einführung in die Technik der Kinderanalyse* (Wien, Internationaler Psychoanalytischer Verlag, 1927) forms the first two sections of the *Psychoanalytical Treatment of Children* which appeared in 1946. In a third

1 *The decision*

Because of his immaturity and his state of dependency on others, the child cannot make a decision as to his need for analytic treatment. It is for the parents to take the initiative. The child, therefore, comes before the analyst as a stranger, feeling no bond with him and without reason for placing any confidence in him.

When adults seek analysis, they are aware that they are mentally ill, although, of course, some are much less objective about this than others. As Michel Foucault (1954) points out: 'There is always an allusive recognition of the situation, a diffuse perception of the morbid backcloth in front of which the pathological scenes are being enacted.' It is, in fact, this ambivalent awareness which brings the adult patient to the analyst.[1]

The decision for analysis never really comes from the child who is to be the patient. The child rarely has a proper awareness of his condition for he cannot really appreciate the difficulties he is going through. He may *feel* anxious, unhappy or abandoned, but he has neither the judgment nor any frame of reference to recognize that he is 'ill'.

The initiative to consult the analyst must therefore come from the parents, whose reasons for consulting him may vary widely. Their disquiet is largely determined by the extent to which they themselves can tolerate the child's disturbances. This tolerance varies and is not so much related to the mode and intensity of the symptoms as to the subject's anxiety and his awareness of his emotional problems. We shall return to this in a later chapter where the question of the parents' demand will be discussed.

The child cannot, of course, have the same motivation as the adult for seeking treatment. *The wish to get well* which is instrumental in bringing the treatment to a successful conclusion, is not essential for the child, at least not in the initial phase of treatment.

[1] These considerations are not quite as straightforward as they may seem. The adult's decision to seek psychoanalytical treatment is not always completely free and he is often influenced by pressures from people close to him. But even in the case of character neurosis—where the pathological aspect of behaviour or of some personality trait is not always obvious—there is always the 'allusive and partial awareness' referred to by Michel Foucault.

---

section, 'Indications for Child Analysis' which first appeared in 1945, in the *Psychoanalytic Study of the Child,* the author picks up many of her original hypotheses and modifies them in the light of certain English and American work. In 1966 Anna Freud, in *Normality and Pathology in Childhood,* partly revised some of her initial statements; but on the whole this work retains the imprint of the writer's former ideas.

2 *Basic principles of child analysis*

'It seemed almost a matter of prestige for child analysts to maintain that they were bound by the same therapeutic principles to which analysis of adults was committed.' Anna Freud's statement is all the more relevant since all child analysts—to whatever group they belong—agree that minimal requirements must be met in order to speak of child *analysis*: one should eliminate suggestion; discard abreaction as a therapeutical tool; keep manipulation to a minimum. Most would also agree to recognize the necessity of interpreting unconscious material and of analysing resistance and transference. But a difference of opinion does exist about how child analysis can comply with these principles and to what extent technical adjustments are necessary. But Anna Freud (1966) sees the difference between child and adult analysis not only in terms of specific technical difficulties and of discrepancies in the analytic situation, but also in the curative process. With adults, psychoanalysis owes its success to the 'liberation of forces which are present normally and work spontaneously in the direction of a cure. The adult strives for normality since this holds out for him the promise of pleasure in sex and success in work.' The situation is quite different as far as the child is concerned: not only the initial demand for help is missing, but also 'getting well' often means having to adjust to 'unpalatable reality' and giving up immediate gratification. Thus the child may seem to be lacking any motivation to get 'better', since this would mainly be a compliance with the adult's demand. Of course, this parental wish may also be an asset, since in terms of a realistic appraisal it might mean an improvement of the parent-child relationship. This unstable balance may seem discouraging in view of the therapeutic enterprise, since the child would have little incentive to co-operate. But Anna Freud also insists on another factor, *the urge to complete development*, which may be part of the process of cure. The fluid state of child's mental structure makes it possible for the libido and the aggressiveness to flow more readily into new channels which are opened up by psychoanalysis. And 'child analysts often will query how much of the improvement is due to their intervention and how much should be ascribed to spontaneous developmental moves' (A. Freud).

Anna Freud thus felt the need to make certain adjustments in the practice of child analysis in order to make the small patient 'analysable': the necessity of an 'introductory period' (or 'dressage' for analysis); technical expedients in the analysis of children; a revision of the problem of transference.

3 *The introductory phase*

Anna Freud suggested that child analysis be preceded by an introductory phase which, in itself, has nothing analytical about it and which she called the 'dressage' for analysis. We might call it a 'conditioning' or 'inducement' period. In this phase the idea is not to get the patient to become conscious of what is unconscious nor to exert any 'analytical influence' over him, but to break down the initial unfavourable attitudes, that is, to motivate the child to enter and maintain a therapeutic relation. During this period, the patient may establish a rapport based on confidence and at the same time sense the usefulness of an analysis by becoming aware of the need to solve certain difficulties.

The therapist should, at the same time, give the impression of being useful to the child, of being someone who is interested in his welfare and of having a certain power. In this way, he will make himself indispensable and prepare the way for a transference relation which makes an analysis possible.

Subsequently, Anna Freud modified some of her formulations and suggested using the introductory phase to interpret the neurotic defences which reveal the child's attitude to the analyst. Although she would deny that she uses these sessions with the patient to interpret unconscious phantasies or the transference, she would advocate an approach to this therapeutic relationship which would involve interpreting the child's 'character' defences.

4 *Technical adjustments*

As the child is usually unable to provide us with any information about his clinical history or his symptoms, we are obliged to resort to information supplied by the parents. We are thus deprived of a valuable source of material; the parents' own emotional reactions must necessarily give a highly coloured picture of their child and their account is accordingly distorted.

Anna Freud therefore feels that she has to dispense with this important source of analytical material which the adult patient usually himself provides in the course of analysis. Instead of the technique of a recall (remembering), the analyst has to use other ways of getting at the unconscious. Anna Freud advocates the use of the interpretation of dreams reported by the child, although the classical method of free association is not always feasible, and interpretation must sometimes be drawn from what is available from the child's daily life or history, and this, more often than not, comes from the version given by those close to, or around, him.

She does not, however, confine herself solely to verbal material but also uses drawings done by the children during sessions. These drawings may sometimes supersede all other forms of communication between patient and therapist.

Nevertheless she emphasises that in this kind of practice we are not making use of the *fundamental rule*: the child, under certain conditions, may indeed supply free associations, but he can *not* appreciate the rule requiring that *all material*, without reservation, must be put into words and that no censorship must come between his phantasies and their verbal expression. His free associations may occasionally conform to this requirement but they are a precarious basis for the conduct of the treatment.

Free association, the mainstay of analytic technique (also called 'the fundamental rule'), had therefore to be ruled out as a method, young children being neither willing nor able to embark upon it. Appropriate substitutes have to be found. Melanie Klein makes use of children's play activities during the sessions and interprets them in the same way as the free associations of the adult. For her all phases of the child's play have a symbolic value and reveal his unconscious phantasies. Anna Freud does not deny that play can be interpreted symbolically, but insists that the child's attitude is not to be compared with that of the adult, for the latter makes, as it were, a powerful effort not to exclude anything consciously in the course of giving rein to his free associations. Furthermore, Anna Freud points out (1966) that even in using play activities, some caution is necessary in order to interpret them, since play therapy leads to the production of symbolic material and thus to symbolic interpretation which is often uncertain and even arbitrary. She also remarks that freedom of verbal association cannot be reproduced by the freedom of behaviour, since at a given point some restraint becomes necessary and the analyst cannot help interfering in spite of his forbearance and his best intentions, sometimes in order to prevent the child from endangering his own or the analyst's safety. Anna Freud also suggests that free associations tend to liberate sexual phantasies, while 'free action' seems to provoke the child's aggressive trends or the aggressive side of his pre-genitality. She says that technical problems are bound to appear since some 'valuable time must often be spent in efforts to check excesses of aggression which analytic tolerance has released initially'.

5 *The problem of the transference*

In Anna Freud's view it is essential for the child to establish an affectionate relation with the therapist; in other words a 'positive transference' must take place. This conception would justify the pre-analytic phase of the therapeutic relation—the one referred to as the preparation period—which should help the child to follow the course of treatment.

She recognizes that the relation between the child and the therapist is emotionally invested with love or feelings of attachment, revolt or antagonism. She nevertheless maintains that these feelings do not constitute a genuine transference neurosis. The adult, during analysis, may withdraw his cathexes from those objects to which his phantasies connect him and may be capable of structuring it around the person of the analyst; for the child, such a transference is not possible for the following reasons:

(a)   The child's relation with his parents persists during the whole course of treatment, for he depends on them for every gratification, real or imaginary. His conflictual objects are external and not yet internalized as in the case of the adult. The analyst may break into the circle but he cannot replace the parents, for the child feels no need to use him as a substitute figure. In the view of Anna Freud, the child's hostile feelings towards the therapist do not indicate that his ambivalent feelings for his mother have been transferred to him; on the contrary, his very attachment to his mother makes it impossible for him, as it were, to establish such relations elsewhere. The child seeks to obtain from the analyst what he feels deprived of in the real situation and not to reproduce that situation.

(b)   The second obstacle has to do with the analyst's position towards the child. In the case of adult patients, the 'neutral' position of the analyst allows the patient to 'project' and inscribe his phantasies on the 'blank screen' presented to him. The children's analyst must, according to Anna Freud, 'be anything but a shadow', for he cannot resign his educational role and the child 'knows very well just what seems to the analyst desirable or undesirable and what he sanctions or disapproves of'. As such the analyst is unfortunately 'a bad transference object', of little use when it comes to interpreting the transference.

Despite all positive or negative feelings towards the analyst, Anna Freud considers that there is no genuine transference neurosis and this because of extrinsic conditions: the effective presence of the parents responsible for the child's upbringing. The analyst must take into account not only what happens during the sessions but also what occurs in the child's home, where the abnormal reactions are often displayed even during the course of the treatment. It would be possible of course to bring about a change in these conditions by, for instance, separating the child from his parents and carrying on the analysis with the child placed in a suitable institution. This kind of change of surroundings would give the necessary conditions for the setting up of a transference neurosis by removing the original conflictual objects from the child's immediate environment. But the separation of the child from his parents cannot be recommended for the sake of psycho-analysis only; one must have imperative and specific reasons to resort to such a solution.

Anna Freud (1966) points out that in child analysis the analyst is used by the patient in various ways:

(a)   Since the 'hunger of new experience' is part of the child's maturational potential, the child who enters analysis sees in the analyst a new object and treats him as such. He uses the analyst for repetition, i.e. transference goes only as far as his neurosis comes into question. Thus many of the child's attitudes to the analyst are not really transferred since the analyst is used as a 'new object'.

(b)   Not all relations between the analyst and the child are object-relations in the sense that the analyst becomes cathected with libido or aggression. 'Many are due to externalization, i.e. a process in which the person of the analyst is used to represent one or the other part of the patient's personality structure.'

By tolerating freedom of thought, phantasy and, to a certain extent, action, the analyst becomes the representative of the patient's *id*. So far as he helps the child to fight anxiety he becomes an *auxiliary ego* to whom the child clings for help and protection. As an adult the analyst is seen by the child as an *external superego*.

> To interpret such externalizations in terms of object-relationship within the transference would be a mistake, even though originally all conflicts within the structure have their source in earliest relationships. At the time of therapy, however, their importance lies in the fact that they reveal what happens in the child's inner world between his internal agencies, as contrasted with the emotional relationship to objects in the external world. . . .
> Understood in this manner, externalization is a subspecies of transference.

Anna Freud also states that experience has taught her to eliminate the introductory phase (except in certain cases) and to use defence analysis as an introduction to treatment (Bornstein, 1949). She says that she has modified her opinion and does no longer believe that transference in child analysis is restricted to single transference reaction. However, she states that she is 'still unconvinced that what is called transference neurosis with children equals the adult variety in every respect'.

Here we meet with a borderline concept, that of *therapeutic alliance* (R. Sterba, 1940), i.e. the patient's capacity to mobilize his conscious desire to co-operate with the therapist: this has been described in terms of ego-functions, since the child's ego would act as a mediating agency between the desire to get well and the outside help provided by the analyst. Thus Marjorie Harley, commenting (1967) on the nature of transference in children, points out that (a) transference is not limited to the extension into the analytic situation of current reactions to the original love objects, but includes earlier libidinal and aggressive strivings reactivated by the analytic process and directed towards the analyst; (b) transference, even with young children, is sometimes observable, albeit in circumscribed forms; (c) therapeutic alliance with the analyst allows the child to withstand negative transference and the stress of analysis. 'Alliance', as referred to by Frankl and Hellman (1962), means that the child must be able to participate in his treatment in an emotionally dynamic way.

Whether or not a transference neurosis is desirable in the case of a child has also been discussed by A. Freud. Once the transference has taken place the problem of its resolution arises: the child is detached from his parents at a time when he is incapable of being completely independent, and when the analysis comes to its end (i.e. after resolving his transference neurosis) he would be in a very difficult situation towards his parents. Anna Freud therefore considers that, in normal circumstances, the transference is neither possible nor desirable; she recommends that the analysis be conducted solely with verbal material and does not encourage a genuine transference involving a shift of the child's total emotional resources. She prefers to concentrate her efforts on the elucidation of the defence mechanisms used by the child to protect himself against anxiety; this she considers possible quite apart from any interpretation of the transference.

6 *The educational point of view and the role of the superego*

Anna Freud's final reservations as to the possibility of conducting a 'genuine' child analysis are based on her view of the formation of the superego. In the adult, the superego becomes the representative of the normal demands made by society; it originates in the introjection of the superego demands of the first love objects, the parents: 'to them, society has transferred the task of establishing its current ethical claims on the child and enforcing the restrictions upon instinct which it prescribes'. What was originally an unconscious obligation towards the parents has turned into a psychic agency, independent of its prototypes.

In the child's case, there is no clear dividing line between the introjected superego and the real parents to which it owes its establishment. The child's superego builds up progressively and for a long time remains weak and unstable. The instability is particularly noticeable when the child loses its parents through separation or when the parental image is depreciated. When these external supports are over-weakened or absent, the rudimentary superego will oppose no inner volition to the instinctual drives demanding immediate satisfaction.

Thus, in case of separation, regressive behaviour patterns may appear, since the demands of the superego can only be sustained to the degree that a compensation emanating from the love object makes the 'sacrifice' bearable by offering gratification. The same applies to certain reaction-formations such as shame or disgust, which manage to restrain the anal and exhibitionist impulses from breaking through to gratification; they depend on the relationship with the parents who are there to maintain the superego by their actual presence. This difference between the adult and infantile superego is of utmost importance. Anna Freud's view is that the infantile superego has not yet become an 'impersonal representative of the obligations undertaken at the behest of the outer world'. The outer world, particularly the child's daily surroundings, plays an important part in the analysis, especially in respect of the child's use of the instinctual drives which have been freed of repression. 'I think that left alone and with any support withdrawn, the child can only find one single short and convenient path—that of direct gratification. We know, however, that it is desirable to avoid too much direct gratification at any stage of a child's necessarily perverse sexuality. Otherwise, fixation on the once-experienced pleasure will prove a hindrance to further normal development.'

For these reasons Anna Freud considers that the analyst must claim for himself the role of guiding the child. The child must be able to learn which impulses are compatible with social life, which gratifications are acceptable and which drives must be suppressed, rejected or sublimated. She asserts that 'the analyst must succeed in putting himself in the place of the child's ego-ideal for the duration of the analysis'. The child's superego is dependent on the outer world, and since the child is himself unable to control his emancipated instincts, the analyst must exert an 'educational' influence.

The analyst combines two diametrically opposed functions: on the one hand he should allow the child to express freely his wishes and phantasies and help him to become conscious of the material that has been repressed. On the other hand, he has to allow (or forbid) certain immediate gratifications, facilitate sublimation and encourage certain behaviour patterns. The analyst must also be able to exert a certain control over the external situation and over the child's inner structure.

It is true that more recently Anna Freud (1966) has somewhat modified her views. The 'position of authority' to which she formerly attached great importance, she no longer seems to think essential. The child analyst can now return to his purely analytic role with the help and co-operation of an enlightened educational milieu. She thinks that the efforts made to gain this assistance from the educational area have borne fruit. It is none the less true that this educational aim, which she strongly advocates, is based on a theory of the late development of the infantile superego; it also has a therapeutic goal in view: the mental and social adjustment of the child.

The analyst's role will thus be to help the child to curb the excessive demands of his superego and to resolve in this way the anxiety arising from the intrapsychic conflict between id, ego and superego. He must at the same time, however, encourage the formation of another superego based on the image of the therapist himself, less tyrannical and closer to social reality.

III. The psychoanalysis of children: the views of Melanie Klein

The controversies between Melanie Klein and her opponents were clearly stated in a series of discussions arranged in 1943 by the British Psychoanalytic Society. Papers were presented then by

Susan Isaacs, Paula Heimann and Melanie Klein.[1] A general characteristic of Melanie Klein's opponents was 'the assumption, not always expressed, but sometimes implied and sometimes expressed with vehemence, that her propositions are "not psycho-analysis". In some quarters it has been assumed *tout court* that her work is an independent variety of psychological theory . . . ' (J. Rivière, 1952).

Melanie Klein and her followers have always claimed that, although there are differences between them and their opponents, their work is a development and an extension of psychoanalytic knowledge and is firmly based on Freud's theory and postulations. In particular Melanie Klein has retained the *instinctual theory*[2] and the basic relations of psychology to the biological core of the human organism.

Here the question of the unconditional acceptance of Freud's theories must be raised. It is true that Freud's statements are not unequivocal, that he revised his views and his 'own supremely scientific quality of mind is exemplified in these very inconsistencies which he openly displays about certain topics. . . . The task of resolving the inconsistency must come from further work, observation and insight; what is important to him is not to deny an element of truth where he sees it' (J. Rivière, 1952). This also applies to Freud's theory of the *death instinct*, which was (and still is) rejected by many analysts, who claim that this part of Freud's theory can be detached from his work. Melanie Klein, for whom the problem of anxiety in all its bearings has been 'the touchstone, the guiding thread which had led her through the maze', was also what made her discover the importance of the aggressive elements in the child's life and the direct link between anxiety and the theory of death instinct. And although the basic assumptions on which the theory of Melanie Klein rests, can claim 'much support in Freud's writing—explicit or implicit—does not signify that her contribution rests on this foundation. . . . Her results stand on their own foundation of independent and un-remitting work in their development.'

All this is indicative enough that theoretical differences exist between A. Freud's viewpoint and Melanie Klein's work. But it is also true that in 'these controversies we at times derive an impression which is farcical in its effects: each side appears to claim

---

[1] These papers have been published in a collective volume, Melanie Klein et al., *Developments in Psychoanalysis* (1952).
[2] It should be stated that all 'neo-Freudian deviations' have always abandoned this fundamental concept (A. Adler, C. Jung, K. Horney et al.).

to be more Freudian than the other, in that each points emphatic-
ally to one aspect of Freud's formulations in support: one to the
earlier, the other to the modified or later terms of his views' (J.
Rivière, 1952). Those points of divergence not only touch upon
matters of theory relating to the child's early development but
carry over to the *practice* of child analysis. And it is of utmost
importance to see how differences in theory determine variations
in the principles underlying psychoanalytic practice.

Melanie Klein followed in the footsteps of Hermine von Hug-
Hellmuth (1921), who made use of toys and drawings to establish
communication with the child and to allow him to express his
phantasies.[1]

1 *Play technique*

Faced with the difficulties involved in verbal communication,
Melanie Klein sought a means by which the child could express
himself and which at the same time could lend itself to an analytical
interpretation. Play, as a child's natural activity, seemed to her to
be the ideal way, all the more so because it is through play that, in
the analyst's presence, the child's phantasy life can express itself.

As far back as 1926[2] she declared that this *technique* did not in
any way conflict with analytical *principles* and was in any case
inevitable, given the special primitive peculiarities of the mental
life of children:

> The criteria of the psychoanalytic method, namely, that we
> should use as our starting point the facts of transference
> and resistance, that we should take into account infantile
> impulses, repression and its effects, amnesia and the
> compulsion to repetition and, further, that we should
> discovered the primal scene . . . all these criteria are
> maintained in their entirety in the play-technique.

In her criticism of this approach Anna Freud (1926) stated that
play is a natural activity of the child and that it provides him with
a situation governed almost entirely by the pleasure principle.

In fact, Melanie Klein emphasized that the child plays *in the*

---

[1] Melanie Klein's first article, 'Infant Analysis', appeared in 1923 and was later
incorporated in her book, *The Psychoanalysis of Children* (1932). Other articles
appearing between 1921 and 1945 were gathered into one volume, *Contributions
to Psychoanalysis* (Hogarth Press, 1948). Further articles by Melanie Klein, Susan
Isaacs, Paula Heimann and Joan Rivière were published in *Developments in
Psychoanalysis* (Hogarth Press, 1952).
[2] 'The Psychological Principles of Infant Analysis' (1926) forms the basis of the
first chapter of *Psychoanalysis of Children* (1932).

presence of the analyst, and his play thus loses its so-called spontaneity; he plays, but he plays *in a given situation*, in the presence of someone who is watching him and talking to him. Under these conditions the child's play is no more 'spontaneous' than the free association of the patient in the presence of the analyst. In analysis, the purely hedonistic quality of the child's play gives way to expression of anxiety. The presence of the analyst is not intended to 'wheedle' the child; on the contrary, it confers on his play a special significance:

(a)   The play expresses, in a symbolic way, the child's unconscious sexual and aggressive phantasies; but Melanie Klein states 'that one of the necessary conditions of a successfully terminated treatment is that the child, however young, should make use of language in analysis to the full extent of its capacity'.

(b)   The play activity in the analyst's presence gives it a new meaning because the analyst is there to show that the child's 'play goes much further than his play' and that it involves his relationship to libidinal objects.

(c)   A relation between the child and his analyst is built up around the play, bearing the characteristic imprint of the transference situation.

The child may have a general preference for games of pretence or make-believe (being at school, seeing or being the doctor, playing at mother and child). Such games are a direct method of representation and consequently they furnish a greater wealth of verbal associations.

Melanie Klein also provides the child with toys representing persons, animals, houses, cars—material which is an effigy of a world for the use of children, a material already symbolized and 'socialized'. The use of playthings represents a more indirect form of expressing unconscious sexual and aggressive phantasies: phantasies of birth, of the primal scene, of destruction, etc. In Melanie Klein's view,

> behind every form of play activity lies a process of
> discharge of masturbatory fantasies operating in the form
> of a continuous impulse to play. . . . And that inhibitions in
> play and work spring from an unduly strong repression of
> these fantasies. This process, acting as a repetition
> compulsion, constitutes a basic mechanism in the child's
> play. The pleasure he gets in this way provides the
> necessary stimulus for him to continue his analysis. But
> this pleasure gain should never be more than a means to
> an end.

When a certain amount of anxiety has been resolved through interpretation, the child experiences a sense of relief which is an incentive to proceed with his 'work'. The child might even gain insight as to the value of his therapy and wish to go on with it.

The function of play, however, is not simply to re-enact the contents of imagination. Since playing takes place in a specific situation, that is, in the presence of a third party—the therapist—it must be interpreted as an attempt to escape his own inner world of phantasy, to establish a way of communicating with the therapist and, by way of transference, to express his phantasies in his relation to a third party. Thus the child transcends the limits of his imaginary, dyadic, relationship and establishes his role more firmly in the triangular situation, in which a symbolic meaning is attached to all relationships with others. The oedipal situation is paradigmatic in this sense. The choice of objects, the way they are handled, the inner organization of the play, the way the various roles are allocated—all this indicates, over and above a simple reproduction of phantasies, the establishment of a specific symbolic pattern and the creation of a personal 'myth'. From there on the child enters society, in which a symbolic—and often unconscious —meaning is attached to any person and any interpersonal situation.

2 The role of phantasy[1]

We have seen how one of Anna Freud's major concerns is to evaluate the role played by reality in the child's life and its importance in child analysis. Melanie Klein takes an almost diametrically opposite view and emphasizes the importance and function of the child's phantasy life.

Play becomes the very core of child analysis, providing an expression for the patient's unconscious phantasies which represent the mental representation of the instinctual *drives*, the defences put up by the ego, as well as the patient's transference neurosis. Thus all these elements can find an expression in the child's activities during the sessions and be interpreted by the analyst. Play provides an indispensable tool which makes interpretation possible.

(a) PHANTASY AND CHILDHOOD EXPERIENCE The psychoanalytic concept of phantasy must be examined in the light of its historical

---

[1] In the pages that follow a distinction will be made between conscious imaginary representations (fantasy) and their latent unconscious content (phantasy). This distinction is not always an easy one to make.

development. It would be easy to define it as a *psychic representation* of the instinctual drive; the unreality of fantasies are recognized by the patient but their intensity may constitute a source of anxiety or satisfaction. Such a definition, which would include day-dreaming, falls short of covering the full meaning of the psychoanalytical concept. Freud made several attempts to assess phantasy in its relation to the unconscious.

In 1919, Freud talked about the two levels of fantasy formation. It should be emphasized that Melanie Klein's approach to *phantasy* (which can be defined as the content of all unconscious processes) differs from the Freud's view on fantasy as it has been pointed out by Sandler and Nagera (1963). In his writings, Freud has described:

(i) *conscious fantasy*, or day-dreaming, which is a reaction to frustrating external reality. 'It implies the creation of a wish-fulfilling situation and thereby brings about a temporary lessening of instinctual tensions.' However, in this situation, the ego remains aware that this fantasy is not reality: thus conscious fantasy differs from hallucinatory wish-fulfilment which is not distinguished from reality;

(ii) fantasies which are *descriptively* unconscious and are either formed in the system Pcs (preconscious), or are relegated into the unconscious by repression. These repressed fantasies function like 'a memory of instinctual satisfaction and can provide the *ideational content of the instinctual drives*. . . . They deserve the name of fantasy only inasmuch as they are *derived* from the content of conscious or preconscious fantasies.' Unconscious fantasies can in turn express themselves through new conscious day-dreams. Sandler and Nagera's main objection to Melanie Klein's concept of phantasy is that she does not distinguish between fantasying as an ego function and hallucinatory gratification (*see also* Glover, 1945).

Obviously, only the conscious level can be apprehended by the patient; the true meaning eludes him because the underlying content has been re-structured and only the final product is admitted to consciousness. The analysis of the 'manifest' content of the fantasy leads to the uncovering of the unconscious phantasy.

The example quoted by Freud in his article, 'A Child is Being Beaten' (1919), enables us to grasp the shift of meaning achieved. The fantasy reported by the patient is a scene in which *a man is beating a child*. The reconstruction of the phantasy under analysis enables us to see the successive transformations that take place.

M

(i)   In the first phase, when the child is under the sway of sibling rivalry, the fantasy represents the harsh treatment which the father metes out to his rival: '*My father is beating the child* whom I hate, he is beating my rival'. It means: 'My father does not love this other child, *he only loves me.*'

(ii)   After these guilt feelings have been released the fantasy takes on an unmistakably masochistic character: '*My father is beating me* because I was pleased when he was beating my rival, and I like him to beat me.' The implicit meaning, 'My father loves me since he is beating me, just as he was beating my rival (whom he loved)', makes clear how the erotic elements participate in masochism. But although this is the most momentous phase, it may be said that in a certain sense it never has a real existence. It is a *construction* of analysis, but nevertheless a necessity on that account.

(iii)   The final working out of the fantasy as it is modified by repression: *a man* (a surrogate for the paternal image) *is beating a child* (surrogate for the fraternal rival) only acquires its true meaning through the reconstruction of its unconscious origin. But the essential characteristic which distinguishes it from the first phase is that it is now attached to an overt sexual excitement and thus provides a means for onanistic gratification.

(b)   IMAGINED RECONSTRUCTION OF THE PAST Freud also sought to establish a relation between the development of a child's sexual life and his fantasies. He finds that these fantasies—fantasy of the phallic mother, the castration fantasy, fantasy of sexual intercourse—are linked with the first phases of libidinal development. The fantasy of the parental sexual intercourse, which Freud calls the *primal scene*, is a dramatization of the oedipal situation, and Freud at first thought it was based on an actual recollection. But in the case history known as the *Wolf-Man* the primal scene in the patient's dream turned out to be the imaginary condensation of two other, more trivial, memories and it was obvious that the primal scene was a fantasy, thus proving that psychic reality was well ahead of physical reality.[1]

To reconstruct the imagined past thus became a necessary part of analysis. It was not so much that past events and the material for fantasy provided by their memory were important; what mattered was a secondary (retrospective) emotional re-evaluation of early events, based on emotional experiences which occurred later in life.

[1] S. Freud, *From the History of an Infantile Neurosis* (1914).

In this fantasy world, the psychic reconstruction of the past plays a much bigger part than the date of experience. Freud had emphasized more than once that all mental processes had their origin in the unconscious and can only become conscious under certain conditions. These processes emerge directly from instinctual needs or appear as a response to external stimuli. We picture, says Freud (1933), the id 'as being open at its end to somatic influences, and there taking up into itself instinctual needs which find their psychical expression in it'.

(c) PHANTASY AS A PRIMARY CONTENT OF UNCONSCIOUS MENTAL PROCESSES Susan Isaacs (1943) defines unconscious phantasy as the psychic representatives of libidinal and destructive instincts; thus the primary content of unconscious mental processes consists of phantasies. 'Phantasy is the mental corollary, the psychic representative of instinct. There is no impulse, no instinctual urge or response which is not experienced as unconscious phantasy.' The Kleinians thus regard phantasy as the basic ingredient of all mental life. As the psychic representative of instinct it is a means of controlling anxiety and of producing a hallucinatory wish-fulfilment, as for instance the phantasy of incorporating the breast, aggressive feelings towards the frustrating mother and the wish to reject the breast when it is felt to be dangerous or persecutory. Phantasies may appear to be contradictory, e.g. phantasies of incorporation and rejection co-exist in the unconscious. They follow no rational pattern since the child does not distinguish wish from deed. The omnipotent character of these early wishes fit in with Freudian conceptions concerning the infant's hallucinatory wish-fulfilment: everything which is desired is simply imagined in hallucinatory form in the same way as happens in dream thought.

These phantasies, as Susan Isaacs points out, are far removed from words or conscious rational thinking. 'There is a wealth of evidence to show that phantasies are active in mind long before language has developed and that even in the adult they operate alongside and independently of words.' They are determined by the 'logic of emotion' and have independent psychic activity: they are an immediate datum of experience.[1] Phantasies represent an

---

[1] 'Some of our dreams show us a world of drama which we can live through in visual terms only. . . . These things, perceived and imagined and felt, are the stuff of experience. Words are a means of referring to experience, actual or phantasied, but they are not identical with it, not a substitute for it' (S. Isaacs, loc. cit., p. 89).

archaic activity of mental life which only finds verbal expression
at a later phase of development.

The earliest phantasies, then, spring from bodily instincts
and are interwoven with bodily sensations and affects. They
express primarily an internal and subjective reality; yet,
from the beginning, they are bound up with an actual,
however limited and narrow, experience of objective reality.
The first bodily experiences begin to build up the first
memories, and external realities are progressively interwoven
into the texture of the phantasy. Before long the child's
phantasies are able to draw upon plastic images as well as
on sensations: visual, sound, kinaesthetic, touch, taste,
smell, images, etc. And these plastic images, and dramatic
representations of phantasy, are progressively elaborated
along with articulated perceptions of the external world.
Phantasies however do not take origin in the articulated
knowledge of the external world; their source is internal,
in the instinctual impulses.[1]

(d) INTROJECTION AND PROJECTION The mechanisms of introjection and projection are considered by Melanie Klein as essential
ego-functions. In so far as the objects are presented to the
ego as a source of pleasure it takes them into itself, 'introjects'
them; and on the other hand the ego expels whatever within itself
becomes a cause of unpleasure (projection).[2]

Introjection and projection thus allow the subject to incorporate all gratifying objects and to attribute to the outside world all
sources of frustration. These two mechanisms are not only two of
the essential functions of the ego, they also play an important
part in ego-formation. Perception is one of the main features of
ego-formation, inseparable from the building-up of object-
relations: 'The first perception of importance must be essentially
the sensations of receiving by mouth, sucking, swallowing,
spewing.'

What is introjected or projected in this way is an 'object' linked
with visceral sensations and closely bound up with the experience
of oral grasping and the general feeding situation. 'Oral experiences
set their stamp on all sensations and experiences, so that at the
beginning all experiences include oral elements. . . . In this sense
one is justified in regarding the oral sensation of feeding as the first
perception' (P. Heimann, 1943).

[1] S. Isaacs, *loc. cit.*, p. 93.
[2] S. Freud, *Instincts and their Vicissitudes* (1915a).

These mechanisms are intimately related to pervasive 'oral' phantasies: the phantasies of incorporation (devouring, absorption and oral destruction) are among the earliest and most deeply unconscious phantasies since they are the psychic representatives of oral impulses, and, as such, play a considerable role:

> It is not an actual bodily eating up and swallowing, yet it leads to actual alterations in the ego. These 'mere' beliefs about internal objects . . . lead to real effects: deep emotions, actual behaviour towards external people, profound changes in the ego character and personality, symptoms, inhibitions and capacities (S. Isaacs, 1943).

(e) PHANTASY AND MENTAL MECHANISMS Introjection and projection are also the basis of phantasy formation. The primary phantasies are closely related to the infant's first sensory experiences, especially those connected with the feeding situation. They concern the relations which the child establishes with the part object of his first instinctual needs and of the oral impulses, that is, first the nipple, then the mother's breast (and later the mother as a whole person) and can be hallucinated by the child in order to find a momentary gratification of his 'need'.

But this hallucination does not stop at the mere picture: it goes on to what he is going to do with the desired object. If one attempts to translate in articulate speech what it is the infant feels one might say that: *I wish to retain my mother's breast inside of me*, would be an expression of his desire, and correspond to the imagined (hallucinated) wish-fulfilment of: *I possess my mother's breast inside me.* The ability to hallucinate is not limited to the wish to take in, to possess, to destroy or to expel, it also fulfils, in phantasy, that very possession or destruction.

But it is important to make a clear distinction between the *phantasy of incorporation* (or of rejection) and the *psychological mechanism of introjection* (or projection). Mental mechanisms refer to ideas or impressions which are either taken into the self or expelled and attributed to some part of the external world: they are ways of functioning in the mental life, as a means of dealing with internal tensions and conflicts.

These mental mechanisms are intimately related to phantasies. Phantasies are, as Susan Isaacs has pointed out, 'primarily about bodily aims, pains and pleasures, directed to objects of some kind. When contrasted with external or bodily realities, the phantasy is a figment; *yet it is real in the experience of the subject*' (my italics). As a mental function phantasies have real effects both on the inner world and on the external world (i.e. the subject's bodily experience and behaviour). Thus since phantasy is at one and the same time the *psychic representative of the instinctual drive* and the *subjective part of a mental mechanism*, it can be defined as a 'link between the id impulse and the ego mechanism'.

The relationship between the process of introjection and the phantasy of incorporation can be stated by saying that 'what *is* introjected is an image or "*imago*"'. Imago refers to an unconscious image and includes all the somatic and emotional elements of the relation to the imagined object: it is a bodily experience, 'scarcely capable of being related to an external spatial object. They give the phantasy a concrete bodily quality, experienced *in* the body.'

But these experiences are not easy to separate from external perceptions, as long as the skin is not felt to be a barrier separating the subject's inner reality from external reality.

It is also important to realize that phantasy is not, at the beginning, a visual experience. The early visual images are 'eidetic', i.e. vivid, concrete and often confused with perceptions, and closely related to the infant's somatic and emotional experience. Up to the third or fourth year there is no clear distinction between the total body experience and the 'visual' representation in the mind, recognized as such. Later on they become *images* in the narrow sense of the word, i.e. mental representations of identifiable external objects.

(f)   PHANTASY AND THE FUNCTION OF REALITY   Phantasy may be regarded as the 'language' by which instincts are expressed. External perceptions (even when, at the outset, they are not appreciated as such) have an effect on mental processes. The psyche has to cope with many stimuli, both instinctual and external, which it does by means of primitive mechanisms of introjection and projection. In so far as the external world does not satisfy, frustrates, or interferes with the infant's needs and desires, it is at once rejected and hated. These early frustrations will involve an attempt to reduce inner tensions by hallucinatory satisfactions which brings into play the primitive phantasies of incorporation or rejection. The *disappointed hallucinatory wish-fulfilment* is the first spur to adaptation to reality and thus has a part to play in ego-development. Hunger is not satisfied by hallucinating the breast or food, though the waiting for satisfaction may be made tolerable by this imagined gratification. 'The pain of frustration then stirs up a still stronger desire, viz. the wish to take the whole breast into himself and to keep it there as a source of satisfaction. . . . We must assume that the incorporation of the breast is bound up with the earliest forms of phantasy-life'.[1] This hallucinatory gratification operates and remains effective as long as the instinctual tension does not reach a certain threshold. Sooner or later, when the wish becomes too strong, the hallucinatory satisfaction fails and it is then replaced either by aggressive phantasies or by adaptation to real external conditions (e.g. by making demands on the environment).

All reality, however, remains permeated by unconscious phantasies. Early development of skills and all early learning based on oral impulses 'are gradually shifted on to other objects, the hand and eye only slowly attaining independence of the mouth, as instruments of exploration and of knowing the outer world' (S. Isaacs). The infant's world is cathected by oral libido; the intellectual and manual activities will retain throughout life an oral significance both in unconscious phantasy and in the metaphorical use of speech.[2]

(g) PHANTASY AND THE TRANSFERENCE SITUATION As already stated, phantasy represents the latent content of the transference situation. In his relation with the analyst, the patient repeats his early desires, his aggressive drives, his fears and all the mental processes previously experienced in his relationship to people. The image of the analyst may undergo changes from day to day according to changes in the patient's mind, whether these changes are brought about by the analytic situation or by outside events. 'The patient's relation with the analyst is almost entirely one of unconscious phantasy.' The emotional state and attitudes connected with transference enable us to decipher the phantasies at work at the present time and to reconstruct the patient's early history. In this way, the paranoid or depressive positions may be understood. 'The repetition of early situations and "acting-out" in the transference carry us back, far beyond the earliest conscious memories . . . and often shows us feelings, impulses and attitudes appropriate not only to the situations of childhood, but also those of the earliest months of infancy' (S. Isaacs, 1943).

3 The transference situation

Anna Freud's reservations concerning the transference neurosis

---

[1] Susan Isaacs, loc. cit., p. 86.
[2] Susan Isaacs and others have remarked on the extent to which expressions like 'to devour with the eyes', 'to take in through the ears', 'to digest information' bear the imprint of the early oral cathexis of many activities.

in child analysis are not held to be valid by Melanie Klein. According to the latter, transference neurosis occurs in child analysis as it does in the analysis of the adult. This contention is based on Melanie Klein's conception of the early stages of the Oedipus complex and the formation of the superego.

In the analyses of very young children (between two-and-a-half and four years of age) Melanie Klein observes that the child is already deeply involved in the oedipal conflict and to a certain extent has already found a partial solution: the love objects which he desired originally have already been *introjected* and the child refers not to real objects, i.e. his parents, but to *images of objects*.

The superego is already functioning autonomously in the form of an unconscious agency and not a mere executive power controlled by parental rule. This proceeds directly from Melanie Klein's conception of the oedipal conflict which develops during the oral phase when the struggle for the possession of the libidinal object—mother or father—is taking place. Part objects (the mother's breast or the father's penis) are the stakes in the conflict.

Melanie Klein considers that the child is involved in a triangular (not a dyadic) relation from the very beginning of life but, however, he is not yet individualized as a person. Not only does he perceive the outer world as being made out of part objects, but he too is only a 'fragmented body' since he has not yet acquired a 'total image' of himself.

The internalization of objects and the formation of a few elements of the early superego make it possible for the child to establish a transference relation with the analyst.

Underlying this difference of approach we find divergent conceptions of the child-parent relationship. Anna Freud, for instance, considers that the child analyst meets dependency as an ongoing process (whereas, in adult analysis, dependency is encountered only as vestigial symptom related to an early developmental phase). The child 'uses' his parents in many ways: for narcissistic fusion with the mother; for leaning on her capacity to control and manipulate external conditions so that the infant's need can be satisfied; to convert narcissistic libido into object libido by establishing a relation to an external object; as a limiting agent for instinctual gratification; for providing him with an identification which is needed to gain emotional and structural independence. Thus the part which parents play in the causation or in maintaining the child's illness is a prevalent factor and Anna Freud (1966) states that: 'in child analysis it is not the patient's ego but the parents' reason and insight on which beginning, continuance and completion of the treatment must rely. It is the task of the parents to help the child's ego to overcome resistances and periods of negative transference without truanting from analysis. The analyst is helpless if they fall down on this task.'

It is noteworthy that Melanie Klein's approach to the same problem is a quite different one. Although she never denies—and probably even emphasizes—the symbiotic character of these early relationships, she however insists upon the child's phantasies rather than ego-functions. The 'real' mother is of lesser importance than the *imago* through which this mother is represented in the infant's phantasy life. Her therapeutic approach is to alleviate the child's anxiety—which is reproduced and sometimes even enhanced in his relation to the analyst—by interpreting the underlying phantasies. Thus Melanie Klein's intervention does not aim at helping the child to improve his ego-functions, but rather to remove the obstacles—i.e. the early intrapsychic conflict and the ensuing anxiety—which prevents the child from using his ego-functions. The parental role is thus restricted as a reality factor but is prevalent in the instinctual conflict and its psychic representative, i.e. phantasy.

Melanie Klein does not rely on parents to facilitate the child's analytic experience. Consequently she considers that the child is able to establish an independent relation with the analyst and that the phantasy content is going to be displayed in a new situation. This in turn is going to foster the building up of transference neurosis.

Melanie Klein believes that the 'breaking-in' period advocated by Anna Freud makes use of the child's anxiety and guilt feeling in order to encourage an emotional attachment to the analyst instead of enlisting the anxiety in the service of analytic work. Melanie Klein, far from avoiding all manifestation of negative transference, attempts to exploit it in order to mobilize whatever sustains the anxiety at this initial phase of treatment. She remarks that symptoms vary as the analysis proceeds and as the transference neurosis appears more clearly. In the course of the analysis, alternating roles which the child casts for the analyst indicate successive identifications with superego.

In addition to all this, the almost inevitable emotional outbursts that occur outside the analysis and particularly within the family circle itself (called 'acting-out'), are a reflection of the shifts in the phantasy-relations with the analyst. These manifestations are not, as Anna Freud claims, the result of the analyst's failure in his educational role, but rather the outcome of his inability to uncover

and resolve the anxiety and guilt feelings behind these manifestations, the early psychic conflict having been reactivated during
transference.

The therapist cannot therefore be *both* analyst and educator
since the latter becomes the representative of the repressing
agencies: one activity would cancel out the other.

> A children's analyst must have the same unconscious
> attitude as we require in the analyst of adults if he is to be
> successful. It must enable him to be really willing *only to*
> *analyse* and not to wish to mould and direct the minds of
> his patients. If anxiety does not prevent him, he will be able
> to calmly wait for the developments of the correct issue
> and, in this way, that issue will be achieved. If he does this,
> however, he will prove the validity of the second principle
> which I represent in opposition to Anna Freud, namely that
> we must analyse completely and without reservation the
> child's relation to his parents and his Oedipus complex.[1]

It is around the question of transference that the difference of
Anna Freud's and Melanie Klein's opinions is most clearly defined.
Anna Freud maintains that although there may be a satisfactory
transference, no 'genuine' transference neurosis appears in the
case of the child. Children are not ready to enter into a new love
relationship, because the original love-objects, the parents, exist
as objects in reality. This statement is the key to the controversy.
In Anna Freud's view, the child's parents are included in the field
of treatment. For Melanie Klein, the *real surroundings play a sub-*
ordinate role in comparison to the importance taken on by the
intrasubjective conflict. Only the projections and introjections of
'good' and 'bad' objects matter in analysis.[2]

Here the real question arises as to the difference between the
early object-relations and the child-analyst relation in the course
of transference. Melanie Klein emphasizes the primal character of
the child's relation to the mother's breast. Objects are thus
included, from the outset, in the child's mental life. *Transference*
has its origin in| the processes which determine object relations in
the earliest phases. In the course of the transference the earliest
anxiety states are revived, those that give rise to repetition-
compulsion. By assigning various roles to the analyst, the child is
repeating the real and imaginary relations which he maintains with
objects. The psychoanalytic investigation of the interaction

[1] Melanie Klein, 'Symposium on Child Analysis' (1927), in *Contributions to*
Psychoanalysis (1948).
[2] See D. Lagache, 'Le problème du transfert' (1952).

between present and past experience shows that the object is split into idealized and persecutory objects; thus is relieved the fantasy-load with which the objects are cathected. The patient's instinctual drives can thus be cathected to other activities.

4 *Melanie Klein's therapeutic interventions*

During the analytic hour Melanie Klein interprets the child's play, his dramatization, his drawings and all that happens during this session between the child and the therapist.[1] It has been said that she only used 'symbolic' interpretations, since she considers that the child's play and behaviour symbolically represent phantasies, wishes and experiences. However, Klein (1926) says that 'symbolism is only part of it' and that, if we are to understand the child's behaviour and the material provided during the session, we must take into account not only the symbolism which appears in the child's game but also 'all the means of representation and the mechanisms employed in dream-work', i.e. all the defensive mechanisms, the various modes of expression and the inhibition caused by guilt encountered during the therapeutic work. Actually, the first interpretations are aimed at relieving the child's anxiety which appears in the course of the very first sessions; these interpretations enable the therapeutic situation to be structured by the gradual solving of resistances and persistent tracing of the transference to earlier situations. These interpretations afford an opportunity to verbalize the child's underlying anxiety and to show the part played by the analytic situation in his anxiety: this implies an interpretation of the transference. Melanie Klein remarks how rapidly the interpretations take effect, even when the child has not seemed receptive of the interpretation. By showing that his play has a (hidden) meaning which is understood, his play will henceforth be taken as a *communication* between him and the therapist, and not merely as a pleasurable, hedonistic activity. This gives a boost, as it were, to the child's play, and the pleasure, which ensues after an interpretation has been given, is due to the fact that the expenditure necessitated by repression is no longer required. 'Only by *interpreting* and so *allaying* the child's anxiety shall we gain access to his unconscious and get him to phantasy.'

Furthermore, interpretations aim at making the child aware that the anxiety mobilized by the therapeutic situation is the reflection of an anxiety related to earlier conflicts. In other words, it is a reproduction of an anxiety stirred up by the child's experience,

[1] See M. Klein's *Narrative of a Child Analysis* (1961).

by his phantasies concerning his relation with his parents. The elucidation of these primitive phantasies takes place through the symbolic interpretation of the child's play, drawings and activities during the sessions.

The lessening of the anxiety must enable the child to evoke and relive unconscious conflicts which had hitherto been repressed. Following on these interpretations, it should be possible to delve into 'deeper' or more archaic strata; this will produce further anxiety which, in turn, will be resolved.

It thus becomes possible to define a specific technique of interpretation as it is practised by Kleinian analysts: (a) interpretations are given at an early phase of the analysis, often in the very first sessions. Interpretations may be necessary at this stage in order to attenuate the inhibiting effects of a negative transference which could possibly slow down or even halt the progress of treatment; (b) interpretations are aimed at uncovering the unconscious content of the child's play and drawings by pointing out the oedipal themes and by interpreting the introjections and projections in the child's phantasy life. But above all the primal scene as well as castration and destruction anxieties, as they express themselves during sessions, will gradually become available for further interpretation; (c) the need to interpret systematically the negative transference (even in its masked or inchoate form) has been emphasized, for without this no analysis could be brought to a successful conclusion.[1]

In Melanie Klein's view the purpose of analysis is to introduce the child to a symbolic order enabling him to gain some insight into the relationship of the self with the outside world. This comes about mainly because the threatening early superego has now attenuated its demands. This early superego appears at an age when the child is dominated by anxiety; the superego derives from parental images, distorted by his phantasies and reflects his fears and aggressiveness. By loosening the ego's pre-genital fixations the libido becomes available for new cathexes and the anxiety, which tied the child down to its early fixations, can thus be relieved.

The therapeutic aim cannot therefore be defined in terms of improved social or family adjustment, which is only one of the consequences brought about by analysis. In this approach,

---

[1] Lebovici (1962), sees yet another advantage in interpreting the negative transference: by, as it were, taking on the responsibility of the negative displacements, the child is able to see the positive aspects of his identification with his parents and, as a consequence, certain family difficulties are reduced. This brings out very clearly the difference between the two aims: the one being the progress of the treatment, the other, a better adjustment to reality.

analysis has no kind of educational aim. The analyst does not put himself forward as a more acceptable 'ego-ideal'; he provides the child with an opportunity to project his phantasies and thus becomes the locus of speech and interpretation. He remains neutral since it is up to the child to play *his part* unrestricted by any latent or explicit disapproval or any directive from the therapist.

By making use of transference and by recommending verbal interpretation of unconscious phantasies which are brought into the open through this transference, Melanie Klein remains close to so-called classical analysis. In spite of certain technical adjustments, she remains faithful to a conception in which 'the individual is defined as history making and unmaking itself'.

IV. Criteria for the termination of treatment

In the analytic sense, 'cured' implies, rather than a disappearance of symptoms, the accomplishment of an essential personality change which is the outcome of redistribution of psychic energy. But in clinical practice analysis achieves various changes in the patient: in some cases the symptoms disappear (although, seemingly at least, no basic modifications have taken place); in other cases the patient learns how to live with his condition and make the best of it, i.e. his neurotic misery seems to have disappeared and, on a dynamic level, he makes a better and more adequate use of his defences; in yet other cases a deep-seated alteration of the patient's style of life is being achieved. In any of those cases termination of treatment is not an easy decision, since the assessment of change should not be merely based on behavioural or adaptative criteria.

There can, of course, be no arbitrary conclusion to the therapeutic relation between analyst and child. The criteria for this are many and they take into account the clinical changes or structural modifications.

(a)   Some authors take into account the disappearance of clinical manifestations which may have been the reason for initiating psychotherapy, and talk in terms of *symptomatic criteria*. Improvement in family relations, resumption of school work, the adjustment into a social group, the disappearance of openly aggressive behaviour or the lifting of inhibitions—any of these may be a valuable indication as to the right time for bringing the treatment to a close. Likewise, the more or less complete disappearance of clinical symptoms (fidgetiness, enuresis, *pavor nocturnus*), obsessions or phobias, may indicate that morbid processes are on the decline. One should be chary, however, of relying too much on purely symptomatic improvements, for behind these apparent 'cures' a neurotic nucleus may be temporarily quiescent and the disappearance of the symptoms may well camouflage new defence mechanisms. These criteria, therefore, need not in themselves be of any value and, to be taken seriously, must be supported by additional evidence.

(b)   The *development of fantasy life* reflects the change in the patient's object-relations. The child's play, and the drawings which he produces during sessions, help the psychotherapist to follow the successive stages of these relations. In the course of treatment, one must assess the gradual lessening of inhibitions, the appearance of archaic fantasies and the increasing variety and freedom of expression in play and word.

During analysis, it should be possible to follow how the 'good' and 'bad' objects are modified by successive introjections and projections as they appear in the context of transference. Through interpretation the child gains insight into the unconscious meaning of his fantasies and their libidinal and aggressive content.

When the destructive fantasies lose their impact, when the child can go beyond his early anxiety to resolve the Oedipus complex, when he can face up to his fantasies in spite of superego demands, he will then be able to abandon the imaginary world built around 'a two-body fantasy' and become able to establish a triangular, and symbolically signifying relationship, and relinquish his dependency in relation to his primary objects.

(c)   Other authors are more concerned with *structural criteria* as an indication for terminating the analysis. They take the view that the ego must be able to tolerate its instinctual drives, i.e. to use them in a socialized way but without being overwhelmed by unacceptable sexual or aggressive demands.

Nevertheless, ego-control should be flexible enough not to reject those instinctual drives essential for the cognitive and creative functions, for the building-up and development of new object-relations, and for the libidinal cathexis of various motor and sensory functions. Furthermore, the ego's defence mechanisms must lose their initial, rigid way of functioning: some would have to disappear (denial) for they are an indication of a very early mode of adaptation which is incompatible with emotional maturity. They must be replaced by others, such as sublimation, in order to allow of certain instinctual drives, which should manifest themselves in a socially acceptable form. It is to be supposed that these structural criteria are an attempt to assess ego-adjustment, since the ego plays the role of a mediator between external, social reality and the instinctual drives. The resolution of the conflict brings with it a lessening of anxiety and frustration, as well as of aggression and of unconscious guilt. Psychoanalytic treatment should culminate in a verbal consciousness of the conflicts and resistance which manifest themselves during treatment.

What may one expect from analytic treatment? When the child has consciously worked out his fantasies, he should be able to break free from the grip of the fantasy world with which all his past has been cathected. The 'imaginary' order should not rule his present and future behaviour. The lifting of the repression, the elucidation of the transference, the sublimation of the aggressive and libidinal drives, should help the patient to face any new situations without any undue anxiety and to establish new relations without resorting to neurotic defence mechanisms.

Even if the ultimate aim of treatment is viewed in terms of 'adjustment', this is not to be understood in the sense of 'social conformity' but rather that the patient should be free to find his own way of life and to speak and act in his own name.

7 Indications for child analysis

Indications and counter-indications for child analysis depend on an assessment of psychopathological factors. In psychiatric practice such an evaluation rests, largely, on the theories and preconceptions of the practitioner, as can be seen clearly in general psychiatry where a diagnostic, and even a therapeutic, bias operates according to the specific and often unstated conceptions of each psychiatrist.

Psychoanalysis has its own coherent theory about mental illness. Even if one disagrees with the general analytic scheme, one must regard psychoanalysis as a systematized approach with its specific methodology. This has its practical consequences, since any general theory about psychic functioning must necessarily come to envisage diagnostic and prognostic problems, and take its stand on therapeutic procedures. Thus a great deal of work has been done about indications of psychoanalytic therapy, the evaluation of results and the appraisal of therapeutic results achieved by analysis as compared with other therapeutic methods (Anna Freud, 1970; Winnicott, 1965).

So far no agreement has been reached as to the results of analytic treatment; no statistical data exist today which allow us to make any significant statement about the comparative value of various procedures. We can thus evaluate only the actual outcomes of therapeutic analyses, compare their successes and failures, but we have no way of knowing what the outcome would have been if . . . But we can more or less predict which cases are likely to be helped by analysis, and which patients cannot reasonably expect to benefit by it. It would be contrary to psychoanalytic thinking to cast those precepts into rigid doctrine: any given case is specifically determined by its own set of innumerable variables and the analyst must, before he starts or refuses treatment, get a more or less precise picture of every patient he sees. Initial interviews yield a great amount of information, but more than that, they make it possible to gain a clinical impression of the patient's underlying motivations, his willingness to co-operate, his intellectual possibilities and his availability to the analytic process. Such an initial assessment often goes a long way and makes it possible to assert with some probability whether or not analysis is indicated (Freud, 1937).

I. Assessment of childhood pathology

In the field of child analysis indications for therapy can be based on two sets of arguments.

(a)   A diagnostic evaluation, i.e. an effort to ascertain (rather than to classify) the pathological state, to evaluate the meaning of the clinical elements along certain lines of psychopathology and to find out the way the patient relates to his life experience: one might thus reach some approximate 'diagnosis', i.e. see the patient as an individual who relates to his inner and outer world along certain patterns (neurosis, psychosis, character disorder, delinquent behaviours, mental retardation, etc.). This first look might provide us with useful information on the level of pathological reaction types and as such is not essentially different from any clinical appraisal in child psychiatry, since through it the practitioner tries to reach an understanding of the child's symptoms, his developmental status, his family situation, his social adjustment, etc. But it must be clear that such a diagnostic evaluation which is, so to speak, an objective appraisal of the child's present situation, is only a first step.

(b)   A 'structural' assessment, i.e. an evaluation of the clinical picture in terms of the psychoanalytic theory. This is more difficult to achieve in the case of children since a child is in the process of development and maturation: the symptoms can have a very different meaning according to the child's maturational level and developmental phase. Symptoms, as well as interpersonal relations, must thus be understood on the level of phase adequate psychic functioning. We have tried in previous chapters to outline the theoretical framework used by psychoanalysts (libido theory, object-relations, metapsychology, etc.). It is along these lines that the patient's symptoms should be approached. The unspoken and subjective clues, underlying the clinical situation, should also be considered: that is, whatever phantasies, unconscious wishes, and wish-fulfilment, as well as defence mechanisms, the analyst does perceive through the patient's words and symptoms.

But in any case the analyst relies on his analytic theoretical framework, his clinical experience and on his expertise in interpreting the unconscious, hidden, content of the manifest objective material. Thus, the use of analytic theory makes it possible to approach the problem of indications in different ways. But before going any further it is necessary to define the concept of infantile neurosis which is one of the key concepts in this context.

In order to ascertain indications for child analysis an assessment must be made of: (a) clinical symptoms which may be indicative of a neurotic nucleus, that is, a pathological structure of the ego and its defence mechanisms; (b) disturbances of libidinal development and emotional cathexes and their repercussions on object-

N

relations and on the child's intellectual and motor development; (c) the disturbing effects of the particular milieu which, by its obvious or underlying pathology, creates, favours, perpetuates or masks the nature of the structural defect.

The ultimate diagnosis will be the result of the confrontation of the various data during examination.

(i) BIOGRAPHICAL DATA, bearing on the personal history and family history of the child, will help to highlight any disharmony in libidinal development. Difficulties of feeding or delayed acquisition of bladder control, sleep-disturbances or delay in mastering motor or verbal skills, etc., may draw attention to certain stumbling blocks in development. Instead of being smooth and progressive, growth is marked by discrepancies or delays in various areas, indicative of the vicissitudes in the libidinal development and pointing to the 'germinal moment', that is, the starting of the neurotic conflict.

(ii) THE NATURE AND INTENSITY OF THE DISTURBANCES, including neurotic symptoms, so often ignored or underestimated by the parents themselves, as well as the more obvious ones which have induced them to come for help, become clearer under clinical investigation. Difficulty in falling asleep, nightmares, *pavor nocturnus*, bed-time ceremonials, tics or phobic behaviour, food fads and certain character traits—all or any of these may have been ignored by the parents, especially if they have occurred in not too blatant a form, or when they meet with their own idiosyncrasies. Shyness, non-participation, passivity, are far better tolerated by parents than more 'obvious' symptoms such as enuresis or aggressive behaviour.

(iii) THE MODE OF RELATIONSHIP between parent and child, and the family structure and marital relations are also the subject of clinical investigation. The solution of the child's disturbances as well as the co-operation to be expected from the family in case of psychotherapy may depend on the status of family relationship.

It is important to distinguish *reactive* behaviour disorders from symptoms revealing a *neurotic structure*.

Here the concept of maladjustment is of no great help. Its value in adult diagnosis is certainly open to criticism; in the case of children, maladjustment points to criteria which belong to norms established by parents, educators or even psychiatrists. The question therefore arises as to what is the true definition of mental illness. Thomas Szasz (1962) and Michel Foucault (1954) have emphasized that it cannot be reduced to one of mere social 'non-integration'.

The term *reactive* (or secondary) disorder has to be clarified. In terms of psychogenesis, all child disturbances are reactions to a conflict and every symptom may be regarded as an ego-defence against intolerable pressures: they need to be no more than a transient appearance of stress which emerges whenever a particular phase of development makes specially high demands (A. Freud, 1968).

In many cases these pressures are external, and more specifically, have their origin in the family environment. They correspond to actual conditions and are often consciously perceived by the child. The conflict indicates, in these instances, a real situation such as, for example, an open antagonism between parent and child; the conflict is a conscious one, recognized and identified as such by both parties. The disturbance is called 'reactive', or secondary, when removal of external difficulties is sufficient in the long run to eliminate and resolve the conflict. These symptoms may disappear again and leave behind an area of heightened vulnerability.

But quite as often the pressures are internal ones and arise from an unconscious internalized conflict—in the psychoanalytic sense of the word—whereas the real situation appears to be devoid of outward conflict or stress. This is an intrapsychic conflict and it defines the neurotic disturbance whose symptoms will not disappear even when external difficulties are put right. Nevertheless, the *real* conflict and the *intrapsychic* conflict may co-exist, intertwine or follow one another. An actual conflict may be used to camouflage an intrapsychic one and may even be its only clinical manifestation. The aim of psychoanalytic therapy being first and foremost to resolve intrapsychic conflicts, it can only work if the 'real' conflicts are a clinical manifestation of an internalized one.

(iv) PROGNOSTIC ASSESSMENT represents an important element when analytic therapy is considered. As we are concerned with children still in their process of maturation and development, we do not always find it easy to assess the potential outcome and make a prognosis accordingly. In fact, certain cases of maladjustment which appear as a major problem may well find a favourable solution, whereas apparently minor symptoms may well be premonitory of subsequent neurosis or psychosis. It is in any case difficult to assert that disorders from which the patient seems to recover do not in fact leave behind serious consequences. The alarming, or reassuring, aspect of a symptom is not enough to determine the prognosis.

It is well to remember that our aim is to state the indications for a psychoanalysis of the child and not for a general psychotherapeutic treatment. In the opinion of some authors, psychoanalysis should be reserved for those patients in whom the reactive aspect is limited and where one feels justified in talking in terms of a 'neurotic structure' since, in this latter case, there is little chance of spontaneous recovery.

II. The problem of infantile neurosis

The very term 'infantile neurosis' has a twofold meaning in psychoanalysis.

(a) In its first meaning, it indicates a morbid condition characterized by symptoms appearing on an underlying neurotic base. To the extent that these symptoms betoken an internalized, and therefore unconscious, mental conflict, there will be disturbances of mental functioning: fixation or regression of libidinal development; inadequacy of the ego to deal with the demands from outside reality; recourse to defence mechanisms as a protection against instinctual drives; manifestations of anxiety which the ego defences cannot control or contain.

It is to be noted that not all affective disturbances at this age necessarily have the structured character of a neurosis. According to the classification suggested by Glover (1953), the symptom may turn out to be a 'functional disorder' or what is usually described as a secondary behaviour disturbance. It may be a manifestation of non-tolerance of environmental conditions which generally disappears when the external causes are removed, provided, that is, the conflict has not been internalized.[1]

Infantile neurosis poses a diagnostic problem which is the more important because, for certain authors such as Anna Freud, it represents the main indication for psychoanalysis proper, whereas the reactive behaviour disorders often call for analytic psychotherapy or psychiatric social work.

[1] A symptom has rarely in itself a specific diagnostic significance. Thus phobic or obsessional symptoms, school difficulties, behaviour problems, enuresis or nail-biting, are not specific enough to diagnose a neurosis, which is a structured morbid state. Those symptoms may just as well be indicative of a primary behaviour disorder or of a pre-psychotic state. Nevertheless, certain psychosomatic illnesses, such as asthma, psychogenetic obesity, mental anorexia, do point to an underlying neurotic (or psychotic) structure.

(b)   In the second meaning of the term, 'infantile neurosis' is a crucial moment in psychological development, which may or may not manifest itself in symptoms. (These symptoms may be similar to those of a real structured neurosis.) In this sense it is an intra-psychic conflict which may find its spontaneous solution but which may also become irreversible or else reappear as a neurosis in the adult.

In his commentary on the *Analysis of a Phobia in a Five-Year-Old Boy* (1909b), Freud says that Hans was not the only child to present a neurotic symptom (in his case a phobia) at some moment in his development:

> The troubles of that kind are extraordinarily frequent. . . .
> In the course of months or years they diminish, and the
> child seems to recover; but no one can tell what
> psychological changes are necessitated by such a recovery,
> or what alterations in character are involved in it. When,
> however, an adult neurotic patient comes to us for psycho-
> analytic treatment (and let us assume that his illness has
> only become manifest after he has reached maturity) we
> find regularly that his neurosis has as its point of departure
> an infantile anxiety such as we have been discussing, and is
> in fact a continuation of it; so that, as it were, a continuous
> and undisturbed thread of psychical activity, taking its
> start from the conflicts of his childhood, has been spun
> through his life—irrespective of whether the first symptom
> of those conflicts has persisted or has retreated under the
> pressure of circumstances.

Thus every neurosis in the adult has its basis in infantile neurosis which has been ignored or neglected and has 'got better' of itself. Freud returns to this same theme in *Inhibitions, Symptoms and Anxiety* (1926) when he is investigating the origins of anxiety in the adult:[1]

> In a great number of cases the old determinants of
> anxiety do really lapse, after having produced neurotic
> reactions. The phobias of very young children, fears of
> being alone or in the dark or with strangers and phobias
> which can almost be called normal, usually pass off later
> on. . . . Animal phobias, which are of such frequent
> occurrence, undergo the same fate and many conversion
> hysterias of early years find no continuation in later life.
> Ceremonial actions appear very often in the latency period,
> but only a very small percentage of them develop later into

[1] Standard Edition, 20, pp.147-8.

a full obsessional neurosis. . . . The neuroses of childhood are in the nature of regular episodes in a child's development. . . . Signs of childhood neurosis can be detected in *all* adult neurotics without exception; but by no means all children who show these signs become neurotic in later life. . . . It must be, therefore, that certain determinants of anxiety are relinquished and certain danger situations lose their significance as the individual becomes more mature. Moreover, some of these danger situations manage to survive into later times by modifying their determinants of anxiety so as to bring them up to date.

The neurotic will differ from the normal person in that his reactions will be unduly strong. Being grown-up affords no absolute protection against a return of the original traumatic anxiety-situation. Each individual has in all probability a limit beyond which his mental apparatus fails in its function of mastering the quantities of excitation which require to be disposed of.

It is certain that neurosis in the adult is never going to recover spontaneously. As Anna Freud points out, the neurosis, which is a compromise between two opposing forces, can only change its course when the balance is upset as a result of the decisive changes in the instinctual drives, or by a rearrangement of pressures from the superego. Neither of these is likely to come about spontaneously in the adult, who remains anchored to the infantile model of his neurosis. This is precisely what distinguishes adult from infantile neurosis. The child's libidinal organization is a developing one, having a certain pliability which enables it to pass from one phase of its development to the next. Any regression is more likely to break loose from its fixation point and the child's development can resume its normal course. This is especially true at certain points in the libidinal development, when the instincts achieve a certain strength, as, for example, at the onset of the phallic phase or at pre-puberty. In the so-called latency period, the attenuation of the neurosis is partly due to a marked lessening of the instinctual forces and also (mainly) to the fact that the desires related to the oedipal situation have been deflected towards other goals.

III. Structural criteria of indications for child analysis (Anna Freud)

The importance of a structural diagnosis of infantile neurosis does not need to be emphasized. To expound this in greater detail I shall follow the main lines of the work of Anna Freud (1945, 1968), in which she investigates the criteria for the diagnosis of childhood neurosis.

1 *Libido development*

One criterion is based on the development of the libido, the norms of which are known. It has been said that every child whose normal libido development is impaired, either through a regression to an earlier phase or a fixation, is neurotic. But the assessment of an impairment of this kind must take into account the normal overlapping of libidinal phases and the persistence during successive phases of manifestations belonging to earlier ones. An oral or anal symptom may well be found in a later phase, but the really important thing is that 'the major part of the libido attains the phase of organization proper to the child's age level', and that the libidinal manifestations of the present phase predominates over the remnants of earlier ones.

To lay bare these sequellae is very often a difficulty in diagnosis because they are expressed in unconscious phantasies and often can only be brought to light in the course of treatment.

In assessing libidinal development, one must take into account the manifestations of component instincts (exhibitionism, scopophilia, cruelty, greed, etc.); their variation and intensity may indicate fixation points in interests and libidinal cathexes and be the starting-point of later neurotic development. Although the mere presence of these component instincts is not in itself indicative of a neurotic process, their complete absence or dominance would suggest an infantile neurosis.

The vicissitudes of libidinal development betray difficulties which the patient has to face as he develops. To escape anxiety, he reverts to a more primitive organization; the libido regresses to a level corresponding to an earlier phase. The child is then faced by oral and anal wishes which set in motion neurotic defence mechanisms. If such defence is unsuccessful, neurotic symptoms arise 'which represent the gratification of the wish distorted in its form by the action of the repressive forces'. The libido is arrested in its course towards the genital phase; it is forced backward to archaic stages of libido development. At the same time, the object-relations that have been established with the desired object revert to an early emotional pattern. A regression to the oral level, for example, in the search for an oral object, is accompanied by a regression in emotional attitudes: the child becomes demanding, insatiable, expecting immediate gratification, etc. This regression, however, must not be regarded as a purely straightforward affair; it is not just a question of a move backwards but of the reappearance of symptoms based on an archaic model. While the child's intellectual and motor development continues and contacts with the outside world are enriched, a discrepancy appears between his feelings and his experiences with the world around him. We then have to make up our minds as to the precise significance of these manifestations. Is it an infantile neurosis, a morbid condition, where the psychological losses will never be made good? Or is this neurosis a 'fruitful moment' in the child's development and as such a spontaneous recovery can be expected? Childhood neurosis or infantile neurosis? An illness or a phase in mental development? This is the question that has to be answered.

Taking her stand upon the criteria afforded by libidinal development, Anna Freud lays down indications for therapy. If the libido organization remains fluid and shows a progressive tendency which can counteract the regression and the neurotic fixation, the infantile neurosis can be considered as a transitory disorder and psychoanalysis will be unnecessary. On the other hand, when the libidinal constellation becomes rigid, when its clinical manifestations are stereotyped and where there is no sign of a future mobilization of the cathexes, one can assume the existence of a morbid condition where analytic treatment would be indicated.

2 *The neurotic interference with ego development*

This is an equally important criterion for assessing whether analysis is indicated. Anna Freud distinguishes the qualitative and quantitative factors in the development.

(a)   Referring to the term 'ego-strength' as a quantitative datum, she discusses 'the relative efficiency of the ego with regard to the id'. Faced with this, the ego has to act as a regulator. The overwhelming strength of the instincts is followed by a period when the child can make use of the outside world for the fulfilment of his wishes. Through identification with parents, the ego attempts to control its wishes and to adopt a critical attitude towards the instinctual demands. The pleasure principle, which controlled the infant's instinctual life, is now gradually replaced by the reality principle by which wish-fulfilment is reconciled with exigencies of the outside world. This is a function of the ego which consequently now finds itself in a new conflict with the id. In Anna Freud's view the establishment of a balance between the instinctual forces of the id and the power of the ego is an essential condition for harmonious development of the personality. This development is only possible if the relation between these two remains fluid, thereby allowing the environment to be correctly exploited for wish-gratification. 'The incidence of an infantile neurosis acts like a calcification in the middle of a living organism. Each neurotic symptom represents an attempt to establish an artificial balance between the instinctual desires and the repressive forces of the ego.' The neurotic symptom tries to achieve this balance which, by its coherent structure, gradually paralyses the dynamic relation between ego and id. This rigidity is reflected in the stereotype of the measures resorted to by the ego to face up to the demands of the instinct; clinically, the manifestations may appear as a 'strong ego'. The neurotic symptom is simply reflecting the delicate balance between the ego deprived of all adaptive powers and the demands of the instincts controlled by the pleasure principle.

(b) Anna Freud also discusses the ego's *defence mechanism as a qualitative factor* in the establishment of the ego's relations with the outside world. It is the task of the ego, as an agency which organizes the patient's relations with the outside world, to test inner and outer reality, to build up memory traces, to co-ordinate and centralize the often contradictory affects *vis-à-vis* demands coming in from the outside, to control their motor expression and to curb their primitive manifestations. It is upon this organising function of the ego that the patient's efficiency depends, in so far as the functioning of this organizing apparatus enables the patient to find gratifications for his wishes and exert his control over his surroundings. The establishment of these functions thus contributes to the patient's emotional maturation.

The child, however, is still confronted by frustrations, dangers and disappointments from the outside world and by the contradictions between his wishes and reality. The need to give up certain libidinally cathected objects, and so to face the real situation, sets him a difficult choice. The motor expression of instinctual urges is inhibited by the controlling ego.

To cope with these difficulties, the child's ego resorts to certain defence mechanisms. As he cannot change the realities of the situation all he can do is to let them filter through to him, as it were, and thus render them bearable. *Denial* allows him not to see reality as it actually is; *repression* enables him to exclude from consciousness all painful memories and perceptions and to forbid the inner urges to have any conscious representation; by *reaction formation* he can turn to their opposites any undesirable tendencies; by *flight into phantasy* he can exchange distressing facts for pleasurable phantasies; and by *projection* he can attribute, as coming from the outside, those feelings or defects which he does not wish to recognize as being his own.

Normally all these mechanisms are used to protect the ego against anxiety arising from confrontation with the outside world. However, they will eventually give way to a more realistic appraisal.

Infantile neurosis is in fact characterized by the ego's intense and prolonged use of its defence mechanisms. They are not in themselves a sign of neurosis. They may have a fleeting existence when the child is faced with a particular conflict, and disappear when the conflict is resolved, or become superfluous when a certain maturational point is reached. It is the extended and permanent use of these defences which stamp them as truly pathological. Thus, permanent clothing of life with phantasy is, in the view of Lebovici (1950), an especially important sign of neurosis.

It should moreover be noted that the impact of the damage suffered by the ego-functions is felt when ego-maturation is in full swing and for that reason the harm can be all the greater. This means that the normal progress of certain functions may be arrested while others continue to develop. The outcome is a disharmony where some factors predominate at the expense of those which are inhibited.

It should further be noted that the particular defence mechanisms which come into play (unless they are unmistakably specific) seem to accompany one neurotic structure rather than another. Repression, for example, is met more specifically in cases of hysteria; denial of aggressive tendencies may be seen in obsessional neuroses. Phobias, on the other hand, go hand in hand with emotional withdrawal and motor inhibitions, as a means of avoiding anxiety arising from phobogenic situations. As a rule, nevertheless, the defence mechanism spills over from its specific area and makes its appearance, particularly in the child, as a character trait, a component of personality, a way of reacting to life.[1]

[1] There are some similarities between character and symptom. In both, regressive elements appear with a discernible diffusion of libidinal and aggressive components. Both afford the child a striking degree of discharge. Both are influenced by the defensive functions of the ego. 'One could certainly say that character trait and symptom arise out of the interplay of impulse, anxiety, conflict and defence.' However, the adaptation value of the character trait is

3 *The clinical issue*

From this structural analysis of the development of the libido, the maturation of the ego and its defence mechanisms, Anna Freud (1945) was able to draw conclusions justifying, in her view, the indications for analytic therapy.

If a child shows a faulty knowledge of the outer world, far below the level of his intelligence; if he is seriously estranged from his own emotions, with blank spaces in the remembrance of his own past beyond the usual range of infantile amnesia, with a split of his personality and with motility out of ego-control; then there can be little doubt that the neurosis is severe and that it is high time to take therapeutic action.

Recently Anna Freud (1968) has re-examined the problem of indications. Infantile neurosis remains the major indication since it has shown itself as eminently amenable to analytic therapy. But in other cases the recommendations for treatment become much more hesitant.

(a)   When internal conflicts are *acute,* caused by *the pressures of the development phase which the child is passing at the time,* the indication for therapy is less clear-cut than in cases of neurosis (where conflicts are internalized and exert their influence from the past). We know that analysis proceeds best when pathogenic experience belongs to the past. In states of acute distress the ego's whole interest is taken up by the present crisis, and is not available for analytic work (S. Freud, 1937).

This is true of the acute phases of development, of the oedipal conflict (which, as Anna Freud remarks, 'is a prototype of an upsetting love affair, complete with hopes, expectations, jealousies, rivalries and inevitable frustrations'), of sibling rivalry, of castration anxiety; finally, this is true of the process of development itself which 'has the characters of an exciting venture' and may deplete the child's energies.

On one hand we know that such difficulties are inevitable and, as A. Freud calls them, *phase-bound,* i.e. they are probably transitory. 'It is a legitimate task for the child's ego to deal with them and the legitimate duty of the parents to support the child in his endeavours.' On the other hand the child's ego might resort to

---

consistently related to reality. The difference between character and symptom is a quantitative rather than a qualitative one; underlying all symptom formtion is a basic character structure. The difference seems mostly related to the degree of developmental internalization of parental ego ideal and superego demands (Lustman, 1962).

unsuitable solutions, and not all parents are able to provide the child with the necessary support. Many analysts consider that the acute crises endanger the child's normal development and that only analytic help will be effective in avoiding crippling solutions.

(b) In other cases children are, quite obviously, victims of external circumstances: damage is caused and maintained by *environmental interferences with development.* In many cases the child's needs are disregarded, mostly by his parents, in such areas as protection against archaic fears, satisfaction of skin and motor erotism, appropriate stimulations of cognitive functions, tolerance of drive activity, etc. These frustrations create basic developmental faults and they may represent a breeding-ground for neurotic conflict. A. Freud insists on the necessity to distinguish between childhood neurosis and this 'deficiency illness', as she calls it, 'which can be traced back to the lack of some external agent that is an essential requirement for normal growth'.

Parents are very insistent in their demands for treatment because the child's impulsive behaviour, poor school performance or aggressiveness often disrupts the whole family life. In such cases therapeutic help cannot be refused since the problems are of an urgent nature, but psychoanalysis can only achieve limited results: it may help to relieve some of the behaviour disturbances, control aggressiveness or improve schooling. But the child's underlying personality defects remain unchanged.

(c) It is even more difficult to decide whether analysis is indicated in the case of children whose life proceeds under the influence of environment obstacles, e.g. disturbed parents whose neurotic needs meet with the child's needs for dependency, or parents whose behaviour appears distorted by their own neurotic traits; some parents are frightening, threatening figures; others may have exhibitionistic tendencies or actually seduce or aggress their children. One must disentangle the 'real' personality of the parents from the projection and phantasies with which their image is overlaid. All parental threats or seductions are not only products of the child's phantasy.

In such cases children have little chance of growing up normally and 'the appeal for help which is implicit in their precarious circumstances is too strong to be dismissed lightly and often brings them into treatment' (A. Freud, 1968). This does not by any means imply that psychoanalysis is indicated for them as the treatment of choice when the aggressor or the seducer are *real people*, when the pathogenic influence is embodied in the very people who are expected to help the child. Here again A. Freud emphasizes the difficulty of deciding about the opportunity of child analysis which might be unable to counteract the real obstacles.

Thus A. Freud's work on indications of child analysis is based on (a) an examination of the *structural elements* in order to affirm which are the obstacles opposed to personality growth in terms of intersystemic conflicts, ego-defences, anxiety, regression, etc.; (b) *a psychopathological discussion* of the case: in her view, the major, if not only, indication is that of childhood neurosis, since we might expect in that case to alter the qualities of defences, to undo regression and alter the balance of forces within the personality structure.

IV. Indications for child analysis: the views of Melanie Klein

Melanie Klein does not use a structural approach; she is mainly concerned with the impact of non-resolved psychic conflicts on the child, that is assessing the pathogenic effect of anxiety and the inhibiting effects of infantile neurosis. Her diagnostic procedures are aimed at uncovering anxiety behind certain symptoms and behaviour patterns.[1]

1 *Neurotic manifestations and inner conflict*

As he grows up every child must come up against difficulties corresponding to inner conflicts. These include the kind which betray the child's inability to solve them and therefore reveal a genuine neurosis.

Melanie Klein emphasizes symptoms of childhood neurosis: feeding difficulties, sleep disturbances and phobic symptoms. In the infant, anxiety can assume various forms. Sleep may be agitated or interrupted, or there may be difficulties in falling asleep, inability to sleep during the day or the habit of waking up too early. All these are equivalents of night terrors (*pavor nocturnus*) and are directly linked with the phantasies which have brought on the anxiety. In the same sort of way, bed-time ceremonial not only serves the purpose of delaying the actual going to bed or falling asleep but has the value of a magic ritual intended to guard the child against an attack of anxiety. Feeding difficulties may likewise be an indication of an infantile neurosis. These include general

[1] See *The Psychoanalysis of Children* (1932), Chapter VI.

loss of appetite, fussiness about eating or refusal to accept specific foods or solids. Food fads may later appear under the guise of lack of appetite, chewing difficulties or bad table manners.[1]

Clinically an anxiety may show itself in so-called 'functional' disturbances such as tics, nail-biting, enuresis or fidgetiness. Most of these manifestations express archaic mental conflicts; they have a symbolic significance and relate to specific stages of development.

Other symptoms of a more obviously 'psychological' nature may claim our attention. Phobias, whether connected with animals or inanimate objects (buttons, scissors, telephone, vacuum-cleaners, etc.) often make their appearance about the age of two or three years. An animal phobia—the fear of horses—was the main symptom of the first case of infantile neurosis studied by Freud (1909), known as 'the Little Hans.'

Melanie Klein's claim to originality comes from her appraisal of the child's everyday difficulties: how far they have to be regarded as a beginning or a sign of serious disturbances. She draws attention to certain inhibitions concerning play activities: refusal or hesitation to take part in games which are attributed to fatigue or clumsiness. Such oddities, peculiarities or apathy, sometimes continue into the adult life. The adult, of course, can always rationalize his dislike by calling certain activities 'boring', 'tiring' or 'in bad taste', whereas, in the child (because of the importance of play activities in his life), dislikes and habits are much more difficult to camouflage behind rationalizations. Inhibition is always an indication of and an attempt to avoid anxiety and guilt feelings, which is why inhibitions, like any other neurotic symptom, are more amenable to psychotherapy than to educative measures.

Some children avoid certain games altogether or, on the other hand, indulge in some stereotyped activity (in a compulsive fashion) to the exclusion of all others. Other children show lack of perseverence and so flit from one game to the next; or appreciate games which must be played according to strict rules. Some children are unable to take any initiative and will play only when someone else will take the lead and allow them to play a minor part. In Melanie Klein's view, these children suffer from a massive repression of phantasy accompanied by compulsive traits.

Refusal to take part in active games or group activities often

---

[1] In the case of a child who prefers a semi-liquid diet or who swallows his food without chewing, refusal of solid food or chewing difficulties may be associated with problems of oral sadism and with phantasies of oral aggression which he is unconsciously trying to deny.

finds expression in clumsiness or lack of interest in sports, particularly those of the team or competitive variety. This attitude toward playing and competing may even colour the child's entire range of school activities. It may show itself in laziness, in a refusal to learn, in a distaste or dislike for certain subjects, in reading difficulties, in an incapacity to work except under authoritarian discipline or coercion or when examinations are imminent. Yet, in some cases, inhibited children become 'good' pupils through overcompensation, though their work will retain an element of compulsiveness which may turn to something more serious. These difficulties will have their impact later in life and may even exert a paralysing effect, particularly when a vocational choice has to be made.

Symptoms of anxiety are also sometimes met in a *child's attitude to gifts*. Some children are never satisfied with gifts. Nothing comes up to their expectations; they always show some disappointment. Others are completely indifferent and show no interest in presents. The symbolic significance of presents comes out clearly in analysis:

> Presents signify to the child all those love gifts which it has had to do without: its mother's milk and breast, its father's penis, urine, stool and babies. Presents also alleviate its sense of guilt by symbolizing the free gift of things which it has wanted to take by sadistic means. In its unconscious it regards not getting presents, like all other frustrations, as a punishment for the aggressive impulses that are bound up with its libidinal desires. In other cases, where the child is still more unfavourably situated in regard to its excessive sense of guilt or has failed to modify it, its fears of fresh disappointment will cause it to suppress its libidinal desires altogether so that the presents it does receive are no real pleasure (Melanie Klein, 1932, p. 147).

Tolerance of frustration may be assessed by the child's attitude towards the goals and desires which have been refused or become unattainable to him. To the degree that he has gradually been able to discard certain libidinal objects and accept other, better adapted ones, to that extent he will bow to the exigencies of external reality. This becomes possible with maturation and also as a result of a complete reshaping of the unconscious phantasies concerning his love objects.

Indications for psychoanalysis have been widened as a result of these theoretical conceptions. As everyone, in the first years of life, has to face up to situations where anxiety plays a very large part and against which pathological defences have to be built up, there will always be sequellae, manifest or latent, of varying intensity. Neuroses, behaviour disorders, cognitive deficiencies, difficulties in adjustment, pre-psychotic states, all these are evidence of repeated attempts to resolve the psychic conflict and therefore justify psychotherapy in order to get at the pathogenic nucleus. The indications, therefore, are wider and, short of an idea limit, Melanie Klein sees no obstacle to the 'prophylactic analysis' of all children.

> There can be no doubt that by diminishing their anxiety and sense of guilt and effecting fundamental changes in their sexual life, analysis can exert a great influence not only on neurotic children but on normal ones as well. . . . At present, owing to practical considerations, it is only possible to submit the neurotic difficulties of normal children to analytic treatment in rare cases. In describing indications for treatment, therefore, it is important to state what signs suggest the presence of a severe neurosis. . . .

Psychoanalysis will thus be confined to those cases of infantile neurosis where there is no chance of spontaneous recovery. The problem, for Melanie Klein, is not so much one of detecting the neurosis as foreseeing the possibility of its spontaneous resolution. This kind of solution may seem improbable and even impossible when neurotic difficulties, anxiety or emotional ambivalence block the way to an adjustment to the outside world, impair the establishment of object-relations and expose the child to undue suffering. In some cases of infantile neurosis 'whose severity is unmistakable owing to the extent and character of the symptoms' analysis is clearly indicated.

There are other neuroses, however, operating surreptitiously which may go undetected or their seriousness may be underestimated by the child's family. The usual criteria for adjustment, which are valid in the case of the adult, may have little relevance for the child.

> In judging what is neurotic in a child we cannot apply the standards proper to adults. It is by no means those children who approximate most nearly to non-neurotic adults who are the least neurotic themselves. Thus, for instance, a small child who fulfils all the requirements of its upbringing and does not let himself be dominated by its life of phantasy and instinct, which is, in fact, to all appearances completely adapted to reality, and moreover, shows little sign of anxiety—such a child would assuredly

be abnormal in the fullest sense of the word. . . . Normally, we should expect to see clear traces of the severe struggle and crises which the child passes in the first years of his life.

Adjustment to the demands of schooling and education generally, which the child apparently seems to cope with without undue difficulty, is not merely a question of adjusting to the real situation. It may well involve a massive curbing of instinctual drives, where phantasies have succumbed to highly 'efficient' repression. Apparent absence of maladjustment does not necessarily mean the absence of all neurotic conflict, for we know from experience that behind a *seemingly* well-adjusted behaviour a silent neurotic process is going on, the prognosis for which, however, is generally much more unfavourable than in cases where the symptoms are obvious.

2 *Diagnostic criteria*

Melanie Klein assesses the gravity of a neurosis by selecting criteria which are indicative of distorted psychological development.

(a)   INHIBITION OF THE EPISTEMOPHILIC IMPULSE shows itself in an unwillingness to know or to learn, not only in school but in any activity where the acquisition of knowledge is involved—reading, creative games, and even enjoying entertainments. Melanie Klein mentions in particular the child's lack of curiosity about sexual matters; he never asks questions and shows a resistance to sexual enlightenment. The reluctance to learn is attributed to a massive repression of normal curiosity under the impact of unconscious phantasies about his parents' sexual life; this inhibition is then displaced on to the process of knowing.

(b)   REPRESSION OF THE IMAGINATIVE LIFE, as shown by children's games, reflects a large-scale repression of phantasies. Stereotyped games or compulsive playing, reduced to constant repetition, are evidence of constraints which the child's phantasy life has to suffer because of restrictions on his libidinal instincts.

(c)   INABILITY TO TOLERATE FRUSTRATION shows the child's immaturity in his relations with people in his environment. It also tells us about his insecurity and his lack of control of his own drives. He sees every refusal or demand coming from the outside

o

as a punishment for his aggressive or libidinal phantasies whose impact he cannot dominate. His inability to adjust his position *vis-à-vis* the coveted object often refers to his unconscious destructive phantasies.

(d)   OVER-ADJUSTMENT TO EDUCATIONAL REQUIREMENTS is evidence of the introjection of a tyrannical and threatening superego. The freedom of the child's imaginative life has been inhibited and repression has superseded instinctual demands. In these cases the child becomes obedient, well-behaved and hard-working but at the cost of abandoning all instinctual gratification, the freedom to express his phantasies and the spontaneity of his imaginative play. 'The child is mainly concerned with fighting off anxiety and feelings of guilt at all cost, even if it means giving up all happiness and all gratification of his instincts.'

(e)   Finally, the way a child relates to his family circle and with other children has to be considered. Melanie Klein regards a too aggressive or too affectionate behaviour as a sign of the child's inability to face up to the anxiety or hostility felt *vis-à-vis* the libidinal object. It would indicate that these relations are being ruled by sadomasochistic interplay which would subsequently affect the child's integration into family and society.

The criteria suggested by Melanie Klein are not, therefore, concerned with adjustment to reality, which may be nothing more than a defence against instinctual drives and primary phantasies. Neither can these criteria be regarded as being based on a 'structural' viewpoint, for they take no account of ego-strength or defence mechanisms. Her criteria are based on the way the child deals with his phantasy life, on the freedom with which he deals with his instinctual demands and with the inhibition which results from the fact that he cannot find a spontaneous solution to the intrapsychic conflicts underlying his phantasies. Melanie Klein seeks to assess, not so much the child's ability to adjust to reality factors, as his potentiality for resolving conflicts, i.e. liberating himself from the inhibiting burden of his phantasy world.

It is clear that whatever the criteria, the indications for therapy cannot be based on descriptive symptomatology. What really matters is the *unconscious symbolic meaning* of the symptom or of the behaviour. The indication for child analysis is based on the evaluation of the child's neurosis:

(a)   its inhibiting effect on emotional and intellectual development resulting from anxiety and from the ego's defences;

(b)   its restrictions on the free play of the child's phantasy life;
(c)   the excessive load of guilt envy and/or depression, as it shows in the child's maladjustment (or overadjustment) to his environment.

It is remarkable that Melanie Klein neglects almost all references to the child's 'real' parents, i.e. she takes little notice of the environmental difficulties or shortcomings. Nor is she seemingly concerned with parental psychopathology: she regards frustration, envy, aggression, i.e the various modes of childhood experience, as causative factors, but seemingly pays little attention to external circumstances as far as the decision for therapy is concerned. Because of the determining role of phantasy, outer reality is only discussed to a minimal extent.

We thus see the difference of approach of Anna Freud and Melanie Klein. To Anna Freud the child's emotional turmoil is only amenable to analysis if the conflict is interiorized; the chances of analytic therapy are poor if a real conflict exists in the child's life. As to Melanie Klein, she considers that the phantasy life of the child is what really determines and causes neurosis, and analysis must be effective whatever the 'real' circumstances might be.

8   The parents

One of the specific problems in child analysis arises from the close link between parent and child. The actual presence of the parents, their part in satisfying the child's needs, and the emotional inter-dependence that goes with it (and from which the child seeks to break loose)—all this will make itself felt in the analytic situation. Any of the child's relations with his environment will have its roots in this primary bond with his parents. Their real presence, their symbolic significance and their phantasy image in the child's mind will also shape the modality of the transference situation during analysis.

In the analysis of adult patients, parents retain an importance as a historical fact with all its symbolic connotations. But in the case of a child, parents are an ever-present reality; they play a promi-nent role as a causative factor of the child's disturbance, but they also influence the present course of the therapeutic process and its final outcome.

The main difference between the two orientations in child analysis revolves round the problem of transference. As we have seen, for Anna Freud, the child is engaged in an actual relation with his parents, who play a real role in the child's everyday life: the child cannot establish a transference relation which would replace the actual relation with his parents. According to her, an analysis in the strict sense (that is, one involving, by definition, the development of a transference neurosis) is impossible, and psychotherapeutic action must look for other means.[1]

Melanie Klein, on the other hand, takes the view that the real and present parental relation is second in importance to the phantasy relation which is established in the child's imagination. The role of the real parents is therefore less important than the role of the imaginary, introjected parents; the child is thus free to re-enact his phantasies and revive his unconscious conflicts in the transference.

Whatever the implications of these theoretical positions, the presence of the parents confers upon child analysis its specific character. Parents must decide or agree to make the initial move by asking the psychoanalyst for advice and/or help. It is with them that the dialogue begins and it is as a result of this that the question of psychotherapy arises. The subsequent course of the treat-ment will depend on their attitude both to the child and to the analysis.

---

[1] Selma Fraiberg, 'Clinical Notes on the Nature of Transference in Child Analysis' (1951).

I. The first interviews

When parents ask for psychological help for their child they initiate a relation between themselves and the analyst. When interviews are conducted freely and not in the form of a rigid enquiry, parents are given an opportunity to talk and gradually to involve themselves personally in what they have to say about their children.

This initial contact between parents and analyst[1] is of crucial importance for an assessment of family dynamics. The early interviews may help the analyst to get a glimpse at the unconscious factors underlying the parent-child relationship but they also throw a light on the concrete facts of the child's development and the family setting. They clarify the unconscious motives for seeking advice or, in some cases, for refusing therapy. In short, these first contacts must help to arrive at an understanding of the move the parents have taken and to decide whether or not psychotherapy is indicated.

1 *The parents' attitude with regard to the child's psychotherapy*

Parental attitudes and prejudices must be evaluated; they represent a great obstacle to treatment because they reflect an unconscious resistance.[2] Behind the distorted ideas or scepticism—and even the grudging and superficial acceptance—in the uninformed public mind *vis-à-vis* the general question of psychoanalysis, lurk deep fears, conscious and unconscious, which are all too often a reflection of the inability of parents to face up to their own emotional problems.

To complicate matters, there is the traditional and widely held idea of childhood purity, based on an image of childhood innocence utterly free of all sexual or aggressive manifestations, which are often interpreted as a sign of perversion or hereditary defect and bear the stigmata of disease. The advent of psychoanalysis has brought about a relative change of certain cultural norms: childhood purity has been largely demystified; sexuality and aggressiveness are recognized as component factors in the child's normal

---

[1] These first interviews may be conducted either by the analyst who is going to be in charge of the child, or with an analyst who will refer the child to somebody else for treatment. Procedures differ according to practical, and sometimes theoretical, principles; but they also vary according to each case, whether it is felt that it might be an advantage or disadvantage for the parents and the child to be seen by the same person.

[2] How widespread these prejudices are has been shown in some detail by S. Moscovici (1961).

development. Our basic attitudes to children have thus been transformed.

Prejudice where sexual matters are concerned, however, dies hard, and parents, because of their own moral principles or emotional conflicts, are afraid lest psychoanalysis make the child aware of problems which they themselves would prefer to ignore or to minimize.[1]

Nevertheless, parents do implicitly recognize the existence of sexual or aggressive impulses in their child. An admission of this can be found in their fear that analysis, which would reveal a child's unconscious wishes to him, would do nothing but exacerbate any existing disorders and possibly weaken the influence of external control. This fear of immorality as a consequence of analytic treatment is somewhat paradoxical, for 'far from gaining strength, unconscious tendencies, on the contrary, are deprived of their power when an outlet into conscious thought is opened up for them. . . . Uncovered and lifted to the conscious level they automatically come under the patient's control and can be dealt with according to his ideal and ideas' (Anna Freud, 1945). Just as the interplay of mental agencies can produce a neurosis, it should also be able to control the instinctual drives when they become conscious. Analysis enables the patient to renounce certain very early libidinal positions and inadequate or neurotic defences and to make use of more economical ones. The result of psychoanalysis, therefore, would not be to leave the patient defenceless in dealing with his instinctual drives but to give him more control over them.

The parental resistances are important in order to determine the possibilities of psychotherapy. In the first interviews the analyst will seek to assess this resistance and he might help the parents to overcome some of it so as to win maximum co-operation; but he will also try to clarify the parents' emotional problems.

2 *Parental pathology*

By consulting the analyst, the parents are indicating their involvement with the child and at the same time questioning their own attitude to the child and his to them.

Through telling the analyst their grievances and disappointment, they establish the child as the object of their own anxiety or

[1] The same fears and prejudices are also to be found in respect of sexual enlightenment, the problems of birth control, pre-marital sexual experience, etc.

frustration. The child's symptoms are the ostensible reason for the consultation, but the child, who is presented as 'difficult', 'maladjusted' or 'odd', reflects, unbeknown to them, the parents' own problems and so becomes an intermediary between them and the analyst. Hence, though the child, initially, may have no demands or expectations, the parents by contrast are the anxiously interested party. In many cases, the child itself is not the sufferer; only the persons around him suffer from its symptoms or outbreaks of naughtiness (A. Freud).

In the first few consultations, the parents may attempt to deny all responsibility for, or share in, the child's disorders; they may boast how well they have brought up their child, assert their moral principles or describe their attitude which they consider to correspond to the image of 'good parents', concerned for their child's well-being, reasonable in their demands on him and scrupulously fair in the rewards and punishments they mete out.

One is tempted to envisage the problem under its two distinct aspects; that of the child on the one hand, and the parents on the other, with a view to establish a division of 'responsibilities'. In fact, the entire family is involved and the situation must be understood in terms of a family neurosis, with each member of the family participating, as it were, in the total clinical picture.

There are, nevertheless, certain cases in which the parental pathology is obvious from the very start. There are irritable, angry or impatient parents; parents overwhelmed by their own aggressiveness towards their child imprisoned in a situation of their own making and which, unwittingly, they are aggravating. There are anxious, over-protective, indecisive parents, parents devoid of any authority, helpless and fearful witnesses of the difficulties of their children who have been thus conditioned by their anxiety. There are the inadequate parents, narcissistically engaged in their social or professional pursuits, unable to face up to their role, offering only a remote parental image and entirely preoccupied by their own, very real problems. There are parents who deceive themselves into thinking that they have found a solution to their difficulties by masking their character neurosis behind social and professional achievements. There are the parents who are obsessional, exacting and fussy, usually inefficient and rigid in their behaviour, who imprison their children in a strict code of rules and manners which is really intended to help them fight against their own anxiety. There are the immature parents, parents who have resigned from their role, the bullying or bullied parents, the hypochondriac parents, and so on, until we have covered the entire gamut of character neurosis. It is important to understand the pathological significance of such character traits and to assess their impact on the child.

As a result of living with parents like this, the child may develop 'reactive' disorders which have set in as a response to their attitude.

A 'reactive' disorder may, however, be rapidly internalized. Whenever an improvement in the parents' attitude (if such an improvement is indeed still possible) is not sufficient to check the child's difficulties, it may be concluded that the disturbance has already been internalized and integrated into a neurotic structure.

The parental pathology is not a simple backcloth against which the child's pathology takes its course. For although the child's behaviour is a reflection of the parents' behaviour, the latter is not fortuitous but arises from past experience and reflects an emotional balance not to be lightly tampered with. Parents will try to maintain this balance and unconsciously resist any attempt to upset it.

Parents often expect the psychoanalyst to find a solution to their child's problems but only if their own way of life is not threatened in the process. Every attempt, therefore, to change parental attitudes will be resisted; an advice or a rational argument will at best bring about superficial changes without getting at the deeper motives behind their behaviour. To tell them that they are the initial cause of the child's difficulties they are complaining about would be to ignore the character structures which are the basis of the family neurosis. Its real root is the parents' unconscious denial, or their ignorance of, the pathological and pathogenic content of their own reactions.

Although in many cases parents' attitudes may at first sight seem gravely impaired, there are others where they may be regarded as normal.[1]

One may ask whether the child's emotional difficulties are not due to some developmental disharmony without the parents themselves being involved in the mental conflict. But even with co-

[1] This means, as pointed out by Diatkine and Favreau (1961), that the psychoanalyst is identifying more readily with the behaviour of the parents, whom he does not find essentially pathological. He may disagree with their educational attitudes, particularly when their views on upbringing and schooling conflict with his more 'liberal' ones. But he does not have to depart from his rule of 'neutrality', which remains essential to his procedure. Nevertheless, it is necessary to know what exact meaning he assigns to this neutrality; he can no more renounce his own convictions than pay lip-service to the opposing view. Neutrality means refraining from *active* criticism or advice; for the analyst knows that parents will only be able to revise the unconscious motivations on which their attitudes are based if he is not judging or advising them, but *listening to* and trying to understand them.

operative and understanding parents we must keep in mind that the child's symptoms have brought with them a certain *modus vivendi* in which the parents have fallen in with the child's difficulties. Therefore, however co-operative they are, two factors must always be taken into consideration: on the one hand, that the manifest adaptation always masks a latent conflict which, however unconscious, remains active, responsible for the origin of the disturbances and conditioning the way the parents react; on the other hand, that any modification (even a cure), will necessarily cause an unbalance of forces which may upset the apparently well-adjusted parental attitude.

3 *Assessment of parental co-operation*

The first interviews will also give the analyst an opportunity of assessing the chances of a change of attitude on the parents' part. Parents can often be induced to take a more objective view of the conflict and to get an insight into their own motives. This, of course, should enable them to get their own infantile experiences into better perspective. This new change of position *vis-à-vis* their child will bring about a *therapeutic deconditioning* (Buckle and Lebovici, 1958). These authors emphasize the ambivalence behind the first consultation; the parents' attitude towards the analyst will be both submissive and aggressive. And because of the emotional components of these interviews it is important not to turn them into a coldly impersonal enquiry.

The parents get some 'narcissistic' satisfaction from being listened to by the analyst: they may feel somewhat reassured in their role as parents, but they also feel encouraged since their difficulties and their demands are being taken seriously. Their confidence, however ambivalent it may be, can be encouraged by occasional words of commendation or even by a smile; this for them is an inducement to proceed. Only the analyst knows that what they have come to ask for in the way of advice or enlightenment can, at best, have only a limited effect. The new conscious awareness which the analyst is trying to get them to achieve will require a considerable effort on their part, the extent of which they cannot measure in advance. Only a satisfactory relation with the psychoanalyst will help overcome these difficulties and enable therapy, in which they must participate, to proceed.

To bring home too suddenly or brusquely their part in the total situation by breaking down the defensive barriers and bringing the repressed conflicts into the open, may well mobilize a sufficient amount of anxiety to make them abandon their request for help. This means, of course, that the situation has to be handled with the greatest tact and caution. There must be no wild[1] interpretation which might confront them with the unconscious meaning of their behaviour which they are not yet ready for. It is here that the 'neutrality' of the analyst assumes its full significance: the analyst's attitude should be neither approving nor critical but an invitation to *carry on.*

At this point, too, the analyst will witness the parents' admission of failure or perceive their complete disarray; he will detect the indirect appeal for personal help for which the child's problems have been only a conscious pretext or an unconscious rationalization. It is important not to misinterpret this appeal nor, for that matter, should the analyst be trapped by the parent's over-aggressive demands: the analyst's field of action is defined by the gap between what he is being asked for and what is in his power to do.

The advice or the information wanted by parents may become the stake in the relation with the psychotherapist. The 'advice' they want is, in fact, a confirmation of their own worth; they want to be recognized as 'good' parents by the specialist.

Any piece of advice will imply a value-judgment, an approval or a criticism of their behaviour or even a plain statement of their inability to accept the responsibility of their role. The ambivalence of the parents' request here becomes obvious. If they are convinced that the analyst possesses a theory on which to base his advice, they are unconsciously committed to make him fail. They may exploit the failure of their over-meticulous (or even ridiculous) application of his advice to prove that nobody, not even the specialist himself, could succeed where they have failed.

4 *Psychoanalysis and education*

To what extent does it make sense to speak of an 'educational system' based on psychoanalysis?

[1] The expression 'wild analysis' was coined by Freud: he was referring to interpretations of the unconscious prematurely hazarded by the therapist, before the patient is 'ripe' for it. Any 'deep' interpretation of latent content or of unconscious attitudes can only be offered after the patient has worked through some of his material. A 'wild' interpretation might of course be a correct one, but is given out of context, regardless of transference or of any historical frame of reference. It is thus felt to be a dangerous intrusion and cannot be integrated by the patient or take its place in his psychic economy. Even when it does not harm the patient, or does not endanger the therapeutic situation, it can neither have a maturing effect nor does it help the patient to gain insight into his difficulties.

Anna Freud (1931) attempted to define the aims of an 'analytical education'. She thought the solution was to find a middle course between the two extremes of coercive punishment and rewards, to achieve a balance between gratification of the instincts and the curb imposed on them. In 1968, she wrote that it seemed a feasible task to remove some of the detrimental influence of parental attitudes

> such as dishonesty in sexual matters, unrealistically high moral standards, overstrictness or overindulgence, frustration, punishments or seductive behaviour. . . . The attempts to reach this aim have never been abandoned, difficult and bewildering as their results turned out to be at times. When we look back over their history now, after a period over more than forty years, we see them as a long series of trials and errors.

Psychoanalysis never has, and probably never will be able to, formulate a set of pedagogical precepts and present them as a body of doctrine. Nevertheless, psychoanalysis certainly has, by throwing light on the multiple factors involved, been able to suggest the framework within which education could be adjusted to meet the needs of the growing child—his maturational readiness, his libidinal phases and the organizational level of his object-relations. In practice, however, education and upbringing are highly individual affairs, not easily amendable to systematization. They must be based on certain principles which govern relations between the child and parents. The latter must be able to perceive and understand the motives underlying the child's behaviour; they must be able to establish with him a communication based on shared emotional experiences and on mutual trust; libidinal gratification must not be forbidden but adjusted to educational aims and must fit in with the different stages of development.

This kind of attitude can only come from parents who have resolved some of their intrapsychic conflicts. They must either have found their own personal solution or have been helped by psychotherapy or analysis to gain insight into the unconscious reason of their conduct.

Some psychiatrists (or pediatricians) try to instruct parents in the principles of child development and parent-child relations. They hope in this way to help them not to behave in a way harmful to their child; not to resort to excessive rewards or harsh punishments (both can cause more harm than good); to become aware of the child's emotional needs; to adopt a logical, liberal way of relating to the child; to be more understanding of

their ambivalent feelings towards the child and not to look for
some unattainably ideal method of bringing up their child. They
may, in this way, eradicate certain prejudices and avoid rigid
attitudes resulting from the parents' identification with their own
parents, whose ideas they may be blindly putting into practice (or
perhaps trying to do the exact opposite).

It is true, though, that psychoanalytic 'enlightenment' has, to a
certain extent, modified general trends of child rearing: sexual
matters are discussed with greater honesty and the child's whims
or aggressiveness are often better tolerated by parents. As Anna
Freud points out:

> Another victory was over the stubborn obstinacy of certain
> early ages which disappeared almost completely after the
> problems of the anal phase were recognized and bowel
> training was carried out later and less harshly. Also certain
> eating disturbances of children ceased to exist after infant
> feeding and weaning were altered to correspond more
> closely to the oral needs. Some sleeping disturbances were
> removed after the struggle against masturbation, thumb
> sucking, and other auto-erotic activities lessened.

But it must be emphasized that this was not only achieved
through direct personal contact between analyst and parents, but
is part of a general education of the public, by means of books,
articles and mass media. This is not 'psychoanalytic' education
but a way of influencing (or even indoctrinating) which may
possibly have some results but with strictly limited objectives.
Psychoanalytic education fell short of becoming the preventive
measure which analysts hoped for in the early 'twenties. Many
children grew up in a different way but, as Anna Freud remarks,
'they were not freer from anxiety or from conflicts and therefore
not less exposed to neurotic or other mental illness'.

Sometimes, so-called modern or progressive ideas about upbringing are misinterpreted by parents and often result in a
kind of anarchic medley of tolerance and freedom. Originally,
'liberal' education was a reaction against coercive disciplinarianism
by which the child was forced into the mould of traditional ideas
and discouraged from having any initiative of his own; all libidinal
gratification, of course, was prohibited and condemned as the
first fatal step towards the whittling away of all moral principles.
Many parents grasped at the letter rather than the spirit behind
this 'new education' and interpreted it as advocating the suppression of all restraint and prohibition. Of course, when the
parental role was thus watered down, the child was free to break

loose from a structured family setting and the internal 'logic' of the situation, and roam around in his own disorganized world. Without any parental image there is no chance of identification and no model by which the child can structure his relations with the outside world. This spurious freedom weakens the sense of reality and brings about anxiety. And sometimes, an authoritarian and implacable superego takes over to replace those barriers which the parents are no longer there to provide. Advice from the therapist could be just about as useful as educational guidance: both are imposed from the outside and have no basis in the unconscious. They are used as 'tricks' while the underlying motivations remain unchanged. Only a real understanding of the unconscious on the part of the parents could lead to a radical change in their attitude.

Moreover, any piece of advice, given and taken, puts the parents in a position of more or less childlike dependence *vis-à-vis* the therapist. And in a situation like this, the therapist's role as parent would emerge most blatantly and culminate in a relation in which any progress or development would be impossible. As they get more and more accustomed to being fed on advice and guidance, parents will resign their proper role, and their behaviour towards the analyst will become more and more like that of a dependent or rebellious child.

The therapist will certainly not achieve his purpose by taking the place of an authoritarian parent (perhaps hated or missed) or by assuming the mantle of a surrogate parent. His efforts will bear fruit only to the extent that he helps the parents to become conscious of the mental conflicts underlying their relation to their child, and then to overcome such conflicts.

II. Psychotherapy for the parent

Psychotherapy with parents is far from being a well-systematized procedure. In some cases parents are already getting therapy and have gained some insight into their child's difficulties, and consult as a result of their own understanding, trying to help their child to get the necessary therapeutic support. In other cases, parents discover their own need for therapeutic help during their interviews with the child analyst. But as often as not they do not realize their own neurotic shortcomings, and therapy is recommended to them although they feel no real need for it. Due to these circumstances the parents' attitude towards therapy runs the whole gamut from a motivated demand to hostile refusal. Accordingly psychotherapeutic measures range from individual analytic therapy to parents' groups. However, indications are based not only on the parental demands for, or resistance to, therapy, but must be envisaged from the point of view of the clinical structure and prognostic appraisal of each case.

1 *Psychoanalytic therapy*

Psychotherapy is an attempt to get at the neurotic nucleus which determines the behaviour of the parent; it may be separated from or coupled with the psychotherapy of the child.[1]

The general problem of indications for analytic therapy for adults cannot be discussed here.[2] We shall only try to present general trends, taking into consideration that analytic therapy is being recommended to parents in relation to the difficulties encountered in their family. Assessment should take account of the clinical features of the family neurosis[3] and include a prognostic evaluation of the short- and long-term possibilities of improvement as well as its influence on the child's behaviour problems. Thus the decision will be dictated by an efficiency factor having regard to:

(a)   accessibility of the parents; their level of intelligence; the pliability of their attitudes and their emotional adaptivity;

(b)   their manifest and unconscious motives for seeking therapeutic help;

(c)   a general clinical picture of the family neurosis.

It should be borne in mind that the incidence of character neurosis is high and that it is almost impossible to evaluate prognosis properly; in such cases psychotherapy is often long and difficult.

Analytic psychotherapy is not aimed at eradicating any specific emotional attitude or getting rid of a particular symptom or behaviour pattern, but to get at the structure of the neurotic personality through the transference situation so that the patient may resolve his intrapsychic conflict.

The transference differentiates analytical psychotherapy from

[1] Its purpose is not merely to persuade the parents to accept treatment for their children or to reduce the frustrations which this is causing them (as in the case of supportive therapy).
[2] The reader is referred to N. W. Ackerman, *Treating the Troubled Family* (1966).
[3] R. Laforgue and J. Leuba (1936) have brought out very clearly the whole notion of *family neurosis* by pinpointing the neurotic factors in the husband-wife relation as well as in their relation with their children. Also see M. Grotjahn, *Psychoanalysis and the Family Neurosis* (1960), and N. W. Ackerman, *The Psychodynamics of Family Life* (1958).

other supportive techniques (e.g. psychiatric case-work). The 'oedipal' transference (Diatkine and Favreau, 1961) should allow the displacement of deep satisfaction, thus providing an indispensable condition for any form of psychotherapy performed on parents. This is not difficult to achieve with co-operative parents whose attitudes can rapidly change when anxiety is reduced, and particularly with parents who derive gratification from improved relations with their children. This shift of their libidinal cathexes calls for emotional flexibility. On the other hand, behind the rationalizations and the rigidity of parents who show considerable resistance before or during psychotherapy, there is a neurotic nucleus which raises serious doubts about any possibility of establishing satisfactory relations with others. These parents, some of whom blame social demands or economic difficulties for not giving their children the attention they need, accept psychotherapy exclusively for their child's benefit under the implicit condition that they should not be asked to participate, in order not to be involved in any major emotional conflict, and that their adjustment should not be questioned.

2 *Supportive psychotherapy*

If the analyst considers that parents are unable to get involved in analytic psychotherapy, but still feels that they should be helped even to a minimal degree, he may suggest supportive therapy. This will entail a limited number of interviews with one or both parents in an effort to keep in touch with them throughout their child's psychotherapy. This will not, of course, solve the parents' neurotic problems but may alleviate the tension arising from the course of treatment which their child is undergoing.

Though this kind of therapy may not seem to go very far, it nevertheless presents considerable difficulties because parents may still get deeply involved in their relationship with the therapist, but the 'transference' cannot be analysed and thus cannot be resolved. Furthermore, sessions often remain focused (as they tend to do) around the child's difficulties and it may be impossible to approach the parents' problem directly; hence these problems remain inaccessible throughout the therapy.

Opposition from the parents, whether hidden or explicit, can impede the endeavours of the child's therapist either by breaking up the relation or by indefinitely postponing any final solution because of their persistently negative attitude. Supportive psychotherapy with parents may explain the meaning the child's therapy has for them, and point out the difficulties and disappointments it may entail. In this way it can help to reduce frustration and guilt feelings and foster a more forbearing attitude to their child's psychotherapy. Although the adult's neurotic structure cannot be expected to be modified from this, there can be a change of attitude great enough for the child's treatment to continue and bear fruit.

All these problems can be invested with anxiety, unleash feelings of hostility against the psychotherapist or instigate dynamic changes in the family.

In the framework of supportive therapies we should mention casework techniques which are becoming more and more important in child guidance where regular interviews can go on for as long as the child's treatment requires them. Case-work not only allows the psychotherapeutic treatment to be geared to the parents' reactions to the child but also, very often, to go beyond them and bring the adult to face his own problems. In this way, many parents who were initially resistant to psychotherapy may be induced, through supportive therapy or case-work, to undergo intensive treatment. For although they may succeed in becoming conscious of their extreme or inadequate attitudes, they may still be quite unable to make the necessary adjustments if the unconscious motivations for their behaviour have not been brought home to them. This, of course, cannot happen without intensive psychotherapy.

3 *Group psychotherapy*

Group psychotherapy and parent groups are another way of helping parents with their psychological problems. These methods are sometimes preferred to individual treatment because they reduce the ambivalent feelings of aggression and submission *vis-à-vis* the therapist. They also sidetrack to a certain extent—by watering them down, as it were—the effects of transference which are sometimes difficult to handle in supportive psychotherapy and in psychiatric case-work.

In most cases, the main benefit is to allow the ventilation of guilt feelings attaching to the child's psychotherapy, to reduce certain aggressive or inhibitory mechanisms connected with questions of education and upbringing, to increase parental tolerance, and to modify some of their own attitudes by the identifications and counter-identifications towards the psychotherapist and the other group members.

Without going into the technical details of handling parent groups, there are nevertheless two techniques which should be mentioned. On the one hand, there are the *discussion groups* under the direction or in the presence of the psychiatrist, where problems of parent-child relations are to be discussed. Valuable information may emerge from these discussions, and changes in relations may be observed to take place inside the group.

The purpose of *group psychotherapies* on the other hand is to bring the parents to an understanding of group dynamics and to achieve structural changes in their personality. They are invited to discuss their personal problems, and the transference between the different members of the group and between them and the therapist is interpreted. These groups are run according to the principles of analytical psychotherapy. They are being used for parents who, because of their anxiety, are reluctant to establish a personal relationship with the psychotherapist but are quite ready to merge with a group where they feel more secure.

III. Indications for parent psychotherapy

There are no rigid criteria for indications of psychotherapy for parents. It would be contrary 'to all psychotherapeutic principle to use diagnosis as a permanent frame of reference' (Diatkine and Favreau, 1961). Over and above any formal diagnosis, account has to be taken of the biographical data and their implications for the existing situation. The underlying character structures and dynamics, as well as the parents' accessibility to analytical psychotherapy, must also be taken into consideration.

Two possibilities then become open to us: either to advise the parents (both or one of them) to start individual psychotherapy, the purpose of which would be to resolve the neurotic element by getting rid of the unconscious elements at the root of the mental conflict; or to start supportive therapy in the hope that certain changes of attitude might alleviate the emotional problems which are the cause of the family disturbances. In one way or another the therapist tries to undo the rigid and repetitive behaviour patterns by interpreting them: those patterns actually exist in the present situation similar to those which the parents came up against in their own childhood. By drawing a parallel between their existing relations and those upon which they have modelled themselves hitherto, they are helped to get a more realistic perspective, both from the genetic and the dynamic point of view. Further, the aim

P

of psychotherapy is to get rid of those infantile patterns of behaviour which have lingered on as early unresolved conflicts, and thereby to achieve *emotional maturity*. Acknowledgment of the existence of these conflicts and recognition that there is a chance of putting them right (which is part of getting the situation into an objective perspective), presupposes emotional resources in the adult who would not seek to reproduce or resolve his neurotic difficulties in his relationship with his own children. Psychotherapy, however superficial, raises the whole question of the therapeutic relation and tries not only to get at the objective situation but also at the imaginary fringe which colours it and at the symbolic significance which is given to it.

Throughout this chapter we have looked at the adult as parent only and have given special consideration to the question of his impaired relations with the child: this approach is justified in so far as the child analyst is dealing here with the total family situation and not isolated elements. (In some cases, of course, a parent might be referred to an analyst quite independently of his child's problems.)

But from the outset, the child analyst will be faced with both children and adults and his work will be concerned with the family unit. Therapeutic work with parents is essential if viewed in this light.

Conclusion

It is quite common to read the conclusion of a book before starting on the book itself. We might just as well take advantage of this possibility and use these pages to serve a dual purpose. Why has this book about child analysis been written?

Over the last fifty years, child analysis has become a highly specialized field. Although it is based on the same basic theories and concepts as the analysis of adults, as we have emphasized throughout this book, technical differences and specific conditions brought about adjustments of the standard analytic technique and raised many problems. It has been sometimes suggested that the practice of child analysis requires special training. This appears obvious since child analysts are confronted with specific problems which are not encountered in the analytic practice with adult patients, and resort to technical parameters which are not part of 'standard' procedures. A similar remark might be relevant concerning the analytic practice with adult psychotic patients, which often requires modifications of the so-called 'classical technique'. It is thus apparent that clinical experience is necessary to deal with such specific problems. But this does not mean that child and adult analysis could, or should, become separate fields.

Although these differences are obvious, they should not obliterate the fact that child analysis does not essentially differ from adult analysis, since the child analyst does use the same methodology and theoretical framework. What differ are the solutions of certain technical issues, not the underlying principles of psychoanalysis. We wish to stress that child analysis is not some subspecies of psychoanalysis as such, but a specialized field of application. Hence we would feel it to be detrimental to the overall concept of analysis if child analysis were to appear as a subspecialized area.

There is another, essential, reason for claiming such a unity. Adult analysis has to deal with the 'child within the adult', and any analyst must be ready and able to listen to the language of childhood, whether he is treating children or adults. Equally, the child is not only confronted with the adult world and language, but is in the maturational and developmental process of attaining, slowly but steadily, his stature as an independent human being. Thus no analyst should be prevented from gaining access to both experiences but in fact should be encouraged to do so. The constant shift between the world and word of the adult and of the child remains one of the conditions on which analytic experience is based.

We would certainly strongly advocate that every analyst should have at least some experience in both areas, both indispensable if he is to see the human person not as a divided self, child on one hand, adult on the other, but as imperatively part of the time-space continuum of the unconscious.

This book was not written for analysts but, as we have already said, for all those who are interested in the 'human sciences', i.e. anthropology, psychology, sociology, and for those who, unconnected with research, do try to understand man's relations to the outer world and to his own self, and their unconscious roots. Today, psychoanalysis is part of our cultural, and sometimes even educational, environment. Whether analysts are happy about this state of affairs; whether they feel that analysis should be kept confined to its own specific areas of research and practice; whether they claim that even the best theoretical exposition of analysis is unable to convey the true stuff of analytic experience; whether they approve of this cultural expansion or not, the fact remains that psychoanalysis is referred to—and sometimes even used—by those who do not have any personal or clinical experience and thus use psychoanalytic theory as a body of science. We feel that we may as well try to diminish certain misunderstandings, show certain limits of its applicability, and to the best of our abilities, bridge the gap.

We have obviously neglected some important issues and have restricted our exploration to 'child' analysis. It should be clear by now that in spite of its limitations we have been speaking of analysis as such and have tried to define its specificity in a given area. A great deal of analytic theory derives from and applies to the child. This can be used as an example for an approach of analytic research to be applied to the psyche *in statu nascendi*. It might be a good starting point for all of us.

Bibliography

Note: Italic figures in square brackets at the end of entries indicate where the work in question is cited in the text.

ABBATE, G. McL. (1967), 'Notes on the First Year of the Analysis of a Young Child with Minimum Participation by the Mother'. In *The Child Analyst at Work*, ed. E. A. Geleerd. New York: International Universities Press.

ABRAHAM, K. (1916), 'The First Pregenital Stage of the Libido'. *Selected Papers on Psycho-Analysis*. London: Hogarth Press, 1927.
— (1921), 'Contributions to the Theory of Anal Character'. *Selected Papers on Psycho-Analysis*. London: Hogarth Press, 1927.
— (1924a), 'The Influence of Oral Erotism on Character Formation'. *Selected Papers on Psycho-Analysis*. London: Hogarth Press, 1927. [*63, 143*]
— (1924b), 'A Short Study of the Development of the Libido'. *Selected Papers on Psycho-Analysis*. London: Hogarth Press, 1927. [*59*]

ACKERMAN, N. W. (1958), *The Psychodynamics of Family Life*. New York: Basic Books. [*208n*]
— (1966), *Treating the Troubled Family*. New York: Basic Books. [*208n*]

AICHHORN, A. (1925), *Wayward Youth*. New York: Viking Press, 1935. London: Hogarth Press, 1957. [*13*]

ALLPORT, G. W. (1937), *Personality; a Psychological Interpretation*. New York: Addison Wesley. [*28*]

AMACHER, P. (1965), 'Freud's Neurological Education and its Influence on Psychoanalytic Theory'. *Psychological Issues*, Monogr. 16. New York: International Universities Press. [*5n*]

ANDERSON, D. (1962), *Studies in the Prehistory of Psychoanalysis*. Norstedts: Svenska Bokförlaget.

ANZIEU, D. (1956), *Le Psychodrame analytique chez l'enfant*. Paris: Presses Universitaires de France.

BALINT, A. (1938), 'Love for Mother and Mother Love'. In M. Balint, *Primary Love and Psychoanalytic Technique*. London: Hogarth Press, 1952. [*140–1*]

BALINT, M. (1968), *The Basic Fault*. London: Tavistock Publications. [*139, 140n*]

BASTIDE, R. (1950), *Sociologie et psychanalyse*. Paris: Presses Universitaires de France.

BENEDEK, T. (1959), 'Parenthood as a Development Phase'. *J. Amer. Psychoanal. Assn.*, 7. [*118*]

BENEDICT, R. (1934), *Patterns of Culture*. New York: Houghton Mifflin Co. [*26*]

BERES, D. and OBERS, S. J. (1950), 'The Effects of Extreme Deprivation in Infancy on the Psychic Structure in Adolescence'. *The Psychoanalytic Study of the Child*, 5. (Currently 24 vols, ed. R. S. Eissler, A. Freud, H. Hartmann, M. Kris. New York: International Universities Press, 1945–69.) [*138n*]

BERGE, A. (1952), *L'Éducation sexuelle des enfants*. Paris: Presses Universitaires de France. [*68–9*]

BERNFELD, S. (1925), *Psychologie des Säuglings*. Wien: Springer. [*13*]

BETTELHEIM, B. (1967), *The Empty Fortress*. New York: Free Press of Glencoe.

BIBRING, E. (1937), 'On the Theory of the Therapeutic Results of Psycho-Analysis'. *Int. J. Psycho-Anal.*, 18.

BIBRING, G. L. et al. (1961), 'A Study of the Psychological Processes in Pregnancy and of the Earliest Mother-Child Relationship'. *The Psychoanalytic Study of the Child*, 16. [*133*]

BLOS, P. (1962), *On Adolescence*. New York: Free Press of Glencoe.

(1967), 'The Second Individuation Process of Adolescence'. *The Psychoanalytic Study of the Child*, 22. [*86*]

(1968), 'Character Formation in Adolescence'. *The Psychoanalytic Study of the Child*, 23. [*28, 86, 87*]

BOLLAND, J. and SANDLER, J. (1965), *The Hampstead Psychoanalytic Index*. New York: International Universities Press.

BONNARD, A. (1950), 'The Mother as Therapist'. *The Psychoanalytic Study of the Child*, 5. [*148n*]

BORNSTEIN, B. (1949), 'The Analysis of a Phobic Child. *The Psychoanalytic Study of the Child*, 3/4. [*156*]

BOWLBY, J. (1951), *Maternal Care and Mental Health*. Geneva: World Health Organization. [*135, 136, 139*]

BREUER, J. and FREUD, S. (1893, 1895), *Studies on Hysteria*. Standard Edition of the Complete Psychological Works of S. Freud, 2. London: Hogarth Press, 1953. [*31n*]

BRODY, S. (1956), *Patterns of Mothering*. New York: International Universities Press. [*29, 61n, 62, 142–3*]

BROWN, J. A. C. (1961), *Freud and the Post-Freudians*. London: Penguin Books. [*25n, 149*]

BRUNSWICK, R. M. (1940), 'The Pre-Oedipal Phase of the Libido Development'. *Psychoanal. Quart.*, 9. [*145*]

BUCKLE, D. and LEBOVICI, S. (1958), *Child Guidance Clinics*. Geneva: World Health Organization. [*203*]

BUXBAUM, E. (1954), 'Technique of Child Therapy'. *The Psychoanalytic Study of the Child*, 9.

CARTER, C. O. (1962), *Human Heredity*. London: Penguin Books. [*19n, 20n*]

CURTIS, S. J. and BOULTWOOD, M. E. A. (1965), *A Short History of Educational Ideas*. London: University Tutorial Press. [*11n*]

DARLINGTON, C. D. (1966), *Genetics and Man*. London: Penguin Books. [*16n, 24n*]

DEUTSCH, H. (1946), *The Psychology of Women*. London: Research Books. [*62, 141n, 144n*]

(1968), *Selected Problems of Adolescents*. London: Hogarth Press. [*81, 82*]

DIATKINE, R. and FAVREAU, J. A. (1961), 'Le psychiatre et les parents'.

La Psychiatrie de l'enfant, vol. 3. Paris: Presses Universitaires de France. [*202n, 209, 211*]

DOLLARD, J., DOBB, L. W., MILLER, N. E. and SEARS, R. R. (1939), *Frustration and Aggression*. New Haven: Yale University Press. [*89n*]

DOLTO, F. (1936), *Psychanalyse et pédiatrie*. Paris: Editions de la Parole, 1961. [*71–4*]

DUFRENNE, M. (1953), *La Personnalité de base*. Paris: Presses Universitaires de France.

EISENSTEIN, V. W. (1956), *Neurotic Interaction in Marriage*. New York: Basic Books.

ERIKSON, E. (1963), *Childhood and Society* (2nd ed.). New York: W. W. Norton. [*26, 118n*]

ESCALONA, S. K. (1963), 'Patterns of Infantile Experience and the Developmental Process'. *The Psychoanalytic Study of the Child*, 18. [*126*]

FEDERN, P. (1932), 'Ego Feelings in Dreams'. In *Ego Psychology and the Psychoses*. New York: Basic Books, 1952. [*46*]

FERENCZI, S. (1927), 'The Adaptation of the Family to the Child'. In *Final Contributions to the Problems and Methods of Psychoanalysis*. New York: Basic Books, 1955. [*69*]

    (1933), 'Confusion of Tongues between Adults and the Child'. *Final Contributions to the Problems and Methods of Psychoanalysis*. New York: Basic Books, 1955.

FILLOUX, J. C. (1947), *L'Inconscient*. Paris: Presses Universitaires de France.

    (1957), *La Personnalité*. Paris: Presses Universitaires de France. [*18*]

    (1968), Preface to French translation of Linton (1945), *Le Fondement culturel de la personnalité*. Paris: Dunod, 1968.

FOUCAULT, M. (1954), *Maladie mentale et psychologie*. Paris: Presses Universitaires de France. [*8, 150, 181*]

    (1961), *Madness and Civilization. A History of Insanity in the Age of Reason* (translated by Richard Howard). New York: Pantheon Books, 1965.

FRAIBERG, S. (1951), 'Clinical Notes on the Nature of Transference in Child Analysis'. *The Psychoanalytic Study of the Child*, 6. [*198n*]

FRANKL, L. and HELLMAN, I. (1962), 'The Ego's Participation in the Therapeutic Alliance'. *Int. J. Psycho-Anal.*, 43. [*156*]

FREEMAN, F. N., HOLZINGER, K. J. and MITCHELL, B. C. (1928), 'The Influence of Environment on the Intelligence, School Achievement and Conduct of Foster Children'. In *27th Yearbook Nat. Social Stud. Education*, Part I. [*19*]

FREUD, A. (1926 [1945]), *The Psychoanalytical Treatment of Children*. London: Hogarth Press, 1946. [*160*]

    (1931), *Introduction to Psychoanalysis for Teachers*. London: G. Allen and Unwin. [*13, 205*]

    (1937), *The Ego and the Mechanisms of Defence*. London:

Hogarth Press. [*117*]

    (1945), 'Indications for Child Analysis'. *The Psychoanalytic Study of the Child*, 1. [*185, 189, 200*]

    (1954), 'Psychoanalysis and Education'. *The Psychoanalytic Study of the Child*, 9. [*145–6*]

    (1958), 'Adolescence'. *The Psychoanalytic Study of the Child*, 13. [*85*]

    (1962), 'Assessment of Childhood Disturbances'. *The Psychoanalytic Study of the Child*, 17.

    (1966), *Normality and Pathology in Childhood*. London: Hogarth Press. [*150n, 151, 153, 155, 158, 170*]

    (1968), 'Indications and Contra-indications for Child Analysis'. *The Psychoanalytic Study of the Child*, 23. [*181, 185, 189, 190, 205*]

    (1970), *Research at the Hampstead Child-Therapy Clinic and Other Papers*. London: Hogarth Press. [*178*]

    and BURLINGHAM, D. T. (1944), *Infants without Families*. New York: International Universities Press.

FREUD, S. (1895), *Project for a Scientific Psychology*. Standard Edition, 2. (*The Standard Edition of the Complete Psychological Works of Sigmund Freud*, 24 vols. Trans. and ed. James Strachey. London: Hogarth Press, 1953.) [*4*]

    (1896), *The Aetiology of Hysteria*. Standard Edition, 3. [*1, 32, 38*]

    (1899), *Screen-Memories*. Standard Edition, 3. [*42*]

    (1900), *The Interpretation of Dreams*. Standard Edition, 4/5. [*xii, 3, 38n*]

    (1901), *Psychopathology of Everyday Life*. Standard Edition, 6. [*38, 42*]

    (1905), *Three Essays on the Theory of Sexuality*. Standard Edition, 7. [*35, 36–41, 42, 55, 58–9, 60, 62–3, 64, 79–80, 121*]

    (1907), *The Sexual Enlightenment of Children*, Standard Edition, 9.

    (1908a), *'Civilized' Sexual Morality and Modern Nervous Illness*. Standard Edition, 9. [*140*]

    (1908b), *On the Sexual Theories of Children*. Standard Edition, 9. [*68*]

    (1908c), *Character and Anal Erotism*. Standard Edition, 9. [*63*]

    (1909a), *Family Romances*. Standard Edition, 9.

    (1909b), *Analysis of a Phobia in a Five-Year-Old Boy*. Standard Edition, 10. [*147, 183, 192*]

    (1912–13), *Totem and Taboo*. Standard Edition, 13. [*5, 76*]

    (1914), *From the History of an Infantile Neurosis*. Standard Edition, 17. [*164*]

    (1915a), *Instincts and their Vicissitudes*. Standard Edition, 14. [*88, 94–5, 166*]

    (1915b), *Repression*. Standard Edition, 14. [*39, 41*]

    (1915c), *The Unconscious*. Standard Edition, 14. [*40*]

    (1916–17), *Introductory Lectures on Psychoanalysis*. Standard

Edition, 15/16. [*31n, 50n*]

(1919), 'A Child is Being Beaten'. Standard Edition, 17. [*163*]

(1920a), *Associations of a Four-Year-Old Boy*. Standard Edition, 18.

(1920b), *Beyond the Pleasure Principle*. Standard Edition, 18. [*30, 57*]

(1921), *Group Psychology and the Analysis of the Ego*. Standard Edition, 18. [*70*]

(1923a), *The Ego and the Id*. Standard Edition, 19. [*38n, 121*]

(1923b), *The Infantile Genital Organization*. Standard Edition, 19. [*66*]

(1924a), *The Resistances to Psychoanalysis*. Standard Edition, 19. [*xiii*]

(1924b), *The Dissolution of the Oedipus Complex*. Standard Edition, 19. [*77, 80*]

(1925a), *Inhibition, Symptom and Anxiety*. Standard Edition, 20. [*47, 50, 93*]

(1925b), *Negation*. Standard Edition, 19. [*48*]

(1925c), *Some Psychical Consequences of the Anatomical Distinction between the Sexes*. Standard Edition, 19. [*74, 75–7*]

(1933), *New Introductory Lectures on Psychoanalysis*. Standard Edition, 22. [*52, 105n, 165*]

(1937), *Analysis Terminable and Unterminable*. Standard Edition, 23. [*178, 189*]

(1938), *An Outline of Psychoanalysis*. Standard Edition, 23. [*xiii, 31, 46*]

(1939 [1934–8]), *Moses and Monotheism*. Standard Edition, 23. [*40, 51–3*]

See also BREUER, J. and FREUD, S. (1895).

FRIEDLANDER, K. (1947), *The Psycho-Analytical Approach to Juvenile Delinquency*. London: Kegan Paul, Trench, Trubner. [*84*]

FURMAN, E. (1957), 'Treatment of Under-fives by Way of their Parents'. In *The Psychoanalytic Study of the Child*, 12. [*148*]

GELEERD, E. R. (1967), 'Intrapsychic Conflicts as Observed in Child Analysis'. In *The Child Analyst at Work*, E. R. Geleerd, ed. [*148*]

(1967), *The Child Analyst at Work*. New York: International Universities Press.

GESELL, A. (1941), *Wolf Child and Human Child*. London: Methuen – New York: Harper. [*18n*]

GLICK, I. D. *et al.* (1967), 'Schizophrenia in Siblings Reared Apart'. *Am. J. Psychiat.*, 124. [*22*]

GLOVER, E. (1932), 'Medico-Psychological Aspects of Normality'. In *On the Early Development of Mind*. London: Imago, 1956.

(1945), 'Examination of the Klein System of Child Psychology'. *The Psychoanalytic Study of the Child*, 1. [*113, 163*]

(1953), *Psychoanalysis and Child Psychiatry*. London: Imago publications. [*182*]

Q

GRANOFF, W. (1956), 'Desire for children, children's desire': (Un désir d'enfant). *La psychanalyse*, 2. [*144n*]

GREENACRE, P. (1953), *Trauma, Growth and Personality*. New York: Norton.

—— (1958), 'Early Physical Determinants in the Development of the Sense of Identity'. *J. Amer. Psychoanal. Assn.*, 6. [*121*]

—— (1960), 'Considerations Regarding the Parent-Infant Relationship'. *Int. J. Psycho-Anal.*, 41.

GRODDECK, G. (1923), *The Book of the It* (trans. M. E. Collins). London: Vision Press, 1950.

GROTJAHN, M. (1960), *Psychoanalysis and the Family Neuroses*. New York: Norton. [*208n*]

GUEX, G. (1950), *La Névrose d'abandon*. Paris: Presses Universitaires de France. [*138*]

HARLEY, M. (1967), 'Transference Developments in a Five-Year-Old Child'. In *The Child Analyst at Work*, ed. E. R. Geleerd. [*156*]

HARLOW, H. F. (1960), 'Primary Affectionate Patterns in Primates. *Amer. J. Orthopsychiatry*, 30.

HARTMANN, H. (1964), *Essays on Ego-Psychology*. London: Hogarth Press.

—— and KRIS, E. (1945), 'The Genetic Approach in Psychoanalysis'. *The Psychoanalytic Study of the Child*, 1. [*89–90*]

—— and LOEWENSTEIN, R. (1946), 'Comments on the Formation of the Psychic Structure'. *The Psychoanalytic Study of the Child*, 3/4. [*17n, 90*]

HECAEN, H. and AJURIAGUERRA, J. (1952), *Méconnaissance et hallucinations corporelles. Intégration et desintégration de la somatognosie*. Paris: Masson.

HEIMANN, P. (1943), 'Certain Functions of Introjection and Projection in Early Infancy'. In M. Klein *et al. Developments in Psycho-Analysis*. London: Hogarth Press, 1952, [*49n, 53n, 166*]

HEUYER, G. (1952), *Introduction à la psychiatrie infantile*. Paris: Presses Universitaires de France. [*138*]

HOFFER, W. (1949), 'Mouth, Hand and Ego-Integration'. *The Psychoanalytic Study of the Child*, 3/4.

—— (1950), 'Development of the Body Ego'. *The Psychoanalytic Study of the Child*, 5.

HORNEY, K. (1937), *The Neurotic Personality of Our Time*. London: Routledge & Kegan Paul.

HUG-HELLMUTH, H. von (1921), 'On the Technique of Child Analysis'. *Int. J. Psycho-Anal.*, 2. [*160*]

ISAACS, S. (1943), 'The Nature and Function of Phantasy'. In M. Klein *et al., Developments in Psycho-Analysis*. London: Hogarth Press, 1952. [*20–1, 165–7, 169*]

ISAKOWER, O. (1938), 'A contribution to the Psycho-Pathology of Phenomena Associated with Falling Asleep'. *Int. J. Psycho-Anal.*, 19. [*43*]

ITARD, J. M. G. (1801), *De l'Éducation d'un homme sauvage* (English

translation: *The Wild Boy of Aveyron*). New York: Appleton
Century Crofts, 1932. [*11, 18n*]

JACKSON, E. D., KLATSKIN, E. H. and WILKINS, L. C. (1952),
'Early Child Development in Relation to Degree of Flexibility of
Maternal Attitudes'. *The Psychoanalytic Study of the Child*, 7. [*137*]

JACOBSON, E. (1964), *The Self and the Object World*. New York:
International Universities Press. [*131*]

JONES, E. (1933), 'The Phallic Phase'. In *Papers on Psycho-Analysis*,
5th ed., London: Baillière, Tindall and Cox, 1948.

(1953–7), *The Life and Work of Sigmund Freud*, 3 vols. London:
Hogarth Press, 1953, 1955, 1957 (*also:* same title, edited and
abridged by L. Trilling and S. Marcus, Hogarth Press, 1962). [*31n*]

KALLMANN, F. J. (1953), *Heredity in Health and Mental Disorder*.
New York: Norton.

KARDINER, A. (1939), *The Individual and his Society*. New York:
Columbia University Press. [*25, 26*]

KHAN, M. R. (1963), 'The Concept of Cumulative Trauma.' *The
Psychoanalytic Study of the Child*, 18. [*33, 129*]

(1964), 'Ego Distortion, Cumulative Trauma and the Role of
Reconstruction'. *Int. J. Psycho-Anal.*, 45.

(1969), 'On Symbiotic Omnipotence'. In *The Psychoanalytic
Forum*, Vol. 3, New York: Science House. [*130*]

KLEIN, M. (1921), 'The Development of a Child'. In *Contributions
to Psychoanalysis*. London: Hogarth Press, 1948.

(1923), 'Infant Analysis'. *In Contributions to Psychoanalysis*.
London: Hogarth Press, 1948. [*160n*]

(1926), 'The Psychological Principles of Infant Analysis'. In
Contributions to Psychoanalysis. London: Hogarth Press, 1948.
[*160, 173*]

(1932), *The Psychoanalysis of Children*. 3rd ed. London:
Hogarth Press, 1949. [*21, 59n, 61n, 160, 191, 193*]

(1957), *Envy and Gratitude*. London: Tavistock Publications.
[*107*]

(1961), *Narrative of a Child Analysis*. London: Hogarth Press.
[*173*]

and HEIMANN, P. ISAACS, S. and RIVIERE, J. (1952), *Developments
in Psycho-Analysis*. London: Hogarth Press.

KLINEBERG, O. (1954), *Social Psychology*. New York: Henry Holt.
[*20n*]

KRINGLEN, E. (1960), 'Schizophrenia in Twins'. *Psychiatry*, 29. [*22n*]

KRIS, E. (1950), 'Notes on the Development and Some Current
Problems of Psychoanalytic Psychology'. *The Psychoanalytic Study
of the Child*, 5. [*89*]

(1951), 'Opening Remarks on Psychoanalytic Child Psychology'.
The Psychoanalytic Study of the Child, 6. [*91*]

(1956), 'The Recovery of Childhood Memories in Psychoanalysis'.
The Psychoanalytic Study of the Child, 11. [*42*]

and GREENACRE, P., FREUD, A. and HARTMANN, H. (1954), 'Problems of Infantile Neurosis: A discussion'. *The Psychoanalytic Study of the Child*, 9.

LACAN, J. (1938), 'La famille'. *Encyclopédie française*, vol. 8: 'La vie mentale'. Paris: Encyclopédie Française. [*61, 65, 75, 77, 78, 98*]
    (1949), 'Le stade du miroir comme formateur de la fonction du Je'. In *Ecrits*. Paris: Le Seuil, 1966. [*123–5*]
    (1953), 'Fonction et champ de la parole et du langage en psychanalyse'. *La Psychanalyse*, 1, 1956. (Eng. trans.: 'The Function of Language in Psychoanalysis'. In Wilden, A. (1968).)
    (1959), 'A la mémoire d'Ernest Jones: sur sa théorie du symbolisme'. In *Ecrits*. Paris: Le Seuil, 1966.
    (1966), *Ecrits*. Paris: Le Seuil, 1966. [*48*]

LAFORGUE, R. and LEUBA, J. (1936), 'La névrose familiale'. *Rev. franç. Psa.*, 9. [*208n*]

LAGACHE, D. (1949), 'De la psychanalyse à l'analyse de la conduite'. *Rev. franç. Psa.*, 14. [*3, 89*]
    (1950), 'Définition et aspects de la psychanalyse'. *Rev. franç. Psa.*, 14.
    (1952), 'Le problème du transfert'. *Rev. franç. Psa.*, 16 [*172n*]
    (1955), *La Psychanalyse*. Paris: Presses Universitaires de France. [*18, 52, 53, 54, 56*]
    (1956), 'Psychanalyse et psychologie'. *Evolution Psychiatrique*, 1956. [*5, 89*]

LAING, R. D. and ESTERSON, A. (1964), *Sanity, Madness and the Family*, 2nd ed. London: Pelican Books, 1970.

LANG, J.-L. (1952), 'L'abord psychanalytique des psychoses chez l'enfant'. *La Psychanalyse*, 4. [*125*]

LAPLANCHE, J. and LECLAIRE, S. (1961), 'L'inconscient'. *Les Temps Modernes*, XVII, July 1961.
    and PONTALIS, J. B. (1967), *Vocabulaire de la psychanalyse*. Paris: Presses Universitaires de France. Eng. trans. London: Hogarth Press, *to be published*. [*6, 56n*]
    and PONTALIS, J. B. (1968), 'Fantasy and the Origins of Sexuality'. *Int. J. Psycho-Anal.*, 49. [*65n, 110n*]

LAUFER, M. (1968), 'The Body Image, the Function of Masturbation and Adolescence; Problems of the Ownership of the Body'. *The Psychoanalytic Study of the Child*, 23. [*83–4*]

LEBOVICI, S. (1950), 'A propos du diagnostic de la névrose infantile'. *Rev. franç. Psa.*, 14. [*50, 188*]
    (1961), 'La relation objectale de l'enfant'. *La Psychiatrie de l'enfant*, vol. 3. [*92, 101*]
    (1962), 'L'oeuvre de Mélanie Klein'. *La psychiatrie de l'enfant*, vol. 4; Paris: Presses Universitaires de France. [*114, 174n*]
    and DIATKINE, R. (1954), 'Etude des phantasmes chez l'enfant'. *Rev. franç. Psa.*, 18. [*113*]

LEUBA, J. (1936), 'La famille neurotique'. *Rev. franç. Psa.*, 9.

LEVINE, R. P. (1968), *Genetics* (2nd ed.). New York: Holt, Rinehart and Winston. [*16n*]

LEVI-STRAUSS, C. (1958), *Anthropologie structurale*. Eng. trans.: *Structural Anthropology*. New York: Basic Books, 1963. London: Allen Lane, 1968. [*25*]

LEVY, D. M. (1934), 'Experiments of the Sucking Reflex and Social Behaviour of Dogs'. *Am. J. Orthopsychiat.*, 4.

——— (1943), *Maternal Overprotection*. New York: Columbia University Press. [*144*]

LEWIN, B. (1946), 'Sleep, the Mouth and the Dream Screen'. *Psychoanal. Quart.* 15. [*43*]

LIDZ, T. (1964), *The Family and Human Adaptation*. London: Hogarth Press. [*22–3, 118*]

LINTON, R. (1945), *The Cultural Background of Personality*. New York: Appleton Century Crofts. [*25, 26n, 27*]

LORENZ, K. (1966), *On Aggression*. London: Methuen.

LUSTMAN, S. L. (1962), 'Defence, Symptom and Character'. *The Psychoanalytic Study of the Child*, 17. [*189n*]

MCDOUGALL, J. and LEBOVICI, S. (1969), *Dialogue with Sammy*. New York: International Universities Press.

MAHLER, M. S. (1958), 'Autism and Symbiosis'. *Int. J. Psycho-Anal.*, 39. [*133n*]

——— (1963), 'Thoughts about Development and Individuation'. *The Psychoanalytic Study of the Child*, 18. [*130, 132*]

MALSON, L. (1964), *Les Enfants sauvages: mythe et réalité*. Paris: Union Général d'Edition, 10/18. [*18n, 19, 27, 57*]

MANNONI, M. (1964), *L'Enfant arriéré et sa mère*. Paris: Le Seuil. [*21, 135, 144*]

MARCUSE, H. (1955), *Eros and Civilization*. Boston: Beacon Press; London: Sphere Books (with Political Preface), 1969. [*81*]

MEAD, G. H. (1934), *Mind, Self and Society*. Chicago: University of Chicago Press.

MEAD, M. (1928), *Coming of Age in Samoa*. New York: William Morrow.

——— (1930), *Growing up in New Guinea*. New York: William Morrow. [*26*]

——— (1935), *Sex and Temperament*. New York: William Morrow.

MITSCHERLICH, A. (1969), *Society without the Father*. Translated from the German by Eric Mosbacher. London: Tavistock Publications. [*81*]

MITTELMANN, B. (1957), 'Motility in the Therapy of Children and Adults'. *The Psychoanalytic Study of the Child*, 12. [*121*]

MORGENSTERN, S. (1927), 'Un cas de mutisme psychogène'. *Rev. franç. Psa.*, 1.

MOSCOVICI, S. (1961), *La Psychanalyse, son image et son public*. Paris: Presses Universitaires de France. [*xiii, 199n*]

MOWRER, O. H. (1950), *Learning Theory and Personality Dynamics*. New York: Ronald Press. [*89n*]

NEUBAUER, L. B. (1960), 'The One-Parent Child and his Oedipal Development'. *The Psychoanalytic Study of the Child*, 15.

NEWMAN, H. H., FREEMAN, F. N. and HOLZINGER, K. J. (1937), *Twins: A Study of Heredity and Environment*. Chicago: University of Chicago Press. [*19*]

NUTTALL, J. (1968), *Bomb Culture*. London: MacGibbon & Kee. *Also* London: Paladin, 1970. [*81n*]

PALMADE, G. (1951), *La Psychothérapie*. Paris: Presses Universitaires de France. [*2*]

POLITZER, G. (1928), *Critique des fondements de la psychologie*. Paris: Presses Universitaires de France, 1969. [*3*]

POLLIN, W. *et al.* (1969), 'Psychopathology in 15,909 pairs of veteran twins'. *Am. J. Psychiat.*, 126, Nov. 1969.

PONTALIS, J. B. (1965), *Après Freud*. Paris: Gallimard, 1968.

RACAMIER, P. C. (1953–4), 'Etude clinique des frustrations précoces'. *Rev. franç. Psa.*, 17–18. [*134, 136–7, 139*]

RANK, O. (1924), *The Trauma of Birth*. London: Kegan Paul, 1929; New York: Harcourt Brace, 1929. [*93*]

RIBBLE, M. (1943), *The Rights of Infants*. New York: Columbia University Press.

—— (1944), 'Infantile Experience in Relation to Personality Development'. In J. McV. Hunt, *Personality and Behavior Disorders*. New York: Ronald Press. [*93, 142*]

RITVO, S. and SOLNIT, A. J. (1958), 'Influences of Early Mother-Child Interaction on Identification Process'. *The Psychoanalytic Study of the Child*, 13. [*131*]

RIVIERE, J. (1952), General Introduction. In M. Klein *et al.*, *Developments of Psycho-Analysis*. London: Hogarth Press. [*159, 160*]

ROBERT, M. (1964), *The Psychoanalytic Revolution: Sigmund Freud's Life and Achievement*. London: G. Allen & Unwin, 1966. [*31*]

ROBERTSON, J. (1962), 'Mothering as an Influence on Early Development'. *The Psychoanalytic Study of the Child*, 17. [*128*]

ROGERS, C. (1951), *Client Centered Psychotherapy*. New York: Houghton Mifflin.

ROHEIM, G. (1950), *Psychoanalysis and Anthropology*. New York: International Universities Press. [*26n*]

ROSENTHAL, D. and KETY, S. S., ed. (1968), *The Transmission of Schizophrenia*. Oxford: Pergamon Press. [*23*]

RUBINFINE, D. L. (1962), 'Maternal Stimulation, Psychic Structure and Early Object Relations with Special Reference to Aggression and Denial'. *The Psychoanalytic Study of the Child*, 17. [*132*]

RYCROFT, C. (1951), 'A Contribution to the Study of the Dream-Screen'. In *Imagination and Reality*. London: Hogarth Press, 1968. [*43*]

—— (1968), *A Critical Dictionary of Psychoanalysis*. London: Nelson. [*4, 6, 50, 52, 54*]

SANDLER, J. and NAGERA, H. (1963), 'Aspects of the Metapsychology of Fantasy'. *The Psychoanalytic Study of the Child*, 18. [*163*]

SCHILDER, P. (1935), *The Image and Appearance of the Human Body*. London: Kegan Paul. [*120*]

SEARS, R. (1944), 'Experimental Analysis of Psychoanalytic Phenomena'. In J. McV. Hunt, *Personality and Behavior Disorders*, New York: Ronald Press. [*89*]

and MACCOBY, E. E. and LEVIN, H. (1957), *Patterns of Child Rearing*. Evanston: Row Peterson. [*143*]

SEGAL, H. (1957), 'Notes on Symbol Formation'. *Int. J. Psycho-Anal.*, 38.

(1964), *Introduction to the Work of Melanie Klein*. London: Heinemann. [*104n, 105, 106n, 108–9, 130*]

SEGUIN, E. (1846), *Traitement moral, hygiène et éducation des idiots*. Paris. [*11*]

SINGH, J. A. L. and ZINGG, R. M. (1942), *Wolf Children and Feral Man*. New York: Harper. [*18n*]

SLATER, E. (1958), 'The Monogenic Theory of Schizophrenia'. *Acta Genet.*, 8.

SMIRNOFF, V. N. (1967a), 'De quelques problèmes que pose au psychanalyste la pratique dispensoriale'. *Rev. Neuro-Psychiat. Infantile*, 15.

(1967b), 'Le souvenir-écran'. *Bull. Association Psychanal. France*, 2. [*42*]

(1969), 'The Masochistic Contract'. *Int. J. Psycho-Anal.*, 50.

and COURTECUISSE, J. (1962), 'De l'anthropologie culturelle à l'observation directe'. *Psychiatrie de l'enfant*, 4. Paris: Presses Universitaires de France.

SPITZ, R. A. (1945), 'Hospitalism'. *The Psychoanalytic Study of the Child*, 1.

(1946a), 'Anaclictic Depression'. *The Psychoanalytic Study of the Child*, 2.

(1946b), 'The Smiling Response'. *Genetic Psychol. Monographs*, 34. [*61*]

(1954), 'Genèse des premières relations objectales'. *Rev. franç. Psa.*, 28. [*100*]

(1955), 'The Primal Cavity'. *The Psychoanalytic Study of the Child*, 10. [*43, 60, 98*]

(1957), *No and Yes*. New York: International Universities Press. [*115*]

(1959), *A Genetic Field Theory of Ego Formation*. New York: International Universities Press.

(1964), 'The Derailment of Dialogue: Stimulus Overload, Action Cycles and the Completion Gradient'. *J. Amer. Psychoanal. Assn.*, 12. [*138n*]

(1965), *The First Year of Life*. New York: International Universities Press. [*88, 92, 93, 117, 138n, 144*]

STERBA, R. (1940), 'The Dynamics of the Dissolution of Transference

Resistance'. *Psychoanal. Quart.*, 9. [*156*]

STIERLIN, H. (1969), *Conflict and Reconciliation: A Study of Human Relations and Schizophrenia*. New York: Doubleday. [*22*]

SZASZ, T. (1962), *The Myth of Mental Illness*. London: Secker and Warburg. [*8, 181*]

TIENARI, P. (1963), 'Psychiatric Illness in Individual Twins'. *Acta Psychiat. Scandinav.*, Suppl. 171; 39. [*22n*]

TYLOR, E. B. (1871), *Primitive Culture*. London.

WAELDER, R. (1960), *Basic Theory of Psychoanalysis*. New York: International Universities Press. [*31, 46n, 50, 105n*]

WALLON, H. (1934), *Les Origines du caractère chez l'enfant*. Paris: Presses Universitaires de France, 1949. [*122*]

WHITING, J. W. M. (1954), *Child Training and Personality*. New Haven: Yale University Press. [*26n*]

WHORF, B. L. (1956), *Language, Thought and Reality*. Cambridge: Massachussets Inst. Technology. [*118n*]

WHYTE, L. L. (1960), *The Unconscious before Freud*. New York: Basic Books. [*3n*]

WIDLOCHER, D. (1962), *Le Psychodrame chez l'enfant*. Paris: Presses Universitaires de France.

WIENER, N. (1954), *The Human Use of Human Beings: Cybernetics and Society*. New York: Doubleday. [*46n*]

WILDEN, A. (1968), *The Language of the Self*. Baltimore: Johns Hopkins Press. [*124*]

WINNICOTT, D. W. (1953), 'Transitional Objects and Transitional Phenomenon'. *Collected Papers*. London: Tavistock Publications, 1958. [*129, 145*]

(1958), *Collected Papers*. London: Tavistock Publications.

(1960), 'The Theory of the Parent-Infant Relationship'. In *The Maturational Process and the Facilitating Environment*. London: Hogarth Press, 1965. [*120–1*]

(1965), *The Maturational Process and the Facilitating Environment*. London: Hogarth Press. [*62, 178*]

(1967), 'Mirror-Role of Mother and Family in Child Development'. In *The Predicament of the Family*. ed. P. Lomas. London: Hogarth Press.

ZEIGARNIK, B. (1927), 'Uber das Behalten von erledigten und unerledigten Handlungen'. *Psychiat. Forsch.*, 9. [*30*]

ZILBOORG, G. and HENRY, G. W. (1941), *A History of Medical Psychology*. New York: Norton. [*7n*]

Index

Note: For references to authors cited, see Bibliography.